PRAISE FOR THE
PBIS Team Handbook

"Through personal anecdotes and helpful tips, Ryan and Baker describe one of the most critical aspects of PBIS implementation: the school team. This revised edition includes cutting-edge research and tools to help teams overcome barriers and improve outcomes for all student groups, including students of color."
> —**Kent McIntosh, Ph.D.,** professor, special education, University of Oregon, Eugene, Oregon

"PBIS is being used in literally thousands of schools across the United States. *The PBIS Team Handbook* provides an accessible description of the key features of PBIS and useful guidance on how a school or district would launch the PBIS adoption process."
> —**Rob Horner,** co-director, OSEP Technical Assistance Center on PBIS, Eugene, Oregon

"This revised edition of *The PBIS Team Handbook* provides the updated practical directions and tools coaches and teams need to implement the framework with fidelity along with tips to deal with real situations that happen within the complex settings of schools. Char and Beth give us important updates about the relationship between MTSS and PBIS. It is also vital to talk about the addition of a new chapter on disproportionate discipline and cultural responsiveness as well as how these affect the data as we learn more about our implicit bias. *The PBIS Team Handbook* highlights this in a very humanistic way. The book continues to be a vital resource for coaches and for those implementing PBIS."
> —**Cristina Dobon-Claveau,** LCSW, PPSC, wellness and prevention coordinator, Roseville Joint Union High School District, Roseville, California

"The second edition of *The PBIS Team Handbook* continues to be an important resource for all schools as they navigate the process of improving outcomes for all students, especially students who struggle with social-emotional learning. The parts of the book that have remained the same provide a solid framework for schools and districts as they work through the process of implementing PBIS, and the addition of a chapter on equity and disproportionality is timely. As a [veteran teacher and administrator], I can attest to the disproportionality which has existed historically and continues to exist despite the good intentions of professionals who support students. Ms. Baker's sharing of her self-reflections related to this topic is courageous and inspiring. I appreciate the referrals to tools that can be used to assess a school's cultural responsiveness as well as to tools to reduce disproportionality. Thank you for providing a user-friendly, real resource for schools!"
> —**Barb Mackey,** assistant special education director, Northern Lights Academy, Cloquet, Minnesota

"*The PBIS Team Handbook* has been an invaluable resource for our school and staff members. It provided us the opportunity to build capacity with not only our teachers, but also our parent community. The authors' ability to provide theoretical and practical information in an engaging format was another reason our school was able to implement PBIS so successfully. Our PLC team used the ideas and information in the handbook to create a much needed plan for our context. *The PBIS Team Handbook* is a critical resource that has assisted our school in creating and utilizing a positive, consistent, and, most importantly, *sustainable* model of behavioral support!"

—**Kelly Kramer, Ed.D.,** director, International School of Dongguan, Dongguan, China

"*The PBIS Team Handbook* is a practical, step-by-step guide to implementing and sustaining a proactive schoolwide PBIS program, while embedding cultural differences, challenges to equity, and tools for teams to consider the disproportionality created in schools today. *The PBIS Team Handbook* is a must-have book for schools to create and sustain a proactive positive behavior support program to meet the needs of each and every student."

—**Amy Piotrowski, Ed.S.,** supervisor, student support services, Burnsville-Eagan-Savage School District, Burnsville, Minnesota

"This revised and updated edition provides a detailed step-by-step how-to guide for the implementation of PBIS from initial consideration to successful practice. Reader-friendly text includes information on essential elements of PBIS, research-based practices with descriptions and examples of team member roles and tools for fidelity and sustainability, and numerous resources and reproducible forms. An important addition is a chapter on how to address issues of disproportionality. It provides practical information for both novice and veteran professionals."

—**Sheldon Braaten, Ph.D.,** executive director, Behavioral Institute for Children and Adolescents, Little Canada, Minnesota

The
PBIS
Team
Handbook

Setting Expectations and Building Positive Behavior

**Revised &
Updated Edition**

Char Ryan, Ph.D., and Beth Baker, M.S.Ed.

free spirit
PUBLISHING®

Library of Congress Cataloging-in-Publication Data
Names: Baker, Beth 1963– author. | Ryan, Charlotte A., author.
Title: The PBIS team handbook : setting expectations and building positive behavior / by Char Ryan, Ph.D., and Beth Baker, M.S.Ed.
Other titles: Positive behavioral interventions and supports team handbook
Description: Revised & updated edition. | Minneapolis, MN : Free Spirit Publishing Inc., [2019] | Authors' names in reverse order in previous edition. | Includes bibliographical references and index.
Identifiers: LCCN 2018038685 (print) | LCCN 2018043613 (ebook) | ISBN 9781631983764 (Web PDF) | ISBN 9781631983771 (ePub) | ISBN 9781631983757 (pbk.) | ISBN 163198375X (pbk.)
Subjects: LCSH: School psychology—United States. | Behavior modification—United States. | School children—United States—Discipline. | Students—United States—Psychology. | School management and organization—United States.
Classification: LCC LB1060.2 (ebook) | LCC LB1060.2 .B34 2019 (print) | DDC 371.7/13—dc23
LC record available at https://lccn.loc.gov/2018038685

Edited by Meg Bratsch and Cathy Broberg
Cover and interior design by Shannon Pourciau

10 9 8 7 6 5 4 3 2 1
Printed in the United States of America

Free Spirit Publishing Inc.
6325 Sandburg Road, Suite 100
Minneapolis, MN 55427-3674
(612) 338-2068
help4kids@freespirit.com
www.freespirit.com

FSC
www.fsc.org
MIX
Paper from responsible sources
FSC® C005010

Dedication

From Char: I dedicate this book to my family, friends, and colleagues who offered their unconditional support, patience, and continual validation. You boosted my confidence and gave me feedback in important ways.

From Beth: I dedicate this book to all practitioners of PBIS—those who are just starting out and those who might be further along in their journeys. Thank you for your work in helping create positive change in our schools. You make a difference.

Acknowledgments

From Char: I want to thank the OSEP Technical Assistance Center on PBIS for the amazing work it has done across the country in creating a clear vision and process for implementing PBIS as well as ways to maintain the process and outcomes. The Center and all its partners do an awesome job of creating and sharing materials and training and of making all the information widely available to schools.

I give special thanks to George Sugai for teaching and modeling and training us in Minnesota. I am also extremely grateful to Rob Horner and Kent McIntosh for the years of collaboration, support, and mentoring and, in particular, for their generous review of and suggestions for this revised edition.

My colleagues at MNPBIS were wonderful in reviewing content and advising about the challenges of making difficult material understandable and accurate. They have done a marvelous job of moving and expanding PBIS in Minnesota from our humble beginnings to a strong statewide program.

Thanks to Judy Galbraith, president and founder of Free Spirit, for believing in us and our idea and ensuring that we had the necessary supports to get it done. The team at Free Spirit is special and did great work in development, design, and outreach.

I owe a particular thank-you to Meg Bratsch, our editor. She has the expertise, skills, organization, and patience that was needed to lead us through the process. She is passionate about the topics and provided us with thoughtful questions to clarify challenging concepts. I cannot imagine completing this project without her support and structure.

Thank you to Norena and Karen, long-time leaders and mentors in Minnesota. They gave me advice, suggestions, and asked for clarifications. They understand the process.

Finally, I want to acknowledge the love and support from family and friends, colleagues, and others in my life. It seemed as if I was always missing things because I was "busy" writing and meeting deadlines. Special thanks to John for your support and to Anne for your indomitable spirit.

It takes a team, both big and small, and with that good things happen.

From Beth: Thank you to all who read the revisions, especially Marquisha Lawrence Scott and Jackie Drolet. Thank you to those who have supported me while pushing through the rewrites: Ani Rubin, Sheryl Tuorila, and Mark Wilde. And a big thank-you to Meg Bratsch for asking the good questions.

Contents

List of Figures

List of Reproducible Forms

See page 201 for instructions on how to download the digital forms.

Introduction

Historically, many educators have relied on reactive practices, responding after behavior occurred, to improve student behavior. We hand out a detention or a visit to the principal for a disruptive behavior. If the behavior doesn't change, maybe the next time we call home and issue another detention. If that still doesn't work, we call home again and issue a suspension. These practices will work for some students, yet others seem unaffected by behavioral "interventions" such as these. After all this work, the behavior isn't improving, and the teacher gives up trying. Given their high number of office referrals and suspensions, these students become what we call "high flyers." Although they've been suspended multiple times, their behavior is still far from stellar. Exclusion does not teach these students new behavior.

Another way to deal with behavior is proactively. Arrange the environment to elicit appropriate behavior and reduce problematic behavior. We teach and model for students exactly how we want them to behave and intervene swiftly and often until they grasp it—thus avoiding the need for harsh punishments. The guidelines provided by Schoolwide Positive Behavioral Interventions and Supports (SWPBIS) were created for this approach. Schoolwide PBIS (hereafter referred to as PBIS) has emerged as a powerful organizing framework that supports school staff in their efforts to move from reactive to proactive behavioral interventions. Supported by decades of research, PBIS is strongly rooted in behavioral theory and practice. By combining evidence-based practices with a systems approach to implementation, PBIS has created a model that has widespread adoption and lasting success.

Using the PBIS framework, schools develop practices to prevent problem behavior and to teach and reinforce expected behaviors consistently across school settings. The system supports all school staff using data to monitor the outcomes.

Consistent data collection enables schools to determine whether the interventions are working for students and whether staff members are receiving the support they need to use the interventions effectively. PBIS, when implemented with fidelity across school systems and grades, has been shown to improve student outcomes (academic skills, prosocial behaviors, graduation rates, attendance, and so on). A school that has fully implemented PBIS will demonstrate a continuum of practices for students with typical needs all the way through practices for students who have high-intensity needs.

> **A Note on Terms**
> Throughout this book, we often refer to students' problem behavior as "disruptive behavior." We do this for brevity. In reality, of course, there are a number of behaviors that constitute minor or major infractions, as defined by schools and districts. We also encourage staff to be mindful of students who may not exhibit disruptive behaviors but rather exhibit depressive (quiet and inward) behaviors that prevent them from engaging in class and with their classmates and teachers. These students may need additional support as well.

PBIS is a three-tiered framework based on the public health prevention model reflecting a continuum of prevention, from universal interventions to intensive ones. Implementation of PBIS occurs in progressive stages, with Tier 1 being fully implemented before Tiers 2 and 3. It may take your school two or three years to firmly establish Tier 1, the universal level. This book will help you develop a sound understanding of PBIS and will walk you through the steps of implementing Tier 1. Though we do not cover Tiers 2 and 3 in this book, we provide a brief description of how to prepare for this expansion.

One of the most valuable elements of PBIS is that it lets teachers do what they do best: *teach*. And it gives administrators more time to lead. Best of all, it gives students more time, confidence, and motivation to learn.

About This Revised Edition
PBIS is a system of evidence-based practices. Since this book was originally published, the field of PBIS has continued to advance in research and in practice. We are committed to keeping pace with improvements, and we strive to reflect and convey the current best practice in PBIS drawn from the field.

At the time of this publication, there are nearly 26,000 schools implementing PBIS in the United States and in 23 countries worldwide. For current numbers, check www.pbis .org. This is exciting news and demonstrates the worldwide movement to improve educational practice and ensure safe and effective learning environments for students.

Specific updates in the book include:
- the integration of MTSS (Multi-Tiered System of Supports) and PBIS
- the most current evaluation tools and how to use them to measure success
- a discussion of PBIS and equity to ensure the framework provides an equitable education and positive behavioral outcomes for all students

The PBIS framework was designed by school leadership teams to address behavioral and disciplinary practices that affect school communities. It is a fluid process that requires not only careful monitoring of data and implementation of strategies and action plans, but also the human capacity for building relationships and committing together, as a school facility, to improve the educational achievements of students.

> This book will help you develop a sound understanding of PBIS and will walk you through the process of implementing Tier 1 of the framework.

Why We Wrote This Book

We wrote this book to explain the components of the PBIS framework and its implementation in user-friendly terms and to offer examples and lessons learned from our experience. The following stories from Char and Beth describe what brought them to PBIS:

From Char: I have spent my entire career working with infants, children, adolescents, and adults with behavior challenges and other special needs. I taught, counseled, coached, trained, and administrated. Over this time I have seen and experienced a lot of trends. For me, PBIS is one of the most significant positive approaches available.

In the early days of my career, now decades ago, we used time-outs and restraint, practices that we steadfastly restrict now. Although I had sound training in behavioral theory and practice, I had a lot to learn and needed to do so early on. One example that stands out was my experience with a student with self-injurious behavior. Briefly, this student banged his head on tables, walls, and any other hard object within reach. The headbanging occurred nonstop at times, perhaps thirty times in a minute; it was stressful to watch. Our team created a plan where we would gently restrain him by holding his arms down. One day his parents said "no more" to restraint practices. At first I was anxious about how we would handle the behavior. The amazing thing was that we became far more proactive and effective. We identified predictable triggers and possible reinforcements for headbanging as well as alternative behaviors. We consequently changed the environment as well as our response, used positive approaches, and kept lots of data. The student's headbanging declined. No injuries occurred to the student or staff, and we resumed teaching. In short, we used positive behavioral interventions. Part of the transition to this PBIS model, for me at least, was overcoming my fear and opening to new ways of practice.

In the 1990s, I was a state specialist for students with emotional-behavioral disorders (EBD), for whom I have always been a strong advocate. The field was working very hard to promote the use of positive behavioral interventions with these students. Sadly, exclusionary and punitive practices were commonplace in those days; seclusion and restraint were frequently implemented and undocumented. There was (and still is) significant stigma and misunderstanding about students with behavior challenges. For one, it was widely assumed by some that students *chose* particular problem behaviors because they wanted to disrupt the school day for everyone else. This belief in negative motives seemed to justify adults' use of harsh punishment and exclusion of these students from school. It was painful to see this happen so often and at the same time talk with students' families, who were desperate for their children to get a good education. While as educators we should not accept problematic behavior, we need to use more positive and effective practices and mental health awareness to restore a healthy school climate.

Throughout these years, we knew that PBIS worked for individual students with challenging behavior. We used

function-based evaluations and positive behavior support plans—what we now consider Tier 3 practices. We had the practices and we had the data, and yet PBIS was still a very hard sell. Our school systems were simply not designed to support the change that was needed. Then in 2002 I attended the first national Schoolwide Positive Behavioral Interventions and Supports (SWPBIS) conference in Chicago. Bingo! It was so inspiring and clearly the right direction to go. Finally we had a model for a continuum of supports for the entire school system.

In 2005, Minnesota began to implement PBIS statewide, starting with nine schools. I was lucky to be the state coordinator for this effort. As change spread in our schools, one of my brightest moments occurred when a talented principal called me and said that with PBIS in place, his school was better able to serve students with emotional-behavioral disorders. He recognized the challenges for these students. This school is a community, and this principal remains one of Minnesota's visionaries.

As I reflect on these educational advances, I see what a significant shift schoolwide PBIS has provided. When Beth asked if I wanted to write a book with her about it, my only answer was "Yes!"

From Beth: I was teaching middle school students with emotional-behavioral disorders, and one day during a math lesson a student said to me, "You're a (insert expletive)." I am not sure why he said it, but I didn't like it. I responded, "That's it! You are suspended! You can go home!" and went to find an administrator. Instead I found the school psychologist and told her what had just happened in my classroom. She asked me, "What do you hope to get by suspending this student?" I told her that he couldn't speak to me that way and he needed to go home. "Do you really think suspending him one more time for the behavior he's been doing for six years is going to change anything?" I thought about it for a minute and then sheepishly replied "No." But I felt exasperated and defeated—what else could I do but suspend him? The school psychologist gave me a social skills curriculum she had received from a mental health treatment center and suggested that it might be helpful to use with my students. She asked her intern to lead the curriculum's lessons with my class.

Over the coming months, the intern taught my students how to use calming strategies, including deep breathing and visualization. He talked with them about different sources of anger and showed them how to release their anger in healthy ways. As a class, we developed common language to discuss feelings and how we react to those feelings. For my part, the curriculum prompted me to work toward understanding my students better and where their behaviors might be originating. As I learned more about my students' backgrounds, families, and school histories, I realized that the feelings and behaviors they demonstrated in class were perhaps a response to me, but could also be a result of much more than my desire to teach them math, for example. Because most of my students were students of color, and all were receiving special education services for emotional-behavioral concerns, perhaps they were frustrated with trying to navigate a system that they were unfamiliar with and that continued to put them in the category of "less than." They were simply displaying the same behaviors they had always used to cope with anger, hurt, and frustration. The student who called me a name wasn't really angry at me—he was angry at the world (and he eventually told me as much when we discussed the

incident). In the past, swearing at a teacher had brought him an automatic suspension, an easy way to escape school. But this consequence had not served to change his behavior. Once I understood this, I wanted to keep the students in the building and work with them on developing better ways of identifying anger and frustration, their root causes, and how to either cope with a situation or use problem-solving to find solutions and change what can be changed.

I remember this incident quite vividly and how it made me rethink my purpose in teaching students with challenging behaviors. It was no longer just about the academics; now I saw how focusing on the social-emotional aspect of my students' lives could also improve their everyday experiences over the long term. I began allowing behavioral "do-overs" in my classroom. We talked about feelings and processed the causes of disruptive behaviors, and I acknowledged and reinforced the new prosocial skills my students were learning. I changed the environment of my classroom from being reactive to proactive to ensure that students felt welcomed and engaged.

With these changes, I no longer felt like a gatekeeper, sending kids back and forth to the behavior room. Now I felt more involved and connected with my students and enjoyed watching them grow emotionally—they could share with me what they were frustrated about and then together we could come up with a solution. The atmosphere in my classroom became calmer. And as a result, we could spend more time on academics.

The changes didn't happen overnight. There was a lot of work involved—relationships built by taking baby steps—and some kids weren't interested in talking about their feelings. Even so, I remember running into a parent of one of these students a few years after the family had moved to a different district. She gave me a hug and told me that her son was doing really well and that his anger was no longer causing him significant trouble. Was it what he had learned in my classroom? Maybe. Was it maturity? Possibly. Does it matter? Not to me. What matters to me is that he figured out a way to cope with his behaviors that worked for him and was not disruptive to everyone around him.

That was my introduction to PBIS, although I was yet to fully understand the theories and principles involved and the potential it had to improve an entire school's culture. Eventually I enrolled in graduate school to earn a master's degree in education, and part of my program required that I do an action research project (implement a project and collect data on it over time). The middle school where I was teaching had just started a schoolwide character education program, and I knew it would be a perfect setting to collect data for my project. While conducting research on social-emotional learning, I kept bumping into articles on PBIS. When I started reading them, I realized that although the program at my school was a great start, it did not include interventions for students who were being continually referred out of class and who were in need of more intensive supports. It also didn't emphasize data collection.

I started looking at our school's data and determined which students were having trouble—not just their names, but also their race and ethnicity, special education services, grades, attendance, behavioral strengths, and patterns. The school's handling of behavior and discipline problems paralleled a scenario that is repeated across the country: A student would get referred out of the classroom and go to the behavior room; here he or she would complete a form agreeing not to do the behavior again, get a lecture, and then return to class. For some students, this process was repeated several times a day, day after day. Teachers were frustrated because behaviors weren't changing. Some students were actually choosing to act out to get sent to the behavior room. Administrators were distressed with the number of students out of class, because we all know that students don't learn unless they are in class.

I began to memorize research and sound bites about PBIS, but I had a hard time really explaining the overall concept and its practices to my colleagues. If only I knew exactly what PBIS meant . . . If only there were a book that spelled everything out in simple language.

Eventually, our principal decided to adopt PBIS in our school. She began by gathering a PBIS team together. We registered for a two-year cohort training with our state department of education. It was at these trainings that I got to know Char, one of the trainers and the coauthor of this book. She was a great mentor to me while I took on the role of a PBIS coach and led my school through the implementation process.

In time, we began talking more about the layers and parts of PBIS and why implementation often seems difficult. By then I had worked as a special education teacher (for students with emotional-behavioral disorders), as a behavior specialist, and as a PBIS coach. Char's expertise in PBIS included serving as the Minnesota PBIS coordinator and working as a coach, as an evaluation specialist, and as a trainer. We decided to collaborate on creating this guide to help educators who are considering PBIS understand how it operates and how to bring it into their own schools with success.

About This Book

The PBIS Team Handbook is written primarily for district PBIS coordinators and teams and new and emerging PBIS coaches—both internal (school-based) and external (district)—and for leadership teams, including administrators and school staff. It is intended for both new and current staff members. We've received feedback from readers who have been involved with PBIS for over a decade and who feel this book provides them with a more complete and detailed understanding of PBIS and how to lead others.

Part One: What Is PBIS? The first five chapters of this book present the components, roles, and expected outcomes of using the PBIS framework.

- **Chapter 1: PBIS 101** provides a detailed overview of PBIS, what it is, how it originated, how the tiers work, who is involved in using the strategies in a school setting, and what steps are necessary to begin implementing it with fidelity. You'll learn what this type of systems change may look like in your building and how these changes will lead to a safer, calmer school climate. This chapter also discusses the fit between PBIS and MTSS.

The sections, chapters, and resources in this book align with the *PBIS Implementation Blueprint* developed by Rob Horner and George Sugai, with support from the US Department of Education's Office of Special Education Programs (OSEP). Throughout this book, we refer to sections of the website for the national OSEP Technical Assistance Center on PBIS (www.pbis.org)—a nationwide network that supports schools throughout the country with SWPBIS resources. Please take a look at the PBIS website to see all the contributors who have helped make PBIS the huge success that it is. Another foundational resource is the *Handbook of Positive Behavior Support*,[1] which details the history, depth, and breadth of this initiative.

- **Chapter 2: The PBIS Leadership Team** details the role of a team in introducing and implementing PBIS, describes how to form an effective team, and identifies key roles and responsibilities for different team members. New research shows the significance of a strong leadership team as a key factor in schools sustaining PBIS.[2] We also discuss how to prepare for, conduct, and evaluate team meetings to ensure that best practices are being followed, and we explore the specific role of administrators in PBIS. We provide suggestions for how to develop and maintain a strong and effective leadership team.

- **Chapter 3: The PBIS Coach** describes the key role and tasks of this important leader in the implementation process, from the knowledge and skills a coach needs to specific steps in guiding the process. Ideas on how to grow and develop as a coach are also covered.

- **Chapter 4: Data and Assessment** includes the newest tools available for monitoring progress, action planning, achieving fidelity, and sustaining practices. It explains the essential assessment and data collection piece of PBIS. It identifies the key components in any behavior monitoring system used to track referrals and summarizes the numerous assessment tools that are commonly used in PBIS. This chapter also highlights the latest changes in the Schoolwide Information System (SWIS) and provides recommendations for setting annual data evaluation schedules.

- **Chapter 5: Effective Data-Based Decision-Making** details a method of data-based problem-solving for PBIS Leadership Teams that can be used with implementation progress, fidelity, and student outcome data. It also briefly introduces the Team-Initiated Problem-Solving (TIPS) model.

1. Sailor, Dunlap, Sugai, and Horner, eds., 2009.
2. McIntosh et al., 2018.

Part Two: Implementing PBIS Tier 1. This section of the book offers a step-by-step guide through the five stages of implementation, explaining the main tasks of each stage, the individuals involved, and how to keep stakeholders informed.

- **Chapter 6: PBIS Stage 1: Exploration and Adoption** explains how to get started with PBIS, including how to determine need, collect baseline data, and take the first steps to get buy-in from school staff and administrators.

- **Chapter 7: PBIS Stage 2: Getting Ready— Installing the Infrastructure** discusses the important task of establishing a PBIS Leadership Team and the initial work of the team as they develop an action plan. At this point, schools typically develop the three to five schoolwide expectations that will serve as the foundation for behavioral change in their school and design an approach to teach and reinforce those expectations.

- **Chapter 8: PBIS Stage 3: Getting Going— Initial Implementation** explains how to put the eight key features of PBIS effectively in place. Special attention is focused on training staff at this stage.

- **Chapter 9: PBIS Stage 4: Up and Running—Full Implementation** explores what PBIS looks like once all the features are in place and the strategies of reinforcement have become automatic to all school staff. The chapter discusses how to ensure that the strategies and principles of PBIS are being used as intended and with fidelity.

- **Chapter 10: PBIS Stage 5: Sustaining and Continuous Improvement** is updated with the most current research on sustainability and looks at how to sustain PBIS over the long term, when leadership and staff turn over and when momentum slows. The discussion includes adapting PBIS to changing circumstances, addressing common barriers at this stage, and identifying what actions will lead to continual improvement and support for PBIS throughout the school. Practical examples are provided.

- **Chapter 11: Equity and Disproportionality: How PBIS Can Help** addresses the importance of reviewing discipline practices that are inequitable to students of color. It is imperative that school discipline practices are fair and just and that learning environments are open and welcoming to all students.

Part Three: Setting the Stage for PBIS Tiers 2 and 3. The final section of this book explores how to know when your school is ready to move beyond the first tier of PBIS and what to do next.

- **Chapter 12: Are You Ready for Advanced Tiers?** offers questions to help you consider whether your school is comfortable enough to advance to the second and third tiers of PBIS to meet the needs of students with more pronounced behavioral challenges. Updates include tools that districts and schools can use to assess their needs and readiness for advanced tiers.

Glossary, Resources, and Appendix. At the end of this book is a glossary of relevant terms, an updated list of references and resources, and an appendix filled with reproducible forms and lists to help you and your school with PBIS implementation. You will also find these forms in the digital content.

Digital Content. The digital content accompanying this book contains customizable versions of all the reproducible forms as well as a PDF presentation that can be modified for use in your school to introduce the PBIS framework to your staff or district. We have done the research and created this tool to help you provide professional development in your school or district. See page 201 for details on how to access the download from Free Spirit's website.

PLC/Book Study Guide. If you wish to use this book in a professional learning community (PLC) or book study group, a PLC/Book Study Guide with chapter-by-chapter discussion questions is available. You may download the free guide at freespirit.com/PLC.

How to Use This Book

Regardless of whether your school is already in the midst of implementing PBIS or has yet to commit to adopting it, you will find information and resources in this book that apply to where you are on your journey. You may choose to read the book straight through or select specific sections or chapters that address where you are right now. We have updated the book to include current evidence-based practice. It focuses on the *how* of thoroughly implementing Tier 1 and is designed to promote the sustainability of the framework as much as the initial implementation.

PLCs and book study groups can use this book in schools exploring or already using PBIS. These chapters will help you get caught up on the terminology and the process. (It took Beth about two years to catch on to some of the nuances of the model.) Also, principals may purchase copies of the book for the PBIS Leadership Team to have on hand during the implementation phase and to walk your team through the process. Staff members who are new to your building may also appreciate having a copy to catch up on what PBIS is all about. Readers tell us that the easy flow and step-by-step guidance are very helpful, even for schools and districts that have already been implementing PBIS.

We welcome you to this wonderful journey. It will likely be filled with pit stops, hills, and valleys. But with patience and perseverance, you can help lead your school to reduced behavioral problems and improved academics, fostering an environment in which teachers are teaching more, administrators are disciplining less, and students are more engaged and productive.

Char Ryan and Beth Baker

PART ONE

What Is PBIS?

CHAPTER 1

PBIS 101

Positive Behavioral Interventions and Supports (PBIS) is now being used in nearly 26,000 schools across the United States and in 23 countries worldwide, across all school settings, from the lunchroom to the library, from the locker room to the individual classroom—and everywhere in between. The PBIS framework has been adopted by rural, suburban, and urban schools; by area learning centers (ALCs), charter schools, and separate-site special education programs; and by preK schools through high schools. Some juvenile justice centers also use PBIS. The framework can be implemented in any school that is interested in improving behavioral and academic outcomes for all students. Many educators and other school staff are witnessing the benefits of this approach and seeing safer, calmer learning environments.

You may be a coach or PBIS team member looking for a way to communicate to others what PBIS represents. Or perhaps you are a staff member trying to figure out just what PBIS means to you. Regardless of your role, this chapter will provide you with a basic understanding of the PBIS approach and how it can be used in your school.

How Was PBIS Developed and How Does It Work?

In the 1980s, researchers at the University of Oregon began to research and develop interventions for use with students who had challenging behaviors in school settings. They noted success with the following practices:

- preventing unwanted behaviors
- using evidence-based practices to teach new behaviors
- teaching the new behaviors explicitly, mindfully, and step-by-step
- keeping data to track progress toward meeting social skills goals

In 1997, Congress reauthorized the Individuals with Disabilities Education Act (IDEA) and secured funding to establish the National Technical Assistance Center on Positive Behavioral Interventions and Supports (www.pbis.org). Researchers from across the country contributed their research and implementation ideas. Finally, all the key studies and research involving behavioral change and supports for students with challenging behaviors were in one spot. The center also created partnerships with university researchers in Oregon, Florida, Missouri, and other states. This led to the expansion of the PBIS framework from special education classrooms to schoolwide programs. In 2002, the center hosted the first PBIS Leadership Forum in Chicago, and in 2004, Rob Horner and George Sugai, with support from the US Department of Education's Office of Special Education Programs, wrote the PBIS blueprints to guide practitioners in implementing PBIS. Updated blueprints can be found at www.pbis.org/blueprint briefstools.

PBIS is an organizing framework for schools to determine how they want to operate as a community—that is, what type of learning environment they want to create and what that means in terms of student behavior and academic achievement. PBIS is grounded in a continuum of evidence-based interventions that are used consistently throughout the school to prevent problematic behavior, to teach prosocial skills, and to reinforce new skills. The framework includes a set of clear practices that are embedded in a three-tiered support system for students. Teachers use specific techniques and procedures, while real-time data provide evidence to determine outcomes. A variety of measurement tools included in the framework are described in chapter 4 and discussed in more detail in later chapters. The framework includes the following eight key features:

1. PBIS Leadership Team that guides the implementation

2. Statement of vision or purpose

3. Three to five schoolwide positive behavioral expectations

4. A continuum of procedures for encouraging the expected behaviors, including a behavioral matrix explaining how those expectations will look in the school

5. Lesson plans that teach the expected behaviors across all classroom and nonclassroom settings

6. Acknowledgment system that recognizes students using expected behavior—both within and outside of the classroom

7. Flowchart of detailed procedures showing how to handle student misbehaviors schoolwide—across all classroom and nonclassroom settings

8. Data-based system for monitoring implementation, fidelity, and outcomes

PBIS is implemented in stages, which enables the school to be fully prepared and trained for the interventions and system changes. The PBIS Leadership Team monitors the fidelity of implementation and completes assessments to ensure the process is on track to success. Staff members

are surveyed to determine what school settings and behaviors may need extra attention (such as hallway behaviors) and what areas may simply need to maintain prosocial behaviors (for example, by posting expectations to remind adults and students about appropriate behaviors).

> Ultimately, PBIS is an organizing framework for schools to determine how they want to operate as a community.

Educators have spent a lot of time, energy, and money figuring out the best way to teach kids reading, math, and other disciplines. PBIS helps schools include social-emotional learning skills. Teachers know that students who regularly interrupt class or who spend a lot of time in the principal's office aren't learning academic or social-emotional skills. What's more, we know that students who are aware of their emotions and can regulate when they are feeling frustrated will do better in school. As a special educator by training, Beth has written many goals for students about self-regulation and then taught those students how to recognize when they are frustrated or anxious and how to handle it in the classroom. We know that students learn the expected school behaviors if they see them modeled and are given time for practice, feedback, and skill reinforcement across school settings. Yet when it comes to social-emotional skills, many teachers aren't comfortable teaching these "soft" skills. Some don't want to spend time teaching behaviors they think their students should already know, despite the evidence that some students haven't mastered the skills we want them to have.

Over the past decade, schools have improved their collaboration with mental health providers. Many districts now have formal agreements with local mental health agencies that provide needed services on-site in the schools. Historically, there have been many barriers to this cooperation. Given that 20 percent of students experience a serious mental health disorder, their success depends on our ability to integrate these systems. For some good examples of integration, see www.pbis.org and look through the sections "School," "Community," and "Research."

PBIS and MTSS

Many schools now implement MTSS, or Multi-Tiered System of Supports, to provide academic support for students. MTSS first appeared in the Every Student Succeeds Act (ESSA) in 2015. The law requires states to ensure the success of all students and all schools. MTSS is not required by this law, per se. It is defined as a "comprehensive continuum of evidence-based systemic practices to support rapid response to students' needs, with regular observation to facilitate data-based instructional decision-making."[1] MTSS is a service delivery framework based on the concept of prevention and increasing levels of supports (tiers) for academic and social behavior.

PBIS was introduced in the 2004 reauthorization of IDEA, in which it was not officially defined or required. However, state departments that accepted federal funds were required to develop their own multi-tiered systems of supports.

Interventions in both MTSS and PBIS utilize evidence-based practices, progress monitoring, and data collection to determine schoolwide, as well as individual student, needs. When combined with MTSS, PBIS provides school teams with tools to create student-centered behavioral interventions and plans. PBIS and MTSS are compatible in their systems approach to practice and implementation.

There is growing discussion and action to integrate MTSS and PBIS into a single unified systemic approach incorporating evidence-based practices to achieve clear academic and social-behavioral outcomes. There are logical reasons for doing so, including:

- Academic and social behavior are related; this is well-known.
- Tiered systems of supports based on a prevention model produce positive outcomes.

- Both PBIS and MTSS have demonstrated widespread application and durability.
- Integrating around common features offers the possibility of increased efficiency.

However, the process of integrating MTSS and PBIS requires a lot of effort and time and needs to be done systematically. There often is confusion about how best to do this or even if these two frameworks are mutually exclusive. The worst-case scenario would be if the strong evidence-based elements of either approach were lost in the process of bringing them together.

In discussions with state MTSS specialists, we agree that the best approach is to clearly recognize the common elements and focus the work on these similarities. Here are a few examples:

1. PBIS focuses on improving student behavioral and, relatedly, academic outcomes. MTSS also focuses on prevention and problem-solving to achieve higher rates of academic proficiency and close the achievement gap.

2. PBIS focuses on evidence-based supports for students across schoolwide, nonclassroom, classroom, and individual student settings. MTSS focuses on academic supports for classes and groups of students.

3. PBIS establishes a continuum of supports in three tiers that is based on screening, progress monitoring, and team-based decision-making for social-behavioral outcomes and improved learning environments. MTSS also focuses on three tiers of academic support for students: core instruction, supplemental instruction, and intensive intervention.

4. PBIS uses data for accurate decision-making and monitoring in a team-based framework. MTSS uses multiple sources of data to define, measure, and improve academic instruction.

We support the effective integrations of these frameworks. Here are some examples of states that have made good progress in doing so:

---

1. Knoff, Reeves, and Balow, 2018.

- **California's Department of Education** provides a good description of MTSS and how it encompasses both PBIS and Response to Intervention (RTI): www.cde.ca.gov/ci/cr/ri.

- **Minnesota's Department of Education** uses MTSS to improve the achievement of students who are not meeting grade-level standards: education.mn.gov/MDE/dse/mtss.

- **Indiana's Department of Education** combines MTSS with Universal Design for Learning (UDL) to enhance learning environments for all students, including those students who have special needs. The website provides many links for further study: www.doe.in.gov /specialed/universal-design-learning -udl-multi-tiered-system-supports-mtss.

This recap is brief and does not detail some of the more complex characteristics of PBIS and MTSS. But it hopefully gives readers a general idea of the commonalities. Our purpose in this book is to provide user-friendly approaches to understanding and implementing PBIS with fidelity.

A Tiered Model

PBIS offers three tiers of support to ensure all students get the help they need. Beginning at Tier 1, or the universal tier, primary prevention interventions for all students are established. Tier 2 involves interventions for students whose behaviors might be considered at-risk. And Tier 3 offers intensive interventions for individual students who have the greatest needs. For teachers and other educators, the PBIS framework guides us to look at the practices we use and to identify new skills we may need to develop in order to fully support all students in an equitable and culturally responsive way.

The three-tiered system of PBIS is based on a model of prevention from public health. The model says that 80 percent of people will respond to general guidance or correction, about 15 percent will need a bit more treatment, and maybe the top 5 percent will need specialized treatment. PBIS replicates that model. The model recognizes that not all problem behavior is the same, nor do all students respond to the same types of interventions. The PBIS framework guides schools in meeting the needs of students at all tiers through a continuum of interventions. This continuum is designed to help staff prevent challenging behaviors by teaching and acknowledging prosocial behaviors.

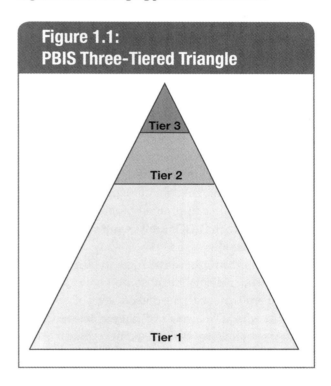

Figure 1.1:
PBIS Three-Tiered Triangle

Tier 3

Tier 2

Tier 1

Figure 1.1 illustrates the PBIS three-tiered triangle. The bottom of the triangle (typically shown in green) represents schoolwide behavioral practices, called Tier 1 interventions. This is the universal prevention of disruptive behaviors by creating quality learning environments for all students across all areas of the school, including nonclassroom settings. This tier includes three to five positively stated schoolwide expectations, lesson plans for teaching expected behaviors to all students, and a practice for monitoring their use. Systems are set up for handling disruptive behavior in the classroom, including when to write an office discipline referral (ODR). Staff may be given professional development in classroom management skills and social-emotional learning.

Tier 2, typically shown in yellow, involves secondary prevention. This is specialized instruction for students who may be considered at-risk and may benefit from small-group instruction in social-emotional skills. For example, during her time as a coach, Beth and the school social worker had a "Lunch Bunch" group of students who were accumulating tardies during the day. After the students finished their lunches, the social worker provided lessons on why it's important to be on time for class and how to get to class on time. Another evidence-based practice at Tier 2 is Check-In Check-Out (CICO) for students who need more assistance beyond Tier 1 interventions. CICO provides more positive adult contact, specific social skills instruction, specific focus on students' achieving schoolwide expectations, and daily contact with adults about progress. Students who succeed with CICO rarely require Tier 3 interventions.

Tier 3 at the top of the triangle (typically shown in red) reflects the most intensive interventions for students with the highest level of need. Students who have behaviors that are deemed to be the most challenging or frequent receive interventions at Tier 3. This tier focuses on one-on-one interventions to help students learn expected school behaviors or on strategies to replace the challenging behavior. Tier 3 interventions require detailed, individual functional behavioral evaluations, behavior support plans, and increased staff involvement.

Outcomes Supported by Three Integrated Elements

The overarching goal for schools is to ensure the academic success and social competence of all students. In the PBIS framework, three integrated elements support the outcomes for social competence:

1. **Data to support decision-making.** Data are used to develop plans and actions that respond to what is really occurring in the school rather than grasping at straws and saying things like, "I am pretty sure most of our students have never had a referral," or "He said at the staff meeting that things are going well, so they must be." Data that are kept current provide a real-time look at your school climate.

2. **Practices to support student behavior.** Expectations for student behavior are developed and clearly communicated and taught to all students. Another essential component involves specifically and systematically acknowledging students for performing expected behaviors. Along with this, practices are in place for preventing students' disruptive behaviors from erupting in class or in the hallways and other settings.

3. **Systems to support staff behavior.** Staff are trained to prevent many student behavioral problems as well as to deal with disruptive behaviors in a more proactive and positive manner. Systems infrastructure includes creating routines that support and sustain new adult behavior.

These three elements are key to having a behavioral model that is effective, efficient, and relevant. **Figure 1.2** illustrates the way they interact to produce positive outcomes.

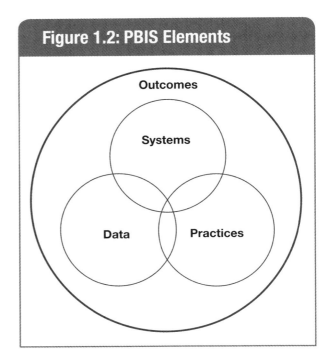

Figure 1.2: PBIS Elements

Outcomes

Systems

Data   Practices

How Is PBIS Implemented?

Anyone who has ever tried to make big changes or adopt new practices in a school knows that it is a complex process. An entire body of science has evolved that studies adoption, implementation, and sustainability of evidence-based practices across the fields of education, social services, medicine, and business. Today, the National Implementation Research Network offers valuable resources to those who want to know more about the implementation science of evidence-based practices.

Implementation science gives us an important perspective regarding the work we are doing. First, the process of adopting a new system of practice—no matter how popular—tends to take up to three to five years or more. From the onset, schools must make a long-term commitment to change.

The second big idea from implementation science is that system change occurs in stages leading to full implementation. The stages portray implementation as a process rather than an event. This means that adoption occurs in a progressive, if not uneven, trend. This dimensional approach has implications for what we do as leaders, coaches, and team members. Understanding this progressive evolution of implementation helps us develop specific tasks for those involved in introducing and using PBIS in schools. The process, then, requires ongoing attention, commitment of resources, and *patience*. In Minnesota, where we work, administrators and schools are advised from the moment of PBIS application that they need to understand and commit to a multiyear process.

The following list summarizes the five stages schools move through as they plan for and then begin using PBIS in their buildings. Each chapter in part 2 of this book details one of the five stages of PBIS implementation.

1. **Exploration and adoption:** Learning more about PBIS and whether it would be a good fit for your school. Does your school need it? How could it be helpful?

2. **Installation:** Getting commitments from your district, your school administration, and your school staff; setting up your PBIS Leadership Team and defining leadership and coaching roles; setting up a data management system such as Schoolwide Information System (SWIS) or another way to track office discipline referrals; choosing a universal, or schoolwide, social skills curriculum or teaching methods.

> The process of adopting a new system of practice—no matter how popular—tends to take up to three to five years or more.

3. **Initial implementation:** Training school staff and students, collecting baseline data, putting minimal features in place—such as identifying your school's vision and purpose, selecting three to five behavioral expectations, teaching behavioral expectations schoolwide, and setting up the behavioral referral process. The PBIS Leadership Team collects baseline data. New schools may start with the Tiered Fidelity Inventory (TFI) as a means of formative evaluation and needs assessment. Some teams may choose to start by completing the Team Implementation Checklist (TIC). Either instrument will help you identify next steps and set action plans. Schools will choose to complete one or the other instrument but not both at this point. The team should also use the Self-Assessment Survey (SAS) to survey the staff and hear their thoughts on how well the school is functioning and on areas of strength and areas in need of modification.

4. **Full implementation:** All universal, or Tier 1, components are now operating completely. Behavioral expectations are taught schoolwide and the PBIS Leadership Team meets on a regular basis. All eight PBIS features (see page 11) are implemented and meet fidelity criteria.

At this point, districts may consider expanding PBIS to other schools.

5. **Sustainability and continuous improvement:** PBIS has become common practice, which is reflected in school or district policy and visibility. Schools have implemented systems that ensure continuous adaptation to fit local contexts and changes while maintaining fidelity. Ongoing fidelity assessment assures the team of their program's sustainability and provides data for continued improvement.

Who Is Involved with PBIS?

PBIS is a schoolwide initiative. This means that every adult on staff who encounters students during the school day—from bus drivers to hall monitors to teachers and administrators—is trained in using PBIS practices so students receive the same message consistently in all school settings. Successful implementation of PBIS relies on at least 80 percent agreement from staff, or what we refer to as staff buy-in. Buy-in is an important and constant consideration, both while PBIS is being implemented and during later stages in which sustainability and improvement are the focus.

When schools decide to implement PBIS, a coach and a representative PBIS Leadership Team are chosen to ensure that the practices of PBIS are being used with fidelity across all school settings. The coach might be a general or special education teacher, behavior specialist, school psychologist, social worker, or counselor. The PBIS Leadership Team should be composed of a cross section of staff in your building. It must be a representative group academically, by grade and curriculum area, and also must reflect the diversity and racial makeup of your school.

Administrators, in particular, play a key role in providing leadership and garnering initial and long-term support for PBIS. This support takes many forms—including a clear vision and purpose, financial support for substitute teachers, full-time equivalent (FTE) staff allocations for coaches

and others in key roles, and public support for the initiative and its success within the district and community. Indeed, systems change becomes possible in a school only when it is backed by a larger network of support.

Figure 1.3 on page 17 identifies the essential components and their organization in a complete PBIS system. The chart can serve as a blueprint for teams at various levels—school, district, region, state, and beyond. This graphic provides a macro look at the various school-based system components that need to be in place to support and sustain PBIS.

So how does this graphic organizer apply to a school team? Notice that the PBIS Leadership Team is at the center. This is consistent with PBIS being a team-implemented framework. As implementation progresses, the PBIS Leadership Team needs to address several supportive systems; these are situated along the top of the diagram:

- **Funding** at the school and district level is critical. The PBIS Leadership Team develops a plan to ensure ongoing funding.

- **Visibility** is crucial to telling your story from beginning to end—to staff in your school, to your district administration, and to the school board, parent-teacher organization, community, and so on.

- **Political support** refers to embedding the PBIS framework into the structure of the school and district so that key stakeholders support it.

- **Policy** includes multiple levels, from revising local school policies around discipline and behavior to districtwide changes. We have seen district PBIS Leadership Teams work to adopt a uniform referral form and policy across all schools, integrating PBIS with other systems such as MTSS and maintaining core features for sustainability.

The bottom set of boxes in figure 1.3 refer to the components that must be developed and maintained at all levels, and particularly at the school level:

- **Training** includes the installation of the framework initially, as well as the development of internal capacity to train new staff and students.

- **Coaching** is essential to ensure that the knowledge acquired through training is applied accurately. We know from research that transfer of knowledge to the classroom level is accomplished most effectively when coaching is part of the process. Administrators need to focus on ensuring that PBIS coaches or those who provide the essential coaching functions are allocated the time, FTE, to accomplish the work, including training and development.

- **Evaluation** is a core feature of PBIS implementation and sustainability. Each school must ensure that routines for collecting and using data accurately in decision-making are established and that they become a permanent feature.

- **Behavioral expertise** is necessary; schools and PBIS Leadership Teams must have staff with the specialist knowledge and skills to apply to all tiers of intervention.

All parts of this system are needed to ensure that PBIS is completely functional and sustainable. At the end of the implementation phase, your school may be the "model or demonstration" site for your district. Keep this graphic in mind as you begin the early stages of implementation, when it is easy to lose sight of the big picture and be consumed by the initial steps.

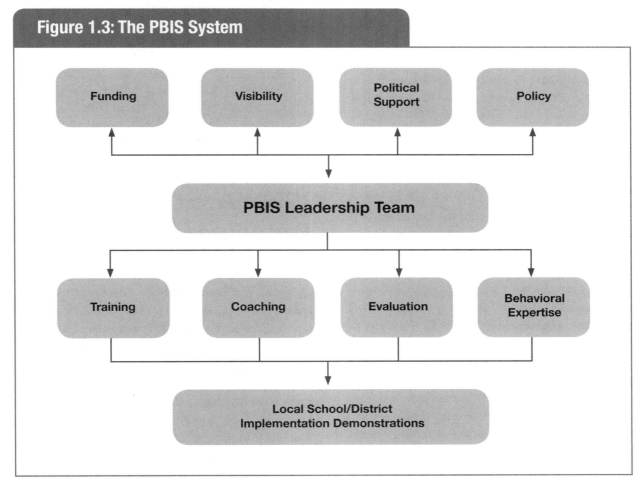

Figure 1.3: The PBIS System

From *Implementation Blueprint and Self-Assessment* developed by the OSEP Technical Assistance Center on PBIS, 2010.

What Type of Training Is Involved?

Most states have PBIS training sites, mostly housed in departments of education or large universities. Some states use the "cohort method," in which districts apply to the cohort and are trained over a one-to-three-year period. Emphasis is on building local capacity and implementing a team-led approach, so audiences are typically school teams. Some states offer a variety of training opportunities for coaches to continue the process of implementing and sustaining PBIS. Still other districts conduct trainings on their own, without the benefit of a large organization to turn to for PBIS training knowledge and experience. If you are interested in formal PBIS training (which we recommend), start with your state department of education or visit www.pbis.org/pbis-network to find your state coordinator. There are also regional PBIS technical assistance centers, including the Midwest PBIS Network, the Mid-Atlantic PBIS Network, the Northeast PBIS Network, and the Northwest PBIS Network.

What Type of Funding Is Required?

Funding needs vary from state to state as well as from district to district. When your school or district makes a decision to implement the PBIS framework, contact the PBIS centers in your state to learn about funding requirements. Some expenses might include the cost of training as well as manuals, guest teachers for the PBIS Leadership Team attending training, planning time for the Leadership Team, release time to prepare lesson plans for teaching schoolwide expectations, incentives for a reinforcement or reward program, and general office supplies. Some schools also purchase a curriculum for Tier 1 schoolwide interventions, such as Second Step or Responsive Classroom, to integrate within the framework. In addition, your school may decide to use a web-based information system, such as SWIS (see pages 71–75), that requires a subscription fee. As you will learn, some expenses are covered by state or regional organizations, while some belong to individual districts. When Char has met with prospective schools or districts, she has used a simple cost-benefit example demonstrating the contributions of each entity. An impressive review of the costs of implementing PBIS versus the costs of suspensions and expulsions for individuals, schools, and communities can be found at the PBIS website. See www.pbis .org/policy-and-pbis under the heading "Evaluation Briefs" for a detailed breakdown of these costs.

> **Resource**
> The PBIS website (www.pbis.org) is developed and maintained by the OSEP Technical Assistance Center on PBIS and offers a wide range of resources, including practice and policy briefs, for schools, districts, states, and regional centers. It houses presentations and training videos you can use for personal and professional development in PBIS. The site also contains information about state coordinators so you can find names and contact information (see www.pbis.org/pbis-network).

What Are the Expected Outcomes of PBIS?

Having good behavioral *systems* and disciplinary *practices* in place and using *data* to confirm or deny your hunches will create outcomes that every school wants to see: improved social and behavioral competence and improved academic achievement. Schools that use the PBIS framework see a decrease in office discipline referrals (ODRs) and suspensions and an increase in academic achievement. Teachers have more time to teach, students have more time to learn, and administrators have more time to run the school rather than spending their days dealing with behaviors. All of this improves favorability with parents and families, stakeholders, and the surrounding community.

Teachers and staff also may experience their schools and students in a different way. Beth recalls talking with a middle school teacher whose school was in its second year of PBIS implementation. She had been ready to resign her position and leave the field of teaching altogether when her school adopted PBIS. But using PBIS completely changed her experience in the classroom and her view of her career by giving her the tools to work with disruptive students. Now she is recommitted to her profession and reenergized in her work with students. Stories like this from teachers and administrators are common and, though anecdotal, they represent the powerful potential of PBIS for preventing or slowing staff turnover, which remains a huge challenge for schools.

The PBIS Leadership Team

Implementing and sustaining PBIS schoolwide occurs through the guidance and actions of a leadership team dedicated to this purpose. It is critical to develop a strong team in which members are knowledgeable about PBIS practices, are enthusiastic and motivated advocates of this behavioral approach, and possess a variety of skills and attributes that will contribute to the team's effective function. You can find a wealth of information on leadership and team functioning within the literature in the fields of education, business, and health care. Leaders, including the PBIS Leadership Team, model commitment to the vision of what a PBIS school will look like and the benefits for all staff and students. This clear vision will draw the school community into action.

> Successful implementation and sustainment require a hands-on PBIS Leadership Team that is dedicated to doing the work involved with PBIS.

When a building's PBIS Leadership Team is well developed and well coached, the tasks associated with initial implementation are divided among team members. In many cases, someone on the building's staff performs the PBIS Leadership Team coaching function; however, this does not mean that the coach becomes the only face of PBIS in the school—nor does he or she do all the work involved. We have seen coaches become experts

in PBIS, and, when their leadership team meets, members remain somewhat dependent on the coach and hesitant to take responsibility for tasks, while the coach's to-do list becomes unmanageable. Then, if the coach leaves the building or burns out from shouldering so much of the responsibility for PBIS, the team flounders. For this reason, successful implementation and sustainment require a hands-on PBIS Leadership Team that is dedicated to doing the work involved with PBIS. Team members must reflect their strong vision for the school, so that not only the team but the whole school community enthusiastically embraces the work.

This chapter provides information on setting up a PBIS Leadership Team in your school. We describe how the team operates to guide the implementation process, and we detail the specific role that administrators play in PBIS implementation. Because the PBIS coach is so critical to success, we devote another whole chapter to this role; see chapter 3 for more information about PBIS coaching.

Role of the PBIS Leadership Team

Although we talk about all the tasks, roles, and responsibilities of the PBIS Leadership Team, we also want to talk about creating true leadership that rises above and beyond simply managing the tasks. An article in *Harvard Business Review* describes leadership as the ability to "influence, motivate, and enable others to contribute toward organizational success."[1] We believe this fits well

---

1. Nayar, 2013.

with the role of the leadership team collectively and the importance of building the capacity of team members and all school staff in PBIS concepts and practices. The PBIS Leadership Team is not a closed group. The administrator, the coach, and all team members have a role in motivating and inspiring staff and students to achieve the shared vision and outcomes.

The PBIS Leadership Team is responsible for implementing PBIS throughout the school. In conjunction with the broader staff, this group tackles many of the foundational, behind-the-scenes tasks and decisions that determine how PBIS will function in a specific school building. For example, the leadership team works with staff to create a list of behavioral expectations for all students and sets the pace of implementation. The process should ensure that behavioral expectations reflect the school's diversity. The team ensures that school staff are trained to teach behavioral expectations and to provide specific acknowledgment to students when they demonstrate these expectations. Teaching and acknowledging behavior is important for staff to ensure they are successfully using PBIS. Team members continually evaluate and improve PBIS practices, and they inform others about their work. At least once a month, the team presents data to staff, gives a general update on PBIS implementation, and solicits input from staff. The team may also communicate outcomes to the school board, the district administration, and the wider school community, including families. In short, the leadership team serves as the public face of PBIS and

provides the momentum to sustain its practices over the long term.

Figure 2.1 illustrates the main goals and tasks of the PBIS Leadership Team. (This graphic is included in the *PBIS Implementation Blueprint* as well as in other resources on the PBIS website, www.pbis.org.) Note the team's primary functions: making agreements, creating a data-based action plan, implementing the plan, and evaluating implementation, fidelity, and outcomes. **Figure 2.2** summarizes the key responsibilities of the administrator, the coach, and the other members of the PBIS Leadership Team.

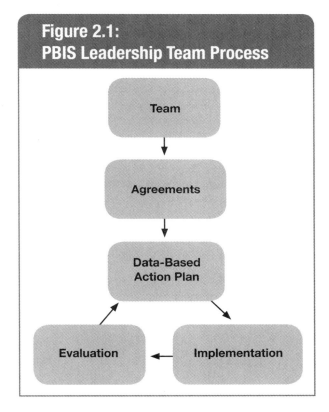

**Figure 2.1:
PBIS Leadership Team Process**

Figure 2.2: Key Responsibilities and Tasks for PBIS Leadership Team Members

Role	Key Responsibilities	Tasks Involved
Administrator	Actively support PBIS	• Communicate the vision and inspire staff buy-in and achievement • Publicly state support for PBIS with stakeholders: entire staff, district, families, and community • Dedicate financial and practical resources to implementing and sustaining PBIS

continued >

Figure 2.2: Key Responsibilities and Tasks for PBIS Leadership Team Members, continued		
Role	**Key Responsibilities**	**Tasks Involved**
Administrator (continued)	Support PBIS as a priority	• Identify PBIS within the top three priorities for school improvement • Document this priority in the written plan, newsletters, etc.
	Attend PBIS Leadership Team meetings regularly	• Attend most meetings • Share leadership • Inspire and motivate staff and students • Support coach and others • Implement decisions • Fund startup costs
	Ensure that the PBIS Leadership Team meets regularly	• Provide resources (release time, paid time, space, and materials) • Encourage team to schedule meetings to present progress to others
Coach	Assist the team's implementation of the elements of PBIS	• Recognize missteps taken by the team and work to get back on course • Collect, understand, and use data • Assess fidelity
Rest of the team	Is organized and meets regularly	• Reflect and model vision for PBIS • Identify essential roles: team lead, notetaker, timekeeper, data resource person, etc. • Set calendar dates and times for a full year's worth of meetings • Use an action plan and determine accountabilities for who, what, how, and when tasks will be completed • Document decisions (in meeting minutes)
	Use data to make decisions	• Access and use data that measure progress toward implementation • Review data at the beginning of each meeting • Use student data (ODRs) to identify school needs, to guide problem-solving and action planning, and to reevaluate actions and outcomes • Adopt a routine for reviewing implementation and outcomes regularly throughout the year
	Present data to staff and community	• Plan frequent opportunities to demonstrate progress and outcomes • Frequently solicit staff and parent input • Set up regular presentations to school board, parent-teacher organization, and other essential groups

Role of Building Administrators in PBIS Implementation

Building administrators are key to successful implementation of PBIS. Research clearly demonstrates how important administrative support is for implementing and sustaining PBIS.[2] What's more, research on staff investment in PBIS tells us that administrator influence is essential if we want staff to adopt PBIS initiatives.[3] Schools trying to implement PBIS without administrative leadership often struggle to get staff members on board. Principals who clearly communicate and model the vision and the value of PBIS to their school community will have a grateful PBIS Leadership Team.

Building administrators and the leadership team will recognize and ensure full-school involvement in PBIS and that all staff and students are involved in a coherent and cohesive manner. Char recalls visiting an elementary school for an onsite PBIS evaluation and discovering that the color-coded acknowledgment tickets implemented by the team actually represented problematic behavior in the kindergarten classes, since the young students often confused the color categories. In other cases, she has seen students with disabilities being excluded from the schoolwide expectations because, as one teacher put it, "they were in special education and had their own rules." We continuously remind the schools we work with that all means *all*.

Commitment and Support

Having the administration on board provides the backbone needed to inspire the staff in using positive behavioral procedures. For some teachers, moving to a proactive behavioral strategy from a reactive one represents a huge shift in the way that they manage challenging behaviors. According to Kevin Filter's research, the level of staff buy-in is directly related to the way in which each staff member perceives the administrator's ability to successfully create and support change.[4]

Administrators can show their commitment to change through their vision and by identifying PBIS as one of the top three priorities for school improvement (in written plans, newsletters, and so on) and by acknowledging that it takes three to five years to fully implement the first tier of PBIS. In addition, budgetary support is essential for success. Administrators must secure adequate full-time equivalent (FTE) staff allocations for a coach and leadership team members. In our experience, many coaches are recruited or assigned responsibilities but nothing is removed from their other assignments. Coaches and team members need their workloads rebalanced in order to successfully carry out their PBIS responsibilities.

One thing that we appreciate about supportive administrators is how their involvement keeps the momentum of implementation rolling. When Beth was working as a coach, decisions could be made easily at her school because the principal was an active participant in PBIS meetings and played a role in the decision-making. Beth knew that PBIS would be in the school for the long haul when the principal took responsibility for announcing to the staff the new practices that were being implemented. Staff could voice their discontent and they would have discussions, but the principal always made the final decision based on what she thought was best for the school.

Support for Coaches

Administrators also need to support coaches by giving them adequate time to accomplish their role. If a coach is a building-based coach, the role and functions will take more time in the early stages of implementation than later, depending on how stable the process is and how well responsibilities are being shared among PBIS Leadership Team members. Though it's difficult to estimate, some

---

2. Coffrey and Horner, 2012.
3. Filter and Sytsma, 2013.
4. Filter and Sytsma, 2013.

coaches have told us they need anywhere from one-third to a full day per week to carry out their assigned tasks and responsibilities for PBIS. In some instances even more time is needed.

District-level coaches (sometimes called external coaches) are often half- to full-time, and they usually manage PBIS implementation in several schools. In addition to the number of schools, district-level staffing decisions should consider the stages of implementation at a coach's various schools. New schools generally require much more time and energy. Keep in mind, however, that schools that have used PBIS for many years may have had significant turnover and fallen off course. Consequently, they may require as much time and effort as a new school, and maybe more. *A word of caution:* Char has seen schools that, after formal training and stable data outcomes, decide they no longer need a full team and could rely solely on the PBIS coach or a dedicated teacher to continue implementation. Nothing could be further from the truth. Schools that are in a sustaining mode and continue to show full implementation and stable student outcomes continue to need support, but the amount and time requirements will vary.

With these factors in mind, we suggest administrators ensure that district-level coaches have a mixed caseload of schools representing a spectrum of needs and intensity. District coaches also need adequate FTE allocations of work hours devoted to the sustainment and improvement stages of PBIS, as well as to initial implementation.

As a coordinator and regional coach, Char worked with new coaches and planned coach trainings each year. One of the biggest obstacles she saw for coaches was the lack of time allocated to learn about PBIS, to develop skills, and to complete their tasks. Coach responsibilities were often add-ons to a full-time job. See chapter 3 for more details about the role of coaches.

Staff Development, Training, and Resources

Another way for the administration to show commitment to the PBIS vision is to provide staff development time for the entire PBIS Leadership Team to attend trainings. Administrators are committed to training the whole staff on Tier 1 universal interventions. When resources are required—such as release time, paid time, space, and materials—administrators take the lead to fulfill these needs. In some instances, staff may wonder why only select people go to the initial training. This is a good opportunity for administrators to explain the overall vision and importance of the prevention approach and to explain the training and level of support that will be provided to all staff.

Presenting the Team's Progress to the School

As implementation continues, administrators encourage the PBIS Leadership Team to present progress to the school faculty. Sharing leadership in this way empowers team members. For example, the team could do a presentation on data findings for office discipline referrals (ODRs). Or team members might present progress to district administration.

Communication

In the first stages of implementation, the administrator models commitment to the vision by supporting the PBIS initiative publicly with verbal, written, and visual statements. This support for PBIS should be evident to the entire staff, to the district, to families, and to the community. As implementation continues, the building administrator also plays a key role in communicating success with PBIS to the district as well as to the community. This means speaking at school board meetings and open houses where the outside community is invited in. It also includes written statements in newsletters and on the school or district website.

Participation

Building administrators may want to create a personal action plan for their participation in the PBIS implementation process. The plan can serve not only to guide their own actions but also to support future administrators who may replace them.

Active participation is a key way for administrators to demonstrate their commitment and support to the team and the entire school community.

The building administrator actively participates in PBIS training and leadership meetings, attending as often as possible. In addition, administrators can help by visiting classrooms and observing the practices of PBIS in action. These visits enable administrators to identify which teachers may be struggling with classroom management and may be in need of coaching. Even more important, it gives administrators the opportunity to acknowledge staff achievements and commitment, thereby increasing staff motivation.

Leadership

Successful implementation of PBIS relies on influence from the building administration, mainly the principal. The role of leadership regarding PBIS is more than merely managing tasks, but uniting staff. The principal guides the school in meeting yearly improvement plans and district-level initiatives. Sometimes principals make choices that are not popular with many staff but are good for the school as a whole. One school social worker told us of a time when her principal freed up a teacher from her daily advisory to do PBIS duties (managing the weekly "Caught You Doing Good" tickets and operating the school reward store). Other teachers thought this was unfair—they had to take on additional advisory students—but the principal felt this was important to keep PBIS on track. In the end, others could see the value of this decision, and to help them feel appreciated, the principal thanked the other teachers publicly for their understanding and their help in taking on the additional work.

Principals inevitably face teachers and other staff members who have philosophical objections to PBIS or who wonder if PBIS is even necessary. Schools that have not successfully implemented PBIS may cite a lack of leadership from building administration, and even district administration, as a reason for its failing. Academic success and test scores often take precedence over other initiatives,

such as reducing suspensions and decreasing challenging behaviors. All these challenges point to the need for administrators to be active leaders in PBIS implementation. Additionally, PBIS presents an opportunity for administrators to unite efforts to integrate academic and behavioral practices. After all, these two things are not independent.

Staff need to feel secure when asked to make a major systems change, going from a punitive discipline structure to one where we teach students not just reading and math skills, but also behavioral skills as a way to prevent disruptions to academic learning. According to researcher Sharon Lohrmann, when principals have difficulty leading a school through systemic changes, staff members often react with defensiveness, passivity, negativity, and unwillingness to collaborate.[5]

Building principals need to be openly committed to PBIS and to staff. Staff members need to see the principal as an active participant on the PBIS team. They also need to see the principal hold all staff members accountable for implementing Tier 1 interventions. The PBIS principles work with adults as they do with students; using a proactive, positive, supportive, and collaborative approach with staff will help. In all these ways, principals set the stage for successful PBIS implementation by being leaders.

Forming the Rest of the PBIS Leadership Team

Once the administrator is on board with PBIS, the next step is to complete an audit of the other teams in your building. This is one way to work smarter, not harder. Consider all of the committees and groups currently meeting in your school to ensure that the PBIS Leadership Team will integrate efficiently with the other teams and not duplicate what they are trying to achieve. For example, take a close look at committees such as the Sunshine Club, Professional Learning Committee, and Character Education Committee, if you have these. Perhaps

5. Lohrmann et al., 2008.

the goals or makeup of some of these groups could be changed a bit, or the group eliminated altogether, to free up staff to join the PBIS Leadership Team.

To help assess the other teams in your building, complete the "Audit of Existing School Committees and Initiatives" matrix on page 33. List all your school's committees and groups and the purpose of each. Consider eliminating committees that no longer support your school vision, mission, and improvement plan. Combine committees with similar functions to free up staff time. *A word of caution:* This process, though logical, takes time to complete in a thoughtful, collaborative way; be sure to gather staff input, buy-in, and support for changes to existing committees.

What Is the Ideal Team Size and Length of Service?

We are often asked how big the PBIS Leadership Team should be. Sometimes the team size is dictated by the training organization. Keep in mind that as group size increases, so do group dynamics and complexity. Here are a few findings from research on group size:[6]

1. Ideal group size is five to seven.

2. Groups that are too small (fewer than five) may have limited viewpoints and lack the critical mass to achieve the best outcome.

3. Ideal size for decision-making and problem-solving may be groups of seven to fifteen.

4. Larger groups require more structure and facilitation.

However large or small you decide to make your PBIS Leadership Team, understand the advantages and disadvantages of various group sizes. If you have a larger team, provide the structure and facilitation needed and consider forming subgroups for specific purposes (for example, a group that tracks the data or organizes student recognitions).

Generally, team members agree to be part of the team for at least three years—long enough to become fluent and effective. You may want to consider a staggered rotation so that the entire team does not turn over at once. Expect, however, that there will also be turnover that is not planned. Be proactive in establishing a plan for who, how, and when new team members will receive essential training to assume new roles. When membership changes, your team may take a step back before progress resumes. Be patient and prepared. And be aware that new teams often need more facilitation than long-standing ones do. See the references and resources for materials on team development and facilitation.

Who Should Be on the Team?

The PBIS Leadership Team typically includes the building administrator, a designated PBIS coach, and other team members. The administrator takes on the task of inviting staff to be on the PBIS team, identifying an effective, representative group of individuals who will work well together. He or she identifies who will be the building's PBIS coach and carefully chooses staff from a wide spectrum of individuals. Because PBIS is a true schoolwide initiative, the team should be made up of a cross section of school personnel and community members including:

- general and special education teachers
- early childhood (including preK and kindergarten) and school-age teachers
- itinerant specialists
- behavior specialists
- paraprofessionals
- school psychologists and social workers
- counselors
- office staff
- hall monitors
- librarians and media specialists
- athletic coaches and directors
- custodians
- food service staff

---

6. Romano and Nunamaker, 2001.

- bus drivers
- students*
- parents and guardians*

Ideally, your PBIS Leadership Team will reflect the races and ethnicities of students and families in your building and community and will represent all grade levels (including preK and kindergarten) and disciplines, male-to-female ratios, cultural and religious backgrounds, and sexual orientations. This is crucial to setting up a system that will support the students and staff in your building who may not be part of the dominant culture, and it creates a climate that welcomes all students and their families. As your school begins implementing PBIS features, it's essential to focus on engaging all stakeholders and representing community values in order to improve the equity in your school discipline policies. In addition to representing a cross section of staff and community, consider individuals based on their skill set, their ability to work together as a group, and their motivation level. Potential team members may volunteer, or the administrator may recruit people according to what and how they will contribute to the purpose and desired outcomes of PBIS. For example, someone might be good with numbers, be loyal to the school, possess excellent classroom management skills, have knowledge of behavioral programs, or be well-connected to students. One administrator invited the teacher who wrote the most office discipline referrals to serve on the PBIS team, and the teacher ended up loving the experience. While the staff was initially surprised to see him on the team, they eagerly welcomed him and he proved to be an invaluable team member. What's more, his response to behavioral disruptions in his classroom became more proactive as a result of his time on the leadership team.

One benefit of having team members from across your school setting is that it increases the buy-in from all areas of the building and ensures that voices from all disciplines will be heard. This is important because you are building a schoolwide system that affects all staff and students. The needs of physical education teachers may be different from the needs of language arts teachers, which may be different from the needs of people who work in the office. The needs and expectations for kindergarteners will differ from those for fourth graders. Never assume that you know the needs of all areas of the school. Always work to bring consensus about what is appropriate for the school as a whole. When having discussions about handling voice levels in the classroom, for example, you may discover that the math teachers want more quiet, while the science, P.E., or kindergarten teachers allow kids to be louder.

> The administrator takes on the task of inviting staff to be on the PBIS team, identifying an effective, representative group of individuals who will work well together.

As you build your PBIS Leadership Team, its membership may change as the school year progresses and certainly from year to year. Building the team is a process that takes time; these teams develop into effective working groups through a series of phases. (For more on these phases, see "Getting Started as a Team" on page 28.)

Key Expertise Needed

Be sure someone on your PBIS team can provide *behavioral expertise*, especially as the team considers interventions that move from Tier 1 to Tiers 2 and 3. This could be the school psychologist, school social worker or counselor, or an experienced special education teacher. The team will benefit from this expertise during discussions of behaviors, such as determining the function of a student's behavior or designing interventions to decrease disruptive behaviors and improve a student's repertoire of acceptable behaviors.

---

*Due to confidentiality, when student or staff names are going to be discussed at a PBIS Leadership Team meeting, parents, guardians, and students should *not* be in attendance.

Your team should also identify someone who will take responsibility for *handling data tasks related to PBIS surveys and other assessments as well as student discipline and achievement data.* Currently, districts are encouraged to identify a person who can fulfill this role and serve as the PBIS assessment coordinator for all schools in the district. Schools interested in using the PBIS assessment tools should contact their state PBIS Leadership Team to identify the local assessment coordinator. The local coordinator will support and facilitate the school's use of assessment tools.

In addition, designate one PBIS Leadership Team member—often the coach—who is willing to take responsibility for *assisting your school in using PBIS assessment tools and data* for active problem-solving, measuring progress, assessing fidelity, and identifying supports needed for sustaining PBIS. We encourage coaches to infect their colleagues with an insatiable curiosity about the data on progress, fidelity, and outcomes so that multiple members of the team become data experts and use data frequently to track their school's implementation.

Getting Started as a Team

Once the PBIS Leadership Team members have been identified and have made a commitment to the process, it's time to build a cohesive group by creating shared agreements, particularly when it comes to running meetings and making decisions. The following ten tasks should be decided at your first meeting.

1. Develop Norms and Decision-Making Procedures

It is helpful for teams to begin with a discussion of the norms that will guide their work together. Set a regular date, time, and place for your meetings (such as every other Monday at 7:00 in Ms. Nelson's room). The facilitator should set the agenda and send it out ahead of time so members can come

prepared. Besides these logistics, decide how you will run your meetings (for example, how to deal with disagreements, keep the workload equitable, and celebrate progress together).

You'll also want to determine how you will make decisions. There are many ways to do this, so be sure to discuss the options as a team. Establish whether you will use full consensus (everyone agrees wholeheartedly), working consensus (everyone agrees but some members may have reservations), majority vote, fist-to-five consensus building, or something else. Each method has pros and cons, but defining how decisions will be made from the start will likely help move your team along when it is faced with making a controversial decision for your school. Allow all voices to be heard, share options and opinions, and resolve to make a decision. To record the norms you establish, see page 38 for a reproducible sample form titled "Routines for Conducting Effective and Efficient Meetings."

At your first PBIS team meeting, you might establish ground rules such as the following:

- Meetings will start and stop on time.
- Facilitator will run the meeting.
- Notes will be taken on action items, not on people.
- Use "I statements."
- Everyone gets a turn to speak.
- Be open to new ideas.
- It's okay to disagree.
- Maintain meeting confidentiality—be careful about sharing staff or student names outside of the meeting.

Some teams create a matrix for detailing members' behavior, which is another way of establishing operating norms and behavioral expectations. Imagine practicing in words and actions what you may be doing with students, as shown in **figure 2.3** on page 29.

Figure 2.3: Sample PBIS Leadership Team Behavioral Matrix	
Respect, Learning, and Responsibility	
PBIS team members model respect.	• Smile, be friendly, and greet each other. • Listen to others' ideas, saving questions and comments until they have finished speaking. • Stay on task. • Be on time and attend at least 80 percent of team meetings.
PBIS team members model learning.	• Be open to new ideas. • Participate in professional development opportunities. • Share articles pertinent to team discussions.
PBIS team members model responsibility.	• Be an active participant—volunteer, offer to help others. • Meet action plan deadlines.

Resource

The Florida PBIS Project has a whole set of resources to help leadership teams and coaches handle the common challenges that arise in group work. Go to flpbis.cbcs.usf .edu/coaching/school.html and scroll down to "Resources to Support Coaching."

PBIS Leadership Teams and the TIPS Model

As you form your PBIS Team, consider adopting Team-Initiated Problem-Solving (TIPS). This research-based approach to problem-solving at the team level includes a model for establishing effective teams, which you can integrate into the development of your PBIS team. A school using TIPS receives additional training on how to follow prescribed meeting foundations, which outline the roles, responsibilities, procedures, and follow-up for effective, efficient meetings. The goal is to ensure that meetings have predictability, participation, accountability, and communication. TIPS also includes an electronic system for recording meeting minutes. For a more detailed discussion of TIPS, see chapter 5.

2. Establish Team Roles and Responsibilities

Team meetings are more effective, efficient, and organized when roles and responsibilities are clearly defined and shared. Begin with identifying team members to take on the following roles:

- **Team leader or facilitator:** someone skilled in running meetings and handling issues that are common in group work.

- **Notetaker (or at least decision-recorder):** someone skilled at taking thorough, accurate notes and who will follow through with sending the notes to all team members in a timely manner—no more than two days after the meeting. These can be shared in a variety of ways, including via Dropbox, wikis, or Google Drive.

- **Timekeeper:** a team member who ensures that meetings start and stop on schedule.

- **Data manager:** a person with data expertise who is responsible for verifying that data are being collected and recorded consistently and accurately. This person should bring current referral data to the meetings. (Alternatively, you might opt to create a subteam to handle the task of managing data.)

- **Archivist:** someone who collects and stores meeting notes and photos to tell the school's PBIS story.

3. Schedule Regular Meetings

Try to schedule meetings for the whole year up front. It's easier to reschedule than to find time once the school year has begun. In our experience, new teams frequently meet every two weeks. Whatever meeting schedule you choose, try to make the process predictable and productive. You are creating the structural support for ongoing action. Start and end on time and take attendance.

4. Establish a Meeting Agenda

Many teams create a standing agenda that reflects regular topics pertinent to early phases of implementation. (For a template, see the reproducible "PBIS Leadership Team Meeting Agenda" on pages 34–35.) Well in advance of each meeting, share the agenda with team members and solicit their input. This allows time to modify the agenda as needed. It may be helpful to differentiate topics on the agenda; for example, some items might be purely informational while others need to be discussed or a decision might be required on the topic. Also consider setting timelines or limits for each topic.

Note to Administrators
Consider adding a PBIS implementation update as a regular agenda item for full-staff meetings each month. This is a good way to inform your colleagues and staff about the progress of PBIS. You may use this time to celebrate successes or to gather new ideas for preventing disruptive classroom behaviors. The PBIS Leadership Team can speak at staff meetings, letting staff know about upcoming new systems or practices and seeking input. For example, if the PBIS Leadership Team would like to implement a monthly honoring ceremony for the whole school, use this meeting time to gauge the interest of staff and get their input to work out some of the details about how to select students. Or team members could lead some professional development by teaching staff a proactive reaction to a disruptive behavior. Beth always had teachers willing to play the disruptive student so she could model to staff how to help a student refocus.

Coach's Tip from Beth

Be proactive in prompting team members about upcoming topics by sending out the meeting agenda well ahead of time. This helps develop continuity and accountability. When team members know that one of the tasks they are responsible for will be discussed at a meeting, they are more likely to come to the meeting prepared to give an update on the item delegated to them.

5. Effectively Facilitate Meetings

Ensure that whoever leads or facilitates PBIS Leadership Team meetings has skills in running meetings and handling common issues in group work. We all know what it's like to be in a meeting that fails to cover the agenda or achieve action items, gets hijacked by off-topic items, or otherwise gets derailed. Establish leadership team norms that emphasize a shared approach with group accountability. For a sample procedural checklist for conducting meetings, see the reproducible "PBIS Leadership Team Meeting Checklist" on pages 36–37. This checklist has been developed to help you prepare for, conduct, and evaluate meetings. In addition, the reproducible "Routines for Conducting Effective and Efficient Meetings" on page 38 helps ensure that meetings are successful. Char, like all educators, has spent a lot of time in meetings. Meetings are costly in terms of staff time, and it is often rare for teams to officially evaluate their process. But ineffective meetings may be recognized by poor attendance and few, if any, positive outcomes.

6. Use Data-Based Problem-Solving at Each Meeting

Using data is an active part of your PBIS Leadership Team meetings and the team's work in general. As noted on page 29, we recommend that you designate a team member to serve as your data manager or assign a subteam to take on this role. However, as a group, you will still be interacting with data and building a decision-making system that relies on data. Indeed, data should inform *all* your PBIS decisions and practices. The team, with help from the coach and data manager, has the challenge of becoming fluent in understanding the various classes of data and the tools that measure progress, fidelity, and outcomes. At all times, team members need to feel that they have ready access to this information.

Effective use of data is a large part of the team's responsibilities from the very beginning, when you collect baseline data about the current state of your school to garner buy-in from other school staff. As the process of implementation moves forward, the team continues to collect, analyze, and use data to determine next steps and to communicate progress to other staff, to administrators, and to the larger community. See chapter 4 to learn about specific data tools and resources.

As you work to improve the behavioral climate in your building, staff will need to have bold conversations about school—the environment, student and staff demographics and relationships,

schoolwide systems and practices, and the values and beliefs of the staff. Looking at data can open some wounds, but it can also eventually heal them. See chapter 5 to learn more about effective data-based decision-making.

7. Develop an Action Plan and Meeting Summary

Be sure to document the decisions and tasks that are generated in team meetings as well as the tasks that have been completed. Having all the activities of your PBIS Leadership Team in one document keeps key players responsible and provides an easy way to monitor and manage the implementation activities. In addition, it can be shared openly with school staff. **Figure 2.4** shows a sample action plan; notice that the first action item lists department chairs as well as PBIS team members as being responsible for establishing professional learning communities (PLCs). Sharing responsibility in this way invests your whole school in PBIS implementation. Also note how this action plan is rooted in the eight key features of the PBIS framework listed on page 11 in chapter 1. This keeps the team focused on PBIS and helps them avoid taking on action

Figure 2.4: Sample PBIS Action Plan

Key PBIS Feature	Action/Activity	Who Is Responsible?	Start Date	Completion Date	Review Date
#3	Create 3–5 schoolwide positive behavioral expectations	PBIS team Dept. chairs Admin.	ASAP	ASAP	Spring—SET evaluation
#6	Acknowledge student behavior in monthly recognition program	PBIS team Admin.	October	End of the year	Each faculty and PBIS meeting
#8	Establish data systems to monitor implementation of PBIS	Coach/data manager PBIS team Admin.	September	Ongoing—end of the year	Monthly PBIS team meetings

items that are not part of that mission. See page 171 of the appendix for a reproducible action-planning sheet.

Coach's Tip from Beth

When I started with PBIS, I tried to implement everything that our school was missing from the list of critical elements all at the same time. Many projects were started, memos were written, promises were made . . . and not much was implemented well. Overloading your team with too many things creates chaos and frustration. Start simple with a couple of items that can be easily accomplished, such as developing the three to five schoolwide positive behavioral expectations or creating the criteria for Student of the Month, and then slowly start adding other items.

---

8. Evaluate Team Meetings and Functioning

Build in a simple process for checking in with team members about meetings, including meeting efficiency and general functionality of the team. This can be as simple as a "thumbs-up–thumbs-down" voting system. The TIPS model discussed earlier includes a very brief member feedback piece on meeting efficacy. Also be sure to have a process for ensuring and reviewing the accomplishment of action steps. Be open to making adaptations to improve the process. Part of this process will undoubtedly include addressing team turnover. Assume turnover will happen on the leadership team and have a plan for preparing and engaging new team members.

9. Follow-Up and Next Steps

At the close of every meeting, review and summarize decisions and next steps, including assignments, due dates, and future meeting dates.

10. Celebrate and Share Successes

Though gratifying, implementing the PBIS framework is a lot of work for everyone involved. It's critical for the PBIS Leadership Team to acknowledge and celebrate the successes achieved as you advance toward full implementation. Plan celebrations to share these successes with the whole school—both staff and students.

Audit of Existing School Committees and Initiatives

List *all* your current building committees and initiatives and fill in the columns for each. Then review the results and answer the questions that follow the chart.

Committee or Initiative Name	Research- or Evidence-Based?	Purpose?	Promotes Safe Schools or Academic Achievement?	Possible to Combine, Tweak, or Eliminate?
	Yes No		Yes No	Yes No
	Yes No		Yes No	Yes No
	Yes No		Yes No	Yes No
	Yes No		Yes No	Yes No
	Yes No		Yes No	Yes No
	Yes No		Yes No	Yes No

What committees or initiatives duplicate efforts?

What committees or initiatives could be combined, refocused, or eliminated?

Make an action plan to track your next steps.

PBIS Leadership Team Meeting Agenda

Date: _____

Meeting facilitator: _____

Notetaker: _____

Timekeeper: _____

Attendees: _____

Review Time Allotted: _____

Things Going Well		Critical Issues and Concerns	
Topic	Data	Topic	Data

continued >

PBIS Leadership Team Meeting Agenda, continued

Action Items Time Allotted: _____

Item	Action Plan/Responsible Person/Due Date
Data review (ODRs, suspensions)	
Progress toward meeting previous action items	
Follow-up from previous action items	
Additional items	

Next meeting date and time: _____

Next meeting facilitator: _____

PBIS Leadership Team Meeting Checklist

Preparing for the Meeting

Person Responsible:

	Review agreements and tasks from previous minutes.
	Identify/review/develop agenda items.
	Invite/remind/prepare participants.
	Prepare/review materials.
	Check/confirm logistics (e.g., room, location, time).
	Other:

Opening the Meeting

Person Responsible:

	Acknowledge/introduce participants.
	Review meeting purpose.
	Review/assign roles.
	Review/modify agenda items (e.g., discussion, decision, information).
	Assign number of minutes for each agenda item.
	Set/review meeting rules and routines.
	Other:

Conducting Business

Person Responsible:

	Follow agenda items.
	Stay within timelines.
	Follow/review rules and routines.
	Restate/review/remind others of each agenda item's purpose or outcome.
	Other:

continued >

PBIS Leadership Team Meeting Checklist, continued

Concluding the Meeting	
Person Responsible:	
	Review meeting purpose.
	Review/summarize agreements and tasks.
	Evaluate extent to which agenda items were addressed.
	Review new agenda items.
	Review compliance with rules and routines.
	Acknowledge/reinforce participation, actions, and outcomes.
	Indicate next meeting date, time, and place.
	Other:

Following Up	
Person Responsible:	
	Distribute minutes.
	Complete agreements and tasks.
	Contact/remind participants.
	Prepare for next agenda.
	Other:

Other Notes/Observations

Routines for Conducting Effective and Efficient Meetings

As you establish group norms, use the following chart to record your team's decisions about how meetings will be conducted and problems solved.

1. How are decisions made?

2. How are problems, conflicts, and disagreements to be resolved or processed?

3. How are roles and responsibilities (such as leadership/facilitation, recording minutes, reporting) assigned and conducted?

4. How is participation encouraged and reinforced?

CHAPTER 3

The PBIS Coach

In the world of PBIS, *coaching* refers to a set of functions that are needed to support and guide the PBIS Leadership Team and school as they work to implement and sustain the key features of PBIS. The research literature indicates that real change in classrooms is related more to coaching than to training alone.[1] Experts Kathy Froelich and Enrique Puig say that both the art and science of coaching are necessary for successful professional learning experiences.[2] The key functions of coaching are described in the *PBIS Implementation Blueprint* (see www.pbis.org) and include the skills and knowledge needed to assist PBIS Leadership Teams during initial training, implementation, and sustaining and continuous improvement phases. PBIS coaches at the school level assist teams in adapting the PBIS framework to their particular school and in using data regularly to ensure fidelity in implementation and in achievement of outcomes.

In many districts, schools have two PBIS coaches: an external coach and an internal coach. External coaches tend to be outside the school at the district or regional level and may coach more than one school building. They are the liaisons between the school and the district, ensuring that school improvement plans are followed and that PBIS teams are completing action plans. External coaches can act as resources for the internal school-level coaches.

The internal PBIS coach is usually a staff member in a specific school who has flexible, limited teaching responsibilities and a solid knowledge of behavior concerns in the building. A school psychologist, school counselor or social worker, or a special or regular education teacher may serve as a school's internal PBIS coach. Occasionally, an assistant principal may serve as the coach. Our caution is that you ensure that whoever functions as the coach has the time and availability to complete the tasks. We have discouraged principals from assuming this role because of their enormous workload. In addition, selecting a peer to perform coaching helps to reduce any perceptions of authority and performance issues that might interfere.

There is typically one internal coach per school, but we have seen instances where two staff members may co-coach. Coaches assist the PBIS Leadership Team with problem-solving tasks, act as a liaison between the school and the district (or external) coach, and can be a resource to other schools' PBIS teams. They can also coach teachers in real time by assisting in their classrooms to model and guide teachers in implementing strategies at each PBIS tier. For small districts, these responsibilities may be assigned to an external district-level coach who serves multiple buildings. See our discussion on pages 23–24 in chapter 2 about coach caseloads.

As Char describes: "When I meet new coaches who are with their teams at the beginning of a two-year training process, I recognize in them both enthusiasm and a sense of anxiety. When I started

---

1. Joyce and Showers, 1995.
2. Froelich and Puig, 2007.

as a PBIS state coordinator, I had to hit the ground running. I knew a lot about PBIS for individual students and as a schoolwide system of practice, but I had a lot to do to pull that together in a meaningful way for coaches and their teams. Early on, my team and I struggled to define what it meant to be a coach: *What did coaches do? Who should be a coach? What was the difference between a coach and a team leader?* In those early days, we offered meetings and networking opportunities for both coaches and team leaders. Today, role descriptions are widely available on state and national websites. Team and coach roles are explained at administrator meetings before schools apply and defined again once schools have been accepted into a cohort. We urge administrators to recruit people whose skills match the role descriptions and strongly advocate for a full-time equivalent (FTE) assignment so that coaches can be successful. Still, coaches often report that they are struggling to understand the scope of their job and what they need to be successful. So we build in ongoing training and support the entire system so that no component is standing on one leg. Now, many states provide regular, structured support for coaches."

> In this chapter, we discuss coaching as a set of PBIS functions performed within the context of the schoolwide system.

In this chapter, we discuss coaching as a set of PBIS functions performed within the context of the schoolwide system. We describe the role and associated responsibilities, explaining the significance of coaching for and within the schoolwide system. We also talk about what knowledge coaches need, how to continually develop as a coach, and where to find resources.

What a Coach Is *Not*

As we clarify the role and responsibilities of a PBIS coach, we believe it is important to identify what is *not* part of the coach's role. First, coaches are not administrators. They do not have responsibility for personnel decisions or staff evaluations. This can get a little murky because sometimes coaches conduct observations within the school and in classrooms around PBIS implementation, but this is not for purposes of evaluating staff. PBIS coaches gather and report data, and sometimes data can be associated with the school staff in sensitive ways that require thoughtfulness. Coaches and other team members may notice staff not following through on aspects of implementation. Reasons for this vary. Regardless, coaches do not handle personnel performance issues. A coach may use this as a prompt to look at the school data with the team to see if there is a training need. Coaches may also encounter staff conflicts and become inadvertently involved. Again, the coach's role is not to serve as a professional mediator but to work with the PBIS team to facilitate compromise, conflict resolution, and consensus building.

Role of the PBIS Coach

The role of the PBIS coach is interesting and challenging—an exciting career opportunity for any educator. Most of us know a little bit about coaching as it relates to sports and perhaps academic or instructional coaching or teacher mentoring. While some of the same skills apply, the PBIS coaching role is quite broad. Recall that the PBIS framework is defined as a set of practices that are applied throughout the schoolwide system. The coach thus serves not only the PBIS Leadership Team, but the entire system of the school as well. Because PBIS aims to change the system, PBIS coaches are considered change agents. Consequently, coaches benefit from a broad understanding of how systems change, from the big picture of PBIS, and from the details of process steps (such as team and action planning), practices, problem-solving with data, and communication.

Basic Knowledge That Coaches Need to Be Successful

There are several possible levels of coaching in PBIS. These include a local, or leadership team, coach, also known as an internal coach, and coaches who work at the district, regional, or state level. We will focus our discussion on the internal, or school-based, coaching role.

Coaches are a primary support to the PBIS Leadership Team in achieving and sustaining the major features of PBIS implementation. To educate others about PBIS, coaches should be able to explain the features and use examples of what they look like in action, across all grade levels and disciplines. For instance, coaches in elementary schools should be able to describe how a calming strategy would work for a kindergartner as well as for a fourth grader. They should also have a bag of tricks for preK teachers. Coaches at the middle school level need to know that eighth graders do not want to be treated the same as sixth graders. And coaches at the senior high level should know how the schoolwide expectations are taught to ninth graders versus to twelfth graders. Examples of PBIS features in action can be collected either from other schools in the area that have already implemented PBIS or from websites. We have found that many coaches underutilize state, regional, and national websites as resources for their schools; numerous helpful websites are available. See the references and resources for some examples. Also check your own state or regional PBIS initiative.

Coaches benefit from developing confidence and gentle assertiveness to nudge team or staff members to follow through with surveys or to redirect a team that gets off course.

One key area of knowledge coaches need to cultivate and pass on to the team relates to data resources. The PBIS initiative provides all the Tier 1 evaluation tools needed for successful implementation at www.pbisapps.org. Chapter 4 discusses these tools and how to use them. As you get started in your new coaching role, take time to learn about these tools and get familiar with their acronyms and abbreviations: TIC (Team Implementation

Checklist), SAS (Self-Assessment Survey), SET (School-Wide Evaluation Tool), BoQ (Benchmarks of Quality), TFI (Tiered Fidelity Inventory), ODR (office discipline referral), and more. Becoming very fluent with acronyms and terminology will help you be a more effective coach who can also help team members develop a deeper understanding of the data and really use them.

Coach's Tip from Beth

Do not get caught up in doing too much too fast or comparing your school to another. Make sure you are monitoring your progress and ensure that your team reviews progress data when action planning and problem-solving. You want to understand what your data mean and distinguish between moving slowly and being stalled.

When I was a PBIS coach, I made sure every form was filled out, every checklist completed in a timely manner; I collected surveys from staff and students to get their opinions; I sorted behavior data eight different ways and still I wasn't sure what the next step should be. I remember talking with Char about this. Char's suggestions were simple—focus on only a couple of things rather than trying to tackle everything at once, and look closely at what the data are telling you.

In short, when it comes to PBIS, you need to be able to explain it, present it, teach it, model it, discuss it, and pass it on.

Skills

PBIS coaching skills include those behaviors necessary to put knowledge into action, which means you will use all the skills you have acquired thus far working in education. In addition, since your coaching role involves coaching a system and a team in addition to individuals, it would be helpful to develop or hone skills in the following areas:

1. Group facilitation (effective meetings, planning, and follow-through; knowledge of group development)
2. Conflict resolution
3. Consensus building
4. Communication (written and oral)
5. System change practices

Attributes or Personal Characteristics

Personal attributes include not only inherited traits but also learned behaviors. Being a good coach is easier if you know your strengths and are willing to build on your needs. Remember that you don't have to be born with the characteristics of a successful leader and change agent—you can actively develop them. As you begin, consider identifying someone in your professional life whom you can count on to be honest with you. Then enroll that person as your personal mentor.

Think about the following characteristics. Which ones best describe you? Which ones do you need to develop? Ask your personal mentor to do this as well and then discuss them together.

- sociable
- patient
- flexible
- able to handle complex and ambiguous tasks
- resilient
- approachable
- trustworthy
- attentive to details
- able to see the big picture

Role of Administrators in Selecting and Supporting Coaches

Of course, prospective coaches need to understand the role, function, and responsibilities of the PBIS coach during the implementation process. Equally important, administrators need to understand the role, responsibilities, knowledge, skills, and competencies of a PBIS coach. Whenever possible, administrators should recruit a staff member who already possesses the knowledge and skills required for this coaching role. It is essential that administrators explain this role and function to the PBIS Leadership Team and staff at the very beginning of implementation. This paves the way for the coach to successfully lead implementation efforts.

Every school and district should ensure that it has a strong PBIS coaching system. If that sounds daunting or unfamiliar, one of the main reasons for this book is to help dispel those obstacles. Coaches can be trained. District and school administrators should commit to ensuring that there is funding available for new internal coaches to attend trainings and opportunities for them to network with other coaches. Creating and sustaining a strong PBIS coach is the responsibility of both the school and the district. (For more information, see the *PBIS Implementation Blueprint* at www.pbis.org.)

Self-Direction

In an emerging field where knowledge and application are constantly changing, professionals such as coaches need to be able to accommodate this change. Adopt the mindset of personal continuous improvement, if you don't already possess this view. The following list will help you discern where you are at as a PBIS coach and where you would like to go.

- Develop a personal mission and vision statement regarding PBIS coaching.
- Assess your knowledge, skills, and attributes (see the appendix on pages 169–170 for coach self-assessments).
- Develop a tangible self-improvement action plan, with goals that are achievable and measurable and with timelines that include benchmarks of achievement.
- Identify and develop resources for your self-improvement (personal, professional, tangible, and shareable).

Responsibilities of Coaches

Guide the Team

Guiding is a key aspect of what coaches do. You will be the one who teaches the PBIS Leadership Team about all aspects of PBIS at each stage of implementation. Guiding a team while you are still learning about PBIS yourself can be a challenge; however, if you participate in an organized training program, you will receive a solid foundation from experienced guides. Many state and regional PBIS agencies offer a multitude of online and onsite resources.

Clarify Concepts

As you learn the meaning of the basic PBIS concepts and terms, you will be one step ahead of your colleagues and can help them learn and integrate these terms as well. Try to describe the concepts in your own words, but know where to find resources that can help you explain difficult concepts and that can serve as resources for your colleagues as well.

Coach's Tip from Beth

Don't be alarmed if you do not understand every concept at the onset. Some of the concepts that confused me in the beginning were implementation with fidelity, data-based decision-making, and how to get the staff involved. Focusing on one aspect of the program at a time from which to build your knowledge base will help you avoid feeling overwhelmed with confusion.

Find Examples

Using examples of PBIS implementation will help bring otherwise dry concepts to life as you convey these new ideas to your team. From the myriad of possible examples, select those that best match your school's unique characteristics. For instance, many states have PBIS websites that can help you explain and define the concepts of PBIS. The national PBIS website (www.pbis.org) has vast resources, including videos, webinars, presentations, and briefs. Check the resource section of this book for more information. The digital content for this book includes a PDF presentation (see page 201 for instructions on how to download).

Model Data-Based Problem-Solving

With your PBIS Leadership Team, select a decision-making model that uses data to guide problem-solving. (See chapter 5 for more on data-based models.) As you learn about various tools and data sources, make sure you understand how to:

- use and interpret the multiple sources of data and tools
- implement and use the school's data system
- support and encourage the data manager or team in data collection
- ensure that behavioral referrals are completed and done with fidelity
- monitor that data are being entered into the data system in a timely manner
- ensure the team has current data
- report the data monthly to the staff
- show the team how to use the data to make decisions and evaluate progress

Once you understand these tools and data, you can gradually pass on this knowledge to your team members. Help them build their own understanding and capacity. Teach team members how to access, retrieve, report, and use the various sources of data.

Pace the Implementation

This is an important part of your role. Sometimes new teams are so enthusiastic that they try to do too much too fast. It's hard to recognize that while you are in the process. Remember that, as you implement each feature, you need to be sure that you have buy-in from the school staff and that you have thought about how each feature will be sustained in the face of any changes. Most teams with whom we have worked realize they need to slow down and make sure these elements are solidly in place. You may need to remind the PBIS Leadership Team that implementation occurs over time and is a long-term commitment.

Check Fidelity

A key part of your work will be using formal assessment tools to measure fidelity. Some teams may use the TIC, TFI, or SET or BoQ (these are covered

Figure 3.1: Sample PBIS Informal Fidelity Report

PBIS Component	Classrooms	Areas	Comments
Expectations are posted and visible (include nonclassroom areas).	Ms. Garcia Mrs. Johnson Ms. Pitt	Hallway 2nd-floor bathroom areas	Missing in media center and cafeteria
ODRs are filled out completely.	70% of random classroom ODR checks	N/A	Missing location and motivation
Teachers are using at least 3 interventions before ODR.	82% of random classroom ODR checks	N/A	Redirection seems to be used without success.
Teachers are actively supervising areas (hallways, entry, cafeteria).	Observed Ms. Olson and Mr. Lang	Morning hallway duty	They engaged with students and walked around the entry area.
4:1 positive to negative comments are used by all staff.	Observed Ms. Garcia and Ms. Pitt for 20 minutes during morning meeting	N/A	Ms. Garcia—15 positive, no negative comments; Ms. Pitt—12 positive, 2 negative comments
Staff reinforce positive behaviors in nonclassroom areas.	N/A	Morning duty	Staff greet students and say, "Thanks for taking your hat off."
Nonteaching staff (cafeteria staff, custodians, office staff) are using positive language with students.	N/A	Cafeteria	At breakfast, food service staff say "good morning" and "thank you."
5–8 students chosen at random can say the expectations.	N/A	Various	Yes—asked 6 students
Posters in the school reflect our student makeup.	Various	Various	Need more posters of Hispanic leaders; add to action plan at next meeting.
Behavior management staff follow school behavioral expectations and continuum for misbehaviors.	N/A	Various	Yes—used processing sheet, reminded students of expectations, referred 2 students who were fighting to administrator. Remind them to say "expectations," not "rules."

PBIS team member: Mr. Jordan

Date: 11/6/18

in detail in chapter 4) during the early implementation stage. Check with your state training center for guidance on using these tools. Some states prefer using the TFI over the other assessment tools because it simplifies the assessment process to one report. Be wary of completing any fidelity assessment in isolation and complete it with other members of your team to get a good measure of different voices. You may also be required to have an external, or district-level, coach complete the assessments with your team. Use this assessment data to action plan next steps for your team. **Figure 3.1** on page 44 shows an example of an informal checklist for fidelity. A reproducible checklist can be found on page 49. This could be used in between formal assessments as a quick check-in for your building. Encourage other PBIS team members to also complete the survey to get a good cross-sectional measure of your school.

Seek Ongoing Buy-In on Each Feature

When staff members buy in to the behavioral expectations and the behavioral learning matrix (detailed in chapter 7), you might assume that they will follow through with all the changes the school adopts when implementing PBIS. However, this is not always the case. Beth worked with a school that insisted on adding the IB (International Baccalaureate) learner profile to the behavioral expectations. Without that, the high school would not adopt the behavioral expectations. So, with a bit of wordsmithing from some of the teachers on the team, the new document was created and teachers were pleased and ready to implement the expectations. Remember, as you implement each feature, you need to be sure that you have buy-in from the school staff. Frequent discussions at staff and department meetings can help elicit staff members' thoughts, concerns, questions, and suggestions.

Coaches can help in many ways with staff buy-in, some similar to how students are supported when asked to change their behavior. Here are some things coaches can do:

- Listen to staff frustrations, validate them (change is hard!), and offer some technical assistance with the problem.

- Celebrate staff successes, even little ones. Honor the changes staff are making to improve the learning environment for students.

- Use data to support your ideas and share data with staff as often as possible.

- Include other staff members when designing posters, taglines, or other marketing tools.

- Make PBIS part of your school culture. Include it on your school's website, email staff simple survey questions to get their opinions, or hang charts and graphs in the staff area.

- Gently nudge staff who do not favor PBIS. Make yourself available, reserve judgments, encourage, and be helpful without pushing.

> Remember, as you implement each feature, you need to be sure that you have buy-in from the school staff.

Communicate

Prompt your PBIS Leadership Team to develop a strategy and plan for communicating PBIS progress and other related news with key stakeholders—the school board, the district administration, and the wider school community, including families. The following questions may help inspire your process of guiding the team's communications:

- What is the message? (key message, right message to right person, right time)

- Who is the audience? (internal, external, community)

- What is the purpose? (increase awareness, inform, engage, promote, foster buy-in)

- How will you do it? (newsletters, posters, workshops, case studies, presentations, videos, face-to-face conversations)

- When will you do it? (beginning: awareness; middle: progress; end: selling achievements)

System Coaching

One unique aspect of PBIS coaching is your role as a system coach. PBIS is a systems approach to changing the school climate. Some other coaching models describe a coaching role as working with individuals, providing guidance, giving performance feedback, and so on. In contrast, a system coach works with the leadership team, staff, and the school as an entire system. While you often support individuals within this system, you are working with your school as a whole and thus supporting the system.

Systems thinking: Let's try a simple description. Think about the system as the "whole," in this case the whole school. Then think about it as made up of interdependent groups of individuals, structures, and procedures. Systems theory predicts that a change in one part of the system will lead to changes in other parts. This approach moves us away from isolated departmental or individual approaches toward an understanding of integrated parts.

> Systems theory predicts that a change in one part of the system will lead to changes in other parts.

In our experience, education continues to be very hierarchical in structure. Initiatives often become associated with a certain branch, department, or administrator. When we visit schools, we sometimes hear staff refer to the PBIS Leadership Team as "those people," or we hear team members talk about feeling as if PBIS is in competition with character education initiatives. These examples suggest that the "whole" has not yet been developed in these schools. The priorities of various initiatives have not yet been integrated. PBIS is a schoolwide system, and if it is to become truly incorporated into the culture of a school, the PBIS team cannot work in isolation and initiatives cannot compete. Again, this requires a big-picture view and thoughtful integration of all parts of the process for the purpose of achieving important shared outcomes.

Developing as a Coach

Few people would argue with the need for education professionals to be on a continuous

improvement plan. Education is, after all, our very business and our raison d'être. We teach, and we are lifelong learners. What may have changed over the last decade is our deeper understanding of how best to foster continuous and deep learning. We laugh often during PBIS team training that we have abandoned the "train and hope" model (in which the building staff sit through a one-day training with hopes that they will buy in and be able to implement it on Monday morning). Instead, administrators have restructured staff training based on a team approach that uses frequent teaching and ongoing coaching. We know, for example, that the "sit and get" model translates to about 1 percent of change in a classroom, while training combined with ongoing coaching leads to a 95 percent change in classroom practices.[3] That's terrific! But how does it work for you? *You* are the coach.

Some of us in the PBIS initiative began our work with little guidance for our coaching roles. When Char began, she struggled some and had several trial-and-error learning experiences. She was lucky to find some of the pioneers around the country from whose experience she learned many lessons, not the least of which was to be patient and accept that everything was not going to unfold simply or quickly. She heard Susan Barrett and her colleagues in Maryland speak at a national conference on PBIS, in which Susan said, "We are building the plane as we fly it." Aptly stated and oh-so-true. Through our collective experience, we have developed the following list of important lessons for those of you taking on the role of a PBIS coach:

1. You have to be comfortable with ambiguity and recognize that it is not necessarily bad.

2. It's important to network with others in similar positions, especially with those who have more experience than you do. Don't be shy about reaching out beyond your district or state. The PBIS community is extremely supportive and welcoming.

3. As a coach, you need to be self-directed, empowered to seek out information, and comfortable with creating some of your own answers and clarity.

---

3. Joyce and Showers, 1995.

This section will provide some shortcuts, tips, and voices of experience to help you move along a continuum of growth.

Training and Resources

As an educator, you already have a rich base of knowledge, skills, and attributes. To that, we add means and resources for enhancing this base. As self-led, lifelong learners who are hungry to master their craft, coaches have several means by which to increase knowledge and skills in PBIS coaching. As we mentioned earlier, the majority of states are involved in some level of statewide implementation of PBIS. Some states have been using PBIS for more than fifteen years. This means that states frequently have a statewide system in place to support coaches. These coaching resources may include special online information, coach training, webinars, coaching conferences, and much more. Coaches can:

1. Participate in a formal team training that introduces a rigorous scope and sequence for PBIS implementation. We highly recommend these formal training processes, which include ongoing training and coaching to both coaches and leadership teams. Team trainings provide a very important source of understanding and team capacity building.

2. Attend specialized training and networking opportunities for PBIS coaches. Often, these are offered by state departments of education. Some states even sponsor statewide conferences for coaches. These events provide opportunities for applied learning and practice.

3. Find and utilize resources.

   a. Contact your district office to see if it has a support system for PBIS and PBIS coaching, including formal team training and coaching support.

   b. Contact your state or regional PBIS office for coaching resources. (For a list of these offices, see the references and resources or go to www.pbis.org/pbis-network.)

   c. Visit the PBIS website (www.pbis.org). It is full of information on PBIS in general; on national presentations, evaluation tools, and blueprints for evaluation, implementation, and training; and on state, regional, and national conferences. These resources offer readily available online material as well as webinars and other forms of technical assistance.

   d. Access other websites that focus on PBIS and the role of coaches.

   e. Use online resources for coaches, which include practice examples, forms, and contact information. These, too, are offered by many state departments of education. Some offer specific "coaches' corners" that focus on issues specific to PBIS coaches.

4. Identify a mentor or coach with whom you can work.

5. Take self-assessments to gauge how you are doing as a coach. These simple tools will help guide your knowledge search. See the following section for details.

The references and resources (page 187) list state PBIS websites and other resources for PBIS coaches.

Self-Assessments

You can find several coach self-assessments at www.pbis.org and state websites. The appendix also offers an example; see pages 169–170. This quick and easy checklist will help you gauge how you are doing by identifying areas of knowledge, skills, and attributes for further development. The action-plan piece allows for self-reflection as you complete the boxes and hold yourself to a timeline for completion. Consider professional development to improve your skills as a coach; there are some terrific trainings available to people who want to be coaches. And we can't say enough about the importance of having a mentor, especially in the early stages as you are finding your way.

Coaching Is an Evolving Process

Many years ago, Char participated in a yearlong leadership fellowship called ARISE. The fellowship was designed to help participants become aware of themselves as instruments of change. Educators serving in leadership roles rarely get systematic training for some of these roles, and all were grateful for this opportunity. The fellowship focused on self-development as well as on leadership and organizational skills. The focus was powerful; the learning priceless. PBIS coaches are in a similar situation—as leaders, coaches, and change agents who need personal, process, and content knowledge to succeed.

As a change agent, you will also benefit from understanding how change occurs within systems and with groups of people. The science and practice of organizational development offers some great resources. Effective leaders (coaches) can and should adapt their leadership style to the readiness of the group they're working with. Move too slow, and you will bore some staff to tears; move too fast, and you will lose others to frustration. A good leader will continue to be aware of and adapt to the group's needs.

The role of the PBIS coach is always changing. One day you are a data analyst, the next, a cheerleader. For example, Beth once got permission to use the office laminating machine to make positive behavior posters for classrooms. Coaches must possess a positive attitude and know when to be firm. Coaches must be respectful of teachers and understand the job-related stressors teachers may be feeling. Coaches must be leaders, but they also must know when to follow. And coaches must face the reality that some staff members are going to love them, while others will want to show them the door.

> Although all team members are highly qualified, credentialed professionals, they may vary greatly in terms of experience, knowledge, and even willingness to participate in PBIS specifically.

The leader's role is a fluid thing. Groups of people come together with various levels of readiness. While the individuals within the group may be experienced and knowledgeable in their professions, the skill sets they possess may be different from what is needed in a new group organized for new purposes. The continuum of groups ranges from those who are unable or unprepared to take responsibility for the task, to those who are willing but lack confidence, and finally, to those who are able, confident, and willing to complete a task and take responsibility.

The same is true when we consider a new PBIS team. Although all team members are highly qualified, credentialed professionals, they may vary greatly in terms of experience, knowledge, and even willingness to participate in PBIS specifically. Frequently, members are willing but do not have a clear idea of how or where to start. In our experience, teams often report that those first few months or longer are like a "maze" where they experience a lot of stimulation and so much information that they sometimes lose track of the road map. In these early stages, coaches can offer more task direction. Coaches must be skilled in PBIS to guide their teams through the maze of implementation and beyond.

PBIS Informal Fidelity Report

PBIS Component	Classrooms	Areas	Comments
Expectations are posted and visible (include non-classroom areas).			
ODRs are filled out completely.			
Teachers are using at least 3 interventions before ODR.			
Teachers are actively supervising areas (hallways, entry, cafeteria).			
4:1 positive to negative comments are used by all staff.			
Staff reinforce positive behaviors in nonclassroom areas.			
Nonteaching staff (cafeteria staff, custodians, office staff) are using positive language with students.			
5–8 students chosen at random can say the expectations.			
Posters in the school reflect our student makeup.			
Behavior management staff follow school behavioral expectations and continuum for misbehaviors.			

PBIS team member: _____

Date: _____

Data and Assessment

Chapter 1 described the purpose of PBIS to achieve important social and academic outcomes for students. This is supported by three integrated systems: evidence-based practices to support students, active and efficient data collection and analysis, and systems to support staff. This chapter focuses on the role of data in achieving implementation, measuring progress, documenting outcomes, and sustaining all gains over time. It also provides recommendations for creating annual schedules to evaluate implementation data.

Role of Data in PBIS
Defining Data

In PBIS, it is essential to efficiently gather and use the right data, at the right time, at the right level, to inform the next right decision. What are data? Here are four viable answers:

A: Data are numbers.

A: Data are bits of information.

A: Data are detailed collections of information that can be queried, used, and grouped to provide answers to various questions.

A: Data are information you collect to learn something. (This is from a group of second graders. We think we like this definition best!)

Simply put: Data help you know where you are. If you don't know where you are, you won't have any idea where to go. Research indicates that fidelity of implementation and better team use of data for decision-making were the strongest indicators for sustained implementation.[1]

School Data

Data collection is the science behind the art of teaching. If you don't review the data collected by your school, you make decisions based on hunches or beliefs. Someone at one school said to us, "We don't want to change our system this year because we have always done it this way and aren't ready to change it." Tradition. The staff at this school also couldn't say what was working well and what needed more work. Consider the assumptions you make about your school or what the community perceives to be true about your school. Data are used to make decisions, evaluate progress, assess fidelity, determine trends, and measure outcomes.

Fortunately, you have easy access to much of the information you'll need. Here are data types that are already tracked at schools, along with descriptions and some ways to analyze them:

- office discipline referrals (ODRs; sometimes referred to as office behavioral referrals)
- suspension rates (What are the problem behaviors and who is getting suspended?)
- grades—midterm and final (Improved behavior generally improves grades.)
- general outcome measures of student learning (Are reading and math scores improving?)
- classroom observations (Are classrooms using similar language for behavioral expectations?)
- attendance and tardy rates (Look for patterns regarding classes and individual students.)

---

1. McIntosh, 2018.

- after-school program attendance (Kids who attend these programs are usually more connected to their schools.)
- meeting minutes (faculty, grade-level, team, other groups and committees that meet on a regular basis)
- nurse log books (Are students leaving the same class on a daily basis?)
- school facility repair reports (Look for vandalism.)
- summative data (collected once per year, usually at the end of a school year)
- number of students receiving free and reduced lunches
- survey results (staff and student climate surveys, parent surveys)
- disaggregated student data (How does your school ensure equity for students by race, ethnicity, and disability status?)
- student enrollment and unenrollment rates (Why are students coming to or leaving your school?)
- staff turnover rates (Why are staff leaving your school?)
- staff sick days used (Staff often use up their sick days at schools that are chaotic and frustrating.)
- summer school attendance (Improved academic skills generally lead to reduced problem behaviors.)
- district testing and year-end statewide testing results (Where is your school doing well and where is it struggling?)

This list illustrates how many data sources you may already have available, while also pointing out that you need to know which data are relevant for which questions before you develop effective solutions. For example, how do attendance patterns affect grades or behavior? How do suspension patterns affect academic performance, behavior, and school completion? Is there a correlation between ODRs in the morning and staff supervision

assignments? So, once you identify your questions, you can gather the right data and summarize trends in charts or graphs. From these charts, you can start to integrate data and begin problem-solving.

Types of Data in PBIS

One of the remarkable aspects of PBIS implementation is the emphasis on data as a key foundation. Remember in chapter 1 we introduced the three PBIS elements—data, systems, and practices—needed to support outcomes (see figure 1.2 on page 14). Not only are the data foundational to PBIS, but PBIS has developed the tools and the guidance to use them correctly so that you can implement the framework as intended. This is called *fidelity*. The tools are free (except for the Schoolwide Information System, or SWIS, suite) online at www.pbisapps.org and readily available to the team 24/7. The Tier 1 tools include the Tiered Fidelity Inventory (TFI), the Team Implementation Checklist (TIC), the Self-Assessment Survey (SAS), the School-Wide Evaluation Tool (SET), and the Benchmarks of Quality (BoQ). This section focuses on three types of data and the tools that measure them:

- implementation progress data
- program fidelity data
- student outcome data

Implementation Progress Data

During PBIS implementation, you will regularly measure implementation progress (also called effort) in two broad areas: attainment of key features and changes in student behavior. Your goal is to get all PBIS features in place. In doing this, your team will create data-driven action plans to guide your work. You track the progress on your action plans by using implementation data from surveys and PBIS assessment tools. These tools help you know where you are with the key PBIS features. Therefore, getting all the data assessments in place is essential.

In addition to implementation data, you will monitor behavioral data using ODRs. ODRs are helpful in determining if there are potential implementation gaps. If ODRs spike, your team can plan interventions strategically and effectively. Assessing progress includes looking at PBIS core features as well as at student behavior data.

Program Fidelity Data

Fidelity refers to the extent and accuracy with which your team and staff are implementing the PBIS core features, how well your plans are consistently followed by staff and students, and how well the framework is being used with integrity. Fidelity assessments are the tools used to answer the questions about accuracy and completeness of implementation: Are you doing PBIS as it was designed? Fidelity data can also help inform areas in your system that could benefit from PBIS coaching or additional training and staff development. Just as students are learning new skills, so are staff teams when implementing PBIS. Fidelity data can help identify areas where progress is going well and where additional support is needed. As noted previously, these measures have already been created and tested and are available online for free. You may also desire to develop or use some additional informal measures, such as observations, staff ratings, and surveys.

> *Fidelity* is the extent to which the core PBIS features are implemented as intended.

Generally, schools implement the PBIS core features gradually over time. Partial implementation means your school has established some but not all features. For example, your school achieves a total score of 50 percent versus 80 percent on a measure. This score might reflect progress in all features or achievement of some but not all features. This is expected. A new school usually achieves partial implementation. It varies how long it takes to achieve full implementation, but we know it is a multiyear process.

Schools that demonstrate all eight features at 70 to 80 percent or higher, depending on the assessment tool, are described as fully implementing PBIS with fidelity. At this level, the team should be seeing positive student outcomes as measured by lower ODR numbers and other indicators. Some specific student behavioral indicators include fewer ODRs from classrooms, during passing time, at recess, on the playground, or at lunch. Another example would be decreased disproportionality by race/ethnicity and disability status, fewer suspensions, improved attendance, improved school climate, and less teacher burnout.[2]

Note that sustained fidelity (fidelity measured over time) leads to measurable outcomes, not a single high score on a single tool at a single time. Fidelity and implementation data vary over time due to natural reasons such as staff and student turnover. The implication for practice is that teams need a routine of regular evaluation in order to identify shifts and make appropriate course corrections. (See pages 77–78 for examples of annual evaluation schedules.)

The goal of implementation is to achieve and sustain all PBIS core features at fidelity. For example, on the TFI, the Tier 1 criterion is 70 percent. Using the TFI is becoming common, and this tool's components are useful for program planning as well as fidelity assessment. Generally, new teams use the TFI at least quarterly.

The SET is an annual assessment for which the gold standard score for fidelity is 80 percent overall and 80 percent on teaching expectations to students. Research has shown that schools that achieve at least 80 percent on the SET total score report will demonstrate changes in student behavior as measured by ODRs.[3] The fidelity criterion on the BoQ, another annual assessment, is 70 percent.

The SAS, which is a measure of systemwide PBIS features based on staff perceptions, is another tool that can be used for measuring fidelity. According to research, in schools with higher levels of fidelity (above 80 percent on other measures), the SAS may actually be more sensitive to

---

2. Mercer, McIntosh, and Hoselton, 2017; Ross, Romer, and Horner, 2011.

3. Horner et al., 2009; Mercer, McIntosh, and Hoselton, 2017.

differences among schools because it represents higher levels of implementation and consensus among staff.[4]

If you have scores below the criterion on any of these tools, it means you have bits and pieces of PBIS in place, but not enough to claim full implementation or fidelity.

We have described several assessments here, but your district and school would not use all these tools simultaneously, only a selection. Research has shown that all the tools have good predictive value and are comparable to one another. Also, total scores versus subscale scores are better for school-wide fidelity measures.

Data Tip from Char

Achieving full implementation is not the finish line. I have seen schools achieve full implementation of Tier 1 in one to two years, but when measured at year three or four, those achievements had declined. Ongoing fidelity assessment is essential to sustainability and maintaining outcomes. Sustaining PBIS with fidelity *over time* is essential to improving student social and academic outcomes.

Student Outcome Data

What are outcome data and how do we measure them? Rob Horner, George Sugai, and other PBIS leaders note that at the end of the day, all the time, money, and human investments related to PBIS are about changing the school culture—improving student social and academic outcomes. Outcome data tell you how well your efforts are paying off toward meeting your desired results. The office discipline referral (ODR) is the most commonly used measure of student behavior across the nation. When PBIS was developed, there was no need to reinvent the ODR model, because ODRs tell you how many

students are leaving the classroom due to behavior problems and, therefore, are missing instruction. (See pages 68–75 for a detailed discussion of ODR data.) ODR data reflect the learning and social environment for students and staff.

PBIS implementation involves multiple and consistent data use for measuring progress, fidelity, and student outcomes to develop action plans and engage in continuous improvement. These same data are useful when communicating with stakeholders about what is going well in your school and what may need improvement. This allows school teams to make their own decisions based on facts. Presenting behavioral data along with academic data offers a complete picture of your school. It can help families decide if your school is a good fit for their child. If your community senses that there are too many fights in your school, see what the data say. Your data may show fights were not nearly as common as the community thought, and sharing that data with the community could help them see your school in a better light. Using your data will increase buy-in and support.

Assessment Tools

This section provides both an overview and a deeper understanding of each of the PBIS assessment tools for Tier 1. We discuss how to use and interpret them and ways to triangulate or integrate these multiple data sources. Developed by the University of Oregon more than a decade ago, PBIS assessment tools help schools through the PBIS implementation process. These tools are available at www.pbisapps.org and are free of charge to schools.

To access the tools, you will get what's called a PBIS assessment coordinator account (also free) at www.pbisapps.org for a team member in your school or district. This coordinator account is a one-time application assigned to an individual. If you have staff turnover and someone new steps into that role, simply submit an application for the new person. By logging into this website, your team

---

4. Mercer, McIntosh, and Hoselton, 2017.

Figure 4.1: PBIS Assessment Tools and Purpose

Tool/Tier	Who Completes	Method	What It Tracks
Tiered Fidelity Inventory (TFI) (Tiers 1, 2, and 3)	PBIS Leadership Team	Self-assessment Interviews Observations Product review	Needs assessment Implementation progress Action planning Implementation fidelity
Team Implementation Checklist (TIC) (Tier 1)	PBIS Leadership Team	Self-report	Progress Action planning Implementation fidelity
Self-Assessment Survey (SAS) (Tier 1)	School staff	Survey	Measure of staff needs Action planning
School-Wide Evaluation Tool (SET) (Tier 1)	Outside evaluator School staff	Interviews Observations Product review	Implementation fidelity
Benchmarks of Quality (BoQ) (Tier 1)	PBIS Leadership Team	Self-report Survey	Action planning Implementation fidelity

can take advantage of the terrific range of support in using these tools, including user manuals, video tutorials, and other resources. **Figure 4.1** above compares the various tools.

All the tools mentioned in figure 4.1 are checks and balances to ensure that the various PBIS features are firmly in place. Remember, research reveals that when schools demonstrate fidelity with all core features of PBIS, there are measurable changes in student behavior through reduced ODRs.

The following sections provide more detail about these five tools.

Tiered Fidelity Inventory (TFI)

At the time of our book's original publication in 2014, the OSEP Technical Assistance Center on PBIS had released the first version of the PBIS Implementation Inventory. After further testing and validation, this inventory is now available and widely used as the Tiered Fidelity Inventory (TFI),

a self-assessment tool that can be used before, during, and throughout sustained implementation of PBIS. This tool assesses all three tiers in PBIS, although schools can use any of the individual scales (tiers) independently. The TFI incorporates many features from other existing tools. You can find the tool online at www.pbisapps.org or at the pbis.org website under "Evaluation."

We are including the TFI in this book because it is an important and effective new tool for schools and districts and has some advantages over the other tools. Many states are now encouraging districts to use the TFI instead of other existing measures. Since we strive to offer our readers the current best practice, we have decided to keep the original Tier 1 tools in this book because they have been widely used and are still used in many schools, districts, and states. We hope our descriptions and recommendations offer schools and districts information to make relevant choices among tools.

The TFI is completed by the school PBIS Leadership Team. The Tier 1 scale of the TFI includes a "walk-through" assessment, similar to the SET, that involves interviews, observations, and product review and is completed prior to the team completion of the TFI survey. New schools can begin with the Tier 1 scale only or use all three; however, the developers recommend completing the full TFI (all three tiers) at the beginning of implementation for baseline purposes. We recommend that schools use the TFI at least quarterly until full implementation is documented. The TFI adds some useful questions and data sources that are more specific than the TIC.

The TFI Tier 1 scale has fifteen items which are represented by three subscales: Teams, Implementation, and Evaluation. These reflect the key features of Tier 1. The assessment also includes an action-planning form. Fidelity criterion for the TFI is 70 percent or greater.

Team Implementation Checklist (TIC)

The Team Implementation Checklist (TIC) is completed by the school PBIS Leadership Team and represents the team's perception of progress at any given time. Some teams review the TIC monthly and some quarterly or annually, depending on what stage of implementation they are in. New schools tend to use the TIC more frequently. The TIC measures progress and provides a historical or chronological record of the school's implementation. It comes with an optional action-plan format (see the appendix on pages 175–176 for a reproducible form you can use) and is a convenient way to keep activity on track. This tool measures progress and achievement in each area by marking as completed, in progress, or not started. (See www.pbisapps.org for an example of the TIC.)

Self-Assessment Survey (SAS)

Another useful tool is the Self-Assessment Survey (SAS). The SAS is used with the entire staff to identify areas they perceive as needing the most attention. Respondents include office support personnel, paraprofessionals, media center specialists, custodians, food service workers, and bus drivers—and all should be surveyed. In this way, the SAS represents a broader staff view of both implementation progress and priorities for change. A very useful way to take the temperature of your school, the SAS measures staff perceptions of the four systems in your building:

1. Schoolwide

2. Classroom

3. Nonclassroom

4. Individual student

The schoolwide component provides a good comparison with the TIC or the TFI. This enables your leadership team to examine whether the staff and the team have similar perceptions about which features are in place. It can be quite informative to compare these views.

The SAS is an online survey that takes about twenty minutes to complete. Staff members rate a number of items according to their implementation phase (complete, in progress, or not started) and then also rate the items' importance (high, medium, or low). We heartily recommend that your leadership team take the SAS before asking staff to take it. Familiarize yourself with the wording to clarify what items mean and with the rating system to understand and advise others how to rate items.

It is important to get a high number of respondents on the SAS to ensure good results. In the PBIS Assessment application, the PBIS assessment coordinator can send staff a survey link to access and complete the SAS. Many schools conduct the SAS during a staff meeting using the computers in the media center. You will have to be more creative to get other staff such as kitchen personnel and bus drivers to participate. (We hear that food reinforcements go a long way!) The pbisapps.org website has great materials under the "Resources" tab. You will find a user guide and materials for the SAS as well as video demonstrations, where you will find help in using the survey (and all PBIS assessments) at your school. It will answer who should complete the survey, when and how it should be completed, and how to summarize the results.

School-Wide Evaluation Tool (SET)

A useful addition to the other data sources (TFI, TIC, SAS, BoQ), the School-Wide Evaluation Tool (SET) is a research-based evaluation tool that measures fidelity of implementation for Tier 1. This tool has seven subscales that correlate with the subscales of the other measures (TFI, TIC, BoQ). The SET is conducted by a trained evaluator who is not part of your school or district. Some states use the SET as part of an overall statewide evaluation of PBIS implementation. The generally accepted criterion for fidelity in initial implementation of PBIS is the "80/80 Rule"—scores of 80 percent on the Teaching Expectations subscale and 80 percent on Overall Implementation. (See www.pbisapps.org for a copy of the SET.)

The SET is considered a research tool. Those of you who enjoy reading original research on PBIS will recognize and understand the importance of this tool in evaluation.

Benchmarks of Quality (BoQ)

The Benchmarks of Quality (BoQ) was developed in the Florida PBIS initiative as a means to evaluate PBIS implementation at Tier 1. This self-assessment tool is completed by the PBIS coach and the leadership team. Online training and resources are available at the PBIS website.

The BoQ has ten subscales that measure fidelity and that also correlate with the other measures we have described. A score of 70 percent or greater on overall implementation is the criterion for fidelity. (See www.pbisapps.org for an example.)

Considerations in Selecting Assessments
This book focuses on Tier 1 assessment tools, but the PBIS Assessment application (www .pbisapps.org) includes tools for each of the three tiers. All tools include multiple types of graphic, tabular, and item reports and all are easily and instantly accessible at the website

through your school PBIS account. Here are some things to consider when selecting assessment tools:

1. **Readiness.** If your school or district is part of a formal statewide or regional training, the sponsor will tell you which tools you will be using during the training period, as well as providing training and coaching support to your team.

2. **Behavior patterns.** Your school and district will want to review student behavior patterns (ODRs), for example, who, what, when, where, why, and any evidence of disproportionality by race/ethnicity and disability status.

3. **TFI.** If your school is not currently in formal training but thinking about it, you could use the TFI as a formative evaluation or baseline to see what PBIS features you may already have in place. This will give you some data as a starting point for discussing the need and desire to pursue PBIS for your school. You may want to check with your state PBIS team to see if you can get assistance in conducting the TFI initially or finding facilitators in nearby districts.

4. **TIC.** Your PBIS Leadership Team could also start by completing the TIC, which provides a snapshot of where the team thinks the school is in the implementation process. The TIC does not offer a school walk-through, unlike the TFI. If you have already selected and used the TFI, you would not need to do a TIC or a SET.

5. **Schedule.** Once you begin formal implementation, start using the PBIS assessment tools on a regular schedule. The tools are listed in figure 4.1 on page 54. You can select certain combinations of tools for value and efficiency. See the end of this chapter for examples of annual evaluation schedules. *Note:* If your district is already using the TIC, SAS, and SET and does not plan to transition to the TFI, follow your district's evaluation plan.

6. **Training.** If your school or district is not affiliated with any formal training program,

your PBIS Leadership Team should look at the assessment tools and determine which ones best meet your needs. The SET and BoQ are high-quality research tools that have been commonly used across the United States. They require formal training for test administrators. If you are not connected to a larger PBIS system, consider reaching out for further training and assistance with these tools.

7. **Other tools.** Also, you can select a different group of assessments that will provide progress monitoring, action planning, implementation fidelity, and communication. Consider whether your district needs to use a research-quality tool to assess fidelity. Whatever you decide, be sure to select tools that are validated for the purpose of the evaluation.

At the end of this chapter, we provide sample annual evaluation schedules. These include different combinations of tools for these purposes.

Coach's Tip from Beth

I remember the first time our team completed the TIC and staff completed the SAS. I tried to create action plans to implement everything that our staff thought was missing from our PBIS plan. Don't try this. Choose a few things that can be easily implemented along with one item that may take a longer time. Consider starting with items that your staff rated as high priority on the SAS.

Integrating Multiple Sources of Data

In addition to thoroughly understanding the purpose and method of each PBIS assessment tool, leadership teams will also integrate these multiple data sources, or "triangulate the data." Triangulation uses multiple data sources to corroborate the results, increase your confidence in their validity, and inform better action planning. For example, when you look at your school's results from both the TIC and the SET, you will gain some insight into whether there are score discrepancies between the two instruments. What you as a PBIS Leadership Team perceive to be in place may not be perceived that way by the rest of the staff. These differences prompt you to ask more questions about the current status of implementation, which will facilitate more precise action planning.

Another example could include a comparison of results for the TFI and the SAS. The TFI is based on the PBIS Leadership Team ratings as well as on the walk-through assessment, which includes observations, interviews, and product review. The SAS is the staff self-assessment, which provides perceptions from a broad group of people in your school. As a new school, you will be comparing results for Tier 1. Both the TFI and the SAS can provide a baseline view and needs assessment as well as progress monitoring. Examine the scales from each to get a more accurate and detailed picture. These two instruments provide a good base of information. Adding the SAS as a staff measure gives the team information about what all staff see as a priority.

Char has known administrators who, upon comparing the results of their spring SAS with the TIC, have revised their implementation action plan based on where staff perceived progress to be. The takeaway of this example is that whether you use the TFI or another tool, the SAS is useful in gathering staff perceptions and, therefore, is not limited to the leadership team's perceptions.

Include multiple assessment tools from the beginning. They are all integral to implementation and are designed to measure Tier 1 implementation. They represent different sources of information (team, staff, outside evaluator) and different methods (self-assessment, interviews, observations, and review of permanent products such as wall posters). They all provide basic evaluation information that, when integrated and summarized, helps you interpret the results. When the same positive results are seen across multiple tools, this convergence of evidence confirms that you are making progress and implementing PBIS with fidelity. As Rob Horner asked, "Did we do what we said we were going to do? Did we implement PBIS with fidelity?" Integrating the data from these tools will help you answer that question with confidence as well as identify areas that need development or tweaking if fidelity weakens over time. **Figure 4.2** on page 59 displays the different tools and their subscales.

> **Caution:** When you can look at your fidelity tools and see that your school has achieved and maintained full fidelity according to the guidelines for the tools, you should also see progress measured by specific ODR improvements based on your action plans across schoolwide systems. If you don't see those corresponding positive changes, then the PBIS Leadership Team needs to go back and take a much closer look at the PBIS features and examine whether fidelity was actually met and whether all features were fully implemented by every staff member, in all settings, with all students.

Assessment Reports in Practice

The purpose of this section is to provide specific examples of the assessment tools. Each PBIS assessment tool produces three downloadable reports that provide various levels of detail:

1. **Total Score Report**—summarizes the overall implementation status. The goal is 80 percent or more on overall implementation (SET, TIC, SAS) or 70 percent (TFI, BoQ). The Total Score Report over time gives your team a general and overall sense of how your implementation varies naturally over the years.

2. **Subscale Report**—reveals the team's progress on the key features of PBIS implementation. This report identifies the small areas on which to focus team action planning. The fidelity criterion score is 80 percent or above on overall implementation (or 70 percent on the TFI); however, this report also allows you to quickly assess progress in each area.

3. **Item Report**—refers specifically to the score for each question on the assessment. This allows teams to determine specifically what has been achieved and what still needs to be done.

The rest of this section shows examples of how some of these reports for the various assessment tools might look for schools at different stages of PBIS implementation.

> **Note:** In the interest of relevance and brevity, we've chosen to include in this book examples of all levels of reports for only the TFI and to show only total score reports for the other four measures. For examples and discussion of subscale and item reports for the TIC, SAS, SET, and BoQ, please refer to the user guides and manuals at www.pbisapps.org.

Sample Reports for the Tiered Fidelity Inventory (TFI)

Total Score Report for the TFI

Looking at the TFI Total Score Report in **figure 4.3** on page 60 gives you the big picture of where this school is in implementation progress for all three tiers after one year. Tier 1 has improved from 47 percent to 73 percent, which is above the fidelity criterion. This is good progress in Tier 1. Deeper examination will provide more details about implementation and specific features established. Tier 2 remains at 42 percent, which is not unusual for a school in the early stages of implementation.

Figure 4.2: PBIS Instruments and Their Subscales*

Tiered Fidelity Inventory (TFI) Tier 1		Team Implementation Checklist (TIC)		Self-Assessment Survey (SAS)		School-Wide Evaluation Tool (SET)		Benchmarks of Quality (BoQ)	
Subscale	Items	Subscale	Items	Subscale	Items	Subscale	Items	Subscale	Items
1. Teams	1–2	**1.** Establish Commitment	1–2	**1.** Expectations Defined	1	**1.** Expectations Defined	1–2	**1.** PBIS Leadership Team	1–3
2. Implementation	3–11	**2.** Establish Team	3–5	**2.** Expectations Taught	2	**2.** Expectations Taught	3–7	**2.** Faculty Commitment	4–6
3. Evaluation	12–15	**3.** Self-Assessment	6–8	**3.** Reward System	3	**3.** Reward System	8–10	**3.** Discipline Procedures	7–12
		4. Define Expectations	9–11	**4.** Violations System	4–8	**4.** Violations System	11–14	**4.** Data Entry and Analysis	13–16
		5. Teach Expectations	12	**5.** Monitoring	10–12	**5.** Decision-Making System	15–18	**5.** Expectations	17–21
		6. Reward Expectations	13	**6.** Management	9, 13–16	**6.** Management	19–26	**6.** Recognition	22–28
		7. Consequences	14	**7.** District Support	17–18	**7.** District Support	27–28	**7.** Teaching	29–34
		8. Classroom System	15–17					**8.** Implementation Plan	35–41
		9. Establish Info System	18–19					**9.** Classroom Systems	42–48
		10. Function-Based Support	20–22					**10.** Evaluation	49–53

*Summaries of the validity and reliability of these tools are available at www.pbisapps.org under the PBIS Assessment resource materials.

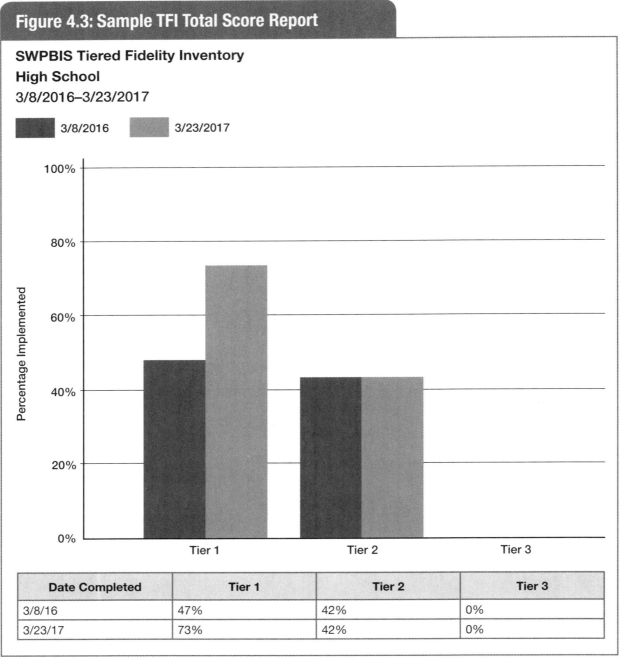

Figure 4.3: Sample TFI Total Score Report

SWPBIS Tiered Fidelity Inventory
High School
3/8/2016–3/23/2017

Date Completed	Tier 1	Tier 2	Tier 3
3/8/16	47%	42%	0%
3/23/17	73%	42%	0%

Subscale Report for the TFI

The report in **figure 4.4** on page 61 breaks down the results in the three subscales of Tier 1: Teams, Implementation, and Evaluation. You can see that this school has improved in all areas. Notably, at Tier 1, the Teams subscale is at 100 percent and Implementation at 78 percent, which is above the fidelity criterion of 70 percent. Finally, the Evaluation subscale has improved, but is still only at 50 percent. We will look deeper to see what specific features need improvement. These data will guide the team in targeted action planning.

Figure 4.4: Sample TFI Subscale Report

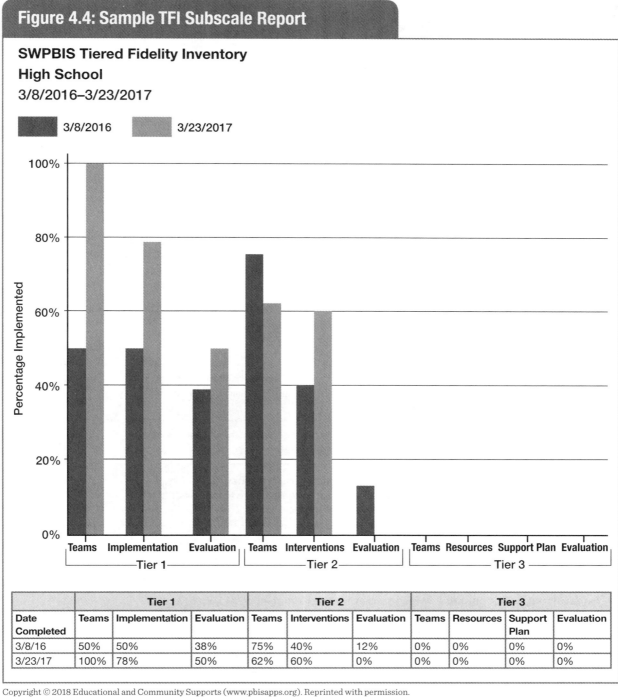

SWPBIS Tiered Fidelity Inventory
High School
3/8/2016–3/23/2017

	Tier 1			Tier 2			Tier 3			
Date Completed	Teams	Implementation	Evaluation	Teams	Interventions	Evaluation	Teams	Resources	Support Plan	Evaluation
3/8/16	50%	50%	38%	75%	40%	12%	0%	0%	0%	0%
3/23/17	100%	78%	50%	62%	60%	0%	0%	0%	0%	0%

Item Report for the TFI

You can review the item report overall to see what's in place and what's in progress. You can look at the scores and also consider the results in terms of priority. For example, when you look at the report in **figure 4.5** on pages 62–63, you quickly see that after one year many items scored a 2, which means the PBIS Leadership Team considers these items in place. You then see that four items were given a score of 1, which means partially in place. And finally, there are two features rated 0, which means nothing is in place. From this you see that future efforts will focus on the areas of implementation and evaluation.

Figure 4.5: Sample TFI Item Report

SWPBIS Tiered Fidelity Inventory
High School

School Year: 2015–16
Date Completed: 3/8/2016–3/23/2017
Scoring Criteria: 0 = Not implemented; 1 = Partially implemented; 2 = Fully implemented

Tier 1: Universal SWPBIS Features

Teams	3/8/16	3/23/17
1. Team Composition: Tier 1 team includes a Tier 1 systems coordinator, a school administrator, a family member, and individuals able to provide (a) applied behavioral expertise, (b) coaching expertise, (c) knowledge of student academic and behavior patterns, (d) knowledge about the operations of the school across grade levels and programs, and, for high schools, (e) student representation.	1	2
2. Team Operating Procedures: Tier 1 team meets at least monthly and has (a) regular meeting format/agenda, (b) minutes, (c) defined meeting roles, and (d) a current action plan.	1	2
Feature 1 Total	2 of 4	4 of 4

Implementation	3/8/16	3/23/17
3. Behavioral Expectations: School has 5 or fewer positively stated behavioral expectations and examples by setting/location for student and staff behaviors (i.e., school teaching matrix) defined and in place.	1	2
4. Teaching Expectations: Expected academic and social behaviors are taught directly to all students in classrooms and across other campus settings/locations.	1	2
5. Problem Behavior Definitions: School has clear definitions for behaviors that interfere with academic and social success and a clear policy/procedure (e.g., flowchart) for addressing office-managed versus staff-managed problems.	2	2
6. Discipline Policies: School policies and procedures describe and emphasize proactive, instructive, and/or restorative approaches to student behavior that are implemented consistently.	1	2
7. Professional Development: A written process is used for orienting all faculty/staff on 4 core Tier 1 SWPBIS practices: (a) teaching schoolwide expectations, (b) acknowledging appropriate behavior, (c) correcting errors, and (d) requesting assistance.	1	2
8. Classroom Procedures: Tier 1 features (schoolwide expectations, routines, acknowledgments, in-class continuum of consequences) are implemented within classrooms and consistent with schoolwide systems.	1	1
9. Feedback and Acknowledgment: A formal system (i.e., written set of procedures for specific behavior feedback that is [a] linked to schoolwide expectations and [b] used across settings and within classrooms) is in place and used by at least 90% of a sample of staff and received by at least 50% of a sample of students.	1	1
10. Faculty Involvement: Faculty are shown schoolwide data regularly and provide input on universal foundations (e.g., expectations, acknowledgments, definitions, consequences) at least every 12 months.	0	1

continued >

Figure 4.5: Sample TFI Item Report, continued		
11. **Student/Family/Community Involvement:** Stakeholders (students, families, and community members) provide input on universal foundations (e.g., expectations, consequences, acknowledgments) at least every 12 months.	1	1
Feature 2 Total	9 of 18	14 of 18
Evaluation	**3/8/16**	**3/23/17**
12. **Discipline Data:** Tier 1 team has instantaneous access to reports summarizing discipline data organized by the frequency of problem behavior events by behavior, location, time of day, and individual student.	1	2
13. **Data-Based Decision-Making:** Tier 1 team reviews and uses discipline data and academic outcome data (e.g., curriculum-based measures, state tests) at least monthly for decision-making.	0	0
14. **Fidelity Data:** Tier 1 team reviews and uses SWPBIS fidelity (e.g., SET, BoQ, TIC, SAS, TFI) data at least annually.	2	2
15. **Annual Evaluation:** Tier 1 team documents fidelity and effectiveness (including on academic outcomes) of Tier 1 practices at least annually (including year-by-year comparisons) that are shared with stakeholders (staff, families, community, district) in a usable format.	0	0
Feature 3 Total:	3 of 8	4 of 8

The PBIS Leadership Team will decide what their priority is. To help, let's apply what we know about the factors that affect sustainability (see chapter 10). Studies show that strong PBIS Leadership Teams, use of data, and classroom implementation are critical. The school in figure 4.5 has good scores for the Teams scale. We notice that there are important aspects from the Evaluation scale that are not in place. Specifically, the school is not using discipline data to make decisions (item 13) or conducting annual evaluations of fidelity and outcomes or sharing these data (item 15). Also, item 10 from the Implementation scale suggests a need to improve faculty involvement and input. With these results, the team can really focus its efforts on building a strong evaluation routine that reviews data monthly. They can also focus on strategies for reporting these data to their stakeholders, including staff.

Classroom implementation is essential. Items 8 and 9 (Implementation scale) indicate a need to improve classroom procedures, student feedback, and consistency among schoolwide and classroom practices. The team will examine what is missing and what is needed. They can look at the walkthrough tools to see if there are particular settings where feedback and acknowledgment procedures need improvement and if there are any classrooms that need additional support implementing these procedures.

Finally, staff and community input and access to evaluation data are important to buy-in and continued support for the school's and district's efforts. Providing data on social and academic improvements goes a long way toward engaging staff. Although it sounds like there is a lot of work to do, these are good results for a high school setting, which often rolls out PBIS at a slower rate than an elementary or a middle school does.

Sample Report for the Team Implementation Checklist (TIC)

Figure 4.6 on page 64 presents a sample TIC Total Score Report from a school that has been implementing PBIS for two years. Notice the steady rising slope. Results are displayed in graphic and tabular form. This gives you the big picture and the percentages of PBIS features that are partially or fully in place. A quick glance tells us this school is making good progress.

Sample Report for the Self-Assessment Survey (SAS)

As we discussed earlier in this chapter, the SAS evaluates the schoolwide systems, classroom and nonclassroom systems, and individual student systems. The Total Score Report for the SAS (see **figure 4.7** on page 65) is based on the eighteen items in the Schoolwide Information System (SWIS) and represents the average implementation score. A score of 80 percent or higher represents a criterion for meeting fidelity at Tier 1. Generally, schools complete a SAS at least once annually. The SAS gives you the opportunity to compare staff perceptions to the PBIS Leadership Team's self-assessment. Examining discrepancies

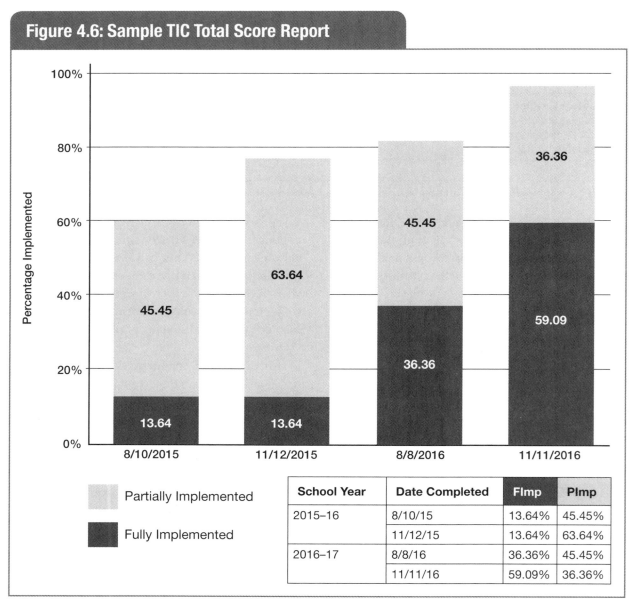

Figure 4.6: Sample TIC Total Score Report

School Year	Date Completed	FImp	PImp
2015–16	8/10/15	13.64%	45.45%
	11/12/15	13.64%	63.64%
2016–17	8/8/16	36.36%	45.45%
	11/11/16	59.09%	36.36%

can be a springboard for great discussion at staff meetings. Disparate findings are not surprising. Defining and implementing consistent practice is an incredible challenge that requires ongoing training, monitoring, and acknowledgment of staff. Not all schools or districts may use this tool, but the value is in comparing this staff survey with self-assessments completed by leadership team members. We have found it useful to create an incentive for staff to complete the survey by setting it up during staff

Figure 4.7: Sample SAS Total Score Report

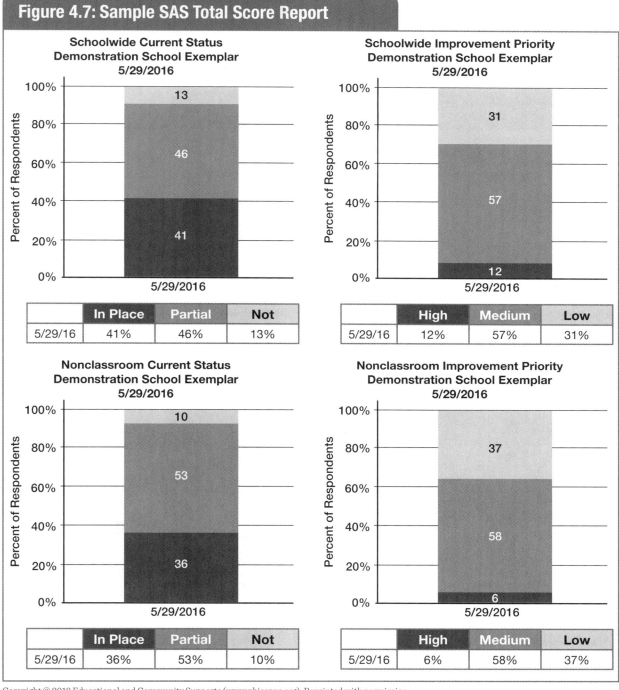

Schoolwide Current Status
Demonstration School Exemplar
5/29/2016

	In Place	Partial	Not
5/29/16	41%	46%	13%

Schoolwide Improvement Priority
Demonstration School Exemplar
5/29/2016

	High	Medium	Low
5/29/16	12%	57%	31%

Nonclassroom Current Status
Demonstration School Exemplar
5/29/2016

	In Place	Partial	Not
5/29/16	36%	53%	10%

Nonclassroom Improvement Priority
Demonstration School Exemplar
5/29/2016

	High	Medium	Low
5/29/16	6%	58%	37%

meetings in the computer lab. Since it's important to get all staff, including unlicensed staff, to complete the survey, some schools use incentives like pizza or other edible treats and even stipends for folks to stay late or come in after the school day. Consistency will pay off; consensus requires patience and commitment from everyone. While the SAS correlates with other Tier 1 measures, it may have even greater advantages for schools that have been achieving implementation for several years.

Sample Report for the School-Wide Evaluation Tool (SET)

When you get your SET results, you will see a display of your scores on the subscales as well as your implementation average. The sample report in **figure 4.8** below represents a school at the end of year one. Notice that the average implementation score (total score) is at 41 percent. The total score is the best view of overall implementation in the school. So

Figure 4.8: Sample SET Subscale and Total Score Report

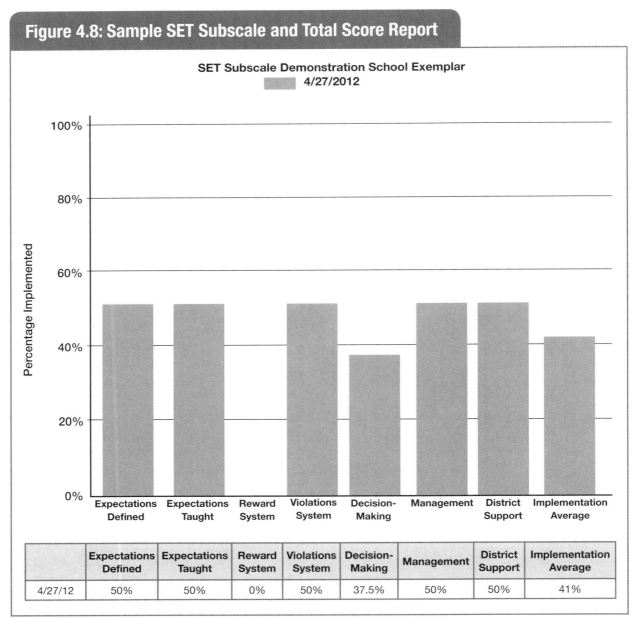

SET Subscale Demonstration School Exemplar
4/27/2012

	Expectations Defined	Expectations Taught	Reward System	Violations System	Decision- Making	Management	District Support	Implementation Average
4/27/12	50%	50%	0%	50%	37.5%	50%	50%	41%

while this school is below the 80/80 criterion (see page 56), this is good progress for year one. Since multiple data sources help the PBIS team gain an accurate understanding, this school might add the TFI for more detail and the SAS as a way of comparing staff perceptions to see the full picture.

Sample Report for Benchmarks of Quality (BoQ)

This school is in its fourth year of implementation, two years out of formal team training. The criterion total score for the BoQ for fidelity purposes is 70 percent or greater. As shown in **figure 4.9** below, this school achieved 81 percent. This means the school is sustaining, over time, with a high level of implementation, which is a good achievement. The BoQ is generally an annual measure. Given new findings, this school might consider adding the SAS every other year, which could provide useful information to see how consistent staff perceptions are. The main question is what student outcomes have been achieved at this level of implementation. In addition, this school will be reviewing and using their ODRs and other student outcome measures.

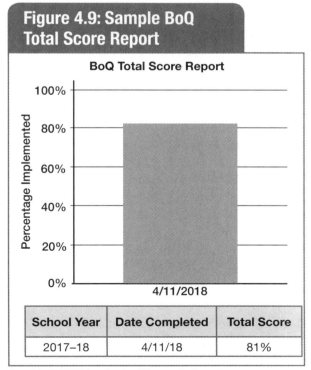

Figure 4.9: Sample BoQ Total Score Report

BoQ Total Score Report

School Year	Date Completed	Total Score
2017–18	4/11/18	81%

A Representative Sample?

When you administer the SAS, you want to secure the highest response rate possible. The sample school in figure 4.7 on page 65 had thirty-four respondents. This number may or may not be representative of that school. A representative response rate depends on the size of the school and number of staff. The PBIS Assessment app allows you to send survey links via email, which is easy but not perfect. Do your best to obtain a high response rate. This takes effort. Set up time during a staff meeting in the computer lab and have everyone do the assessment. Or challenge each grade or department to get the most staff members to complete the assessment. Do not assume this will occur without a lot of prompting and encouragement. Be sure to get unlicensed staff involved. You can model the importance of staff input by presenting results and discussing them at faculty meetings.

Reminder: Your school is not going to use all these tools. We are describing them here so you have an idea in case your district is using a particular combination for measuring implementation progress and fidelity.

Tips for Evaluating Any Type of PBIS Progress Report

We'd like to offer some tips for evaluating various assessments of PBIS implementation.

- First, it is best to use more than one tool, at more than one time, as you progress from implementing to sustaining.

- In the beginning, you will use frequent progress-monitoring reports, such as the TFI or TIC. Using a tool that assesses staff perceptions provides an additional set of data about where you are in relation to implementation. A SAS report might be done once per year early on, and perhaps every other year as schools achieve and maintain solid implementation. Many districts prefer to add an additional external evaluation to the mix, such as the SET, which would be done annually.

- Total scores on instruments are often the best measure of overall implementation, and most studies use total scores rather than subscale scores for this purpose.

- Once you have the big picture in your school, you can use a variety of subscale and item reports to "drill down" to specific actions for planning.

- All these tools relate to fidelity of implementation and are based on the measured presence of the eight key features of PBIS (see page 11). In addition to these tools, it is important to include student outcome data as measured by ODRs. Research shows that once schools have fully implemented and sustained PBIS, changes occur in student behavior. However, fidelity scores alone will not reflect this most important outcome. Therefore, you need to integrate the ODR data into the full picture. If your ODR numbers are high (compared to your baseline) or spiking in some settings, use your data to double-check fidelity and problem-solve.

Remember that scores and implementation fidelity vary over time, and that is normal. It's important to watch for drift and stagnation.

Baseline Data

Baseline data are supposed to reflect where a school is prior to implementation, to give schools a starting point. We have noticed, however, that some administrators and leadership teams are extremely sensitive about baseline scores. Team trainers are sometimes reluctant to share the data with schools out of fear that it will be too discouraging. This line of thinking can have the unfortunate consequence of reinforcing the notion that only top scores should be shared or reported. We know that schools begin implementation at

different points and with different experiences; however, we want to foster comfort with data and an attitude of data being a key resource for success and not the basis of negative judgment.

Try this informal observation: The next time you are present when someone teaches a module or segment on data, pay attention to the presenter's choice of words for introducing the topic. Is the presenter apologetic? Enthusiastic? Does the presenter set the tone of being excited or bored? What message sets the stage? When schools begin PBIS implementation, they enter a cycle of continuous improvement, which is discussed in more detail in the next chapter. Grasping the significance of this approach may help change the views about the meaning and use of baseline data (and other data) before administering assessments. Such reframing might prevent a lot of unnecessary stress.

Student Outcome Data

Office discipline referrals (ODRs) are often used as one measure of student outcomes, though by no means the only one. It is common practice to send students out of class for various behavioral issues, and schools have used out-of-school suspensions for decades. Many educators question these practices, and for good reason. There is no evidence that such exclusionary practices teach students anything. In fact, students who miss class also miss learning opportunities and may become alienated from peers and adults. Ample evidence suggests that suspensions lead to higher dropout rates and lower graduation rates.[5] There is also strong evidence that exclusionary practices are flawed, ineffective, and biased (see chapter 11 for more details). ODRs must be used thoughtfully by teachers and schools, as outlined by your PBIS Leadership Team and according to your school's discipline policy.

Despite concerns, ODRs are also valuable measures of both progress and outcomes in the PBIS implementation process. ODR data can

5. Noltemeyer, Ward, and Mcloughlin, 2015; Fenning and Rose, 2007; Balfanz, Byrnes, and Fox, 2015.

be used in different ways at different times. For example, ODR data may be part of the initial discussion of whether a school has a problem, part of problem-solving, and part of evaluating outcomes and effectiveness.[6] In this section, we'll look at ways to track and organize ODR data so that your team can make the best use of it. These methods include the Schoolwide Information System (SWIS), other student information systems, and systems you can develop on your own to track data, such as spreadsheets.

ODR Data for Screening, Progress Monitoring, and Outcomes

The ODR is not only a strong measure of outcomes, but also can be used for screening and for monitoring progress of individual students and schoolwide PBIS efforts. How can ODRs be useful for screening? In chapter 1 we discussed the conceptual basis of PBIS as a triangle. (See figure 1.1 on page 13.) Recall that a successful Tier 1 system includes easy and efficient interventions that result in 80 percent or more of students having zero to one ODR per school year. As you move up the triangle, Tier 2 interventions target students with two to five ODRs, approximately 15 percent. Using the criterion of two or more ODRs represents a screening of those students who need this extra assistance. At the top of the triangle is Tier 3, which includes the most intense interventions. These interventions are specific and time consuming and are typically appropriate for students who have six or more ODRs.

Using ODR data for screening can identify students who need extra help early and can potentially change the course of their school year. A great example is the October Catch. ODR data can be used as a screening process to begin early intervention for individual students. Researchers Kent McIntosh, Jennifer Frank, and Scott Spaulding found that students who had six or more referrals by the end of the school year typically had two referrals in the fall. This finding is the basis of

what has been called the October Catch, which demonstrates how we can change the trajectory of students by using Tier 2 interventions after two ODRs. The research demonstrates how monitoring ODRs and intervening early, after students receive two referrals, can stabilize behaviors earlier in the school year.[7] This finding supports the importance of using ODR data early and often and demonstrates the significant effects of early intervention. This means more instructional time, less time out of the classroom, and more efficient use of resources.

On a schoolwide level, the leadership team can look at ODR patterns to guide systemic interventions. Here are some ways to interpret the data:

Example 1: When your data show ODRs across many different settings (hallways, bathrooms, library, classrooms), this can indicate that core features of PBIS are not uniformly in place. The PBIS team can look at broader strategies to increase implementation schoolwide.

Example 2: If the team finds a high number of referrals in a few settings, then interventions can be tailored for those settings and not implemented schoolwide. This is more efficient and accurate.

Example 3: When the PBIS Leadership Team's data show a small number of students making up a high number of referrals, the team can look at providing more intensive and targeted interventions for these students. This might mean Tier 2 and 3 interventions. As we know from research, intervening with students who have two or more ODRs at the start of the school year may prevent them from ending up with six or more ODRs by year's end.

The process of examining ODR data in specific ways is often called a "drill down." The benefit of this specificity is that the PBIS team and school staff can use their time and effort more efficiently. We will talk more about the drill-down process in later chapters.

ODR data are useful in monitoring progress. When schools implement Tier 1 PBIS with

---

6. McIntosh, Frank, and Spaulding, 2010.
7. McIntosh, Frank, and Spaulding, 2010.

fidelity, they see decreases in ODRs. Fewer ODRs translate into increased instructional time, academic improvements, saved administrative time, improved social climate, and decreased burnout. A new brief, *What Are the Economic Costs of Implementing SWPBIS in Comparison to the Benefits from Reducing Suspensions?* provides some interesting data on the cost-benefit of implementing PBIS and reducing suspensions. You can find it online at www.pbis.org.

ODRs and Disciplinary Procedures

ODRs can only help you monitor progress and outcomes if they contain accurate data, collected on a consistent basis and immediately available for problem-solving. We recommend that you work with staff to operationally define each behavior so that you increase consistency in identification.

What Char did with school teams beginning SWIS was start with a list of behaviors, each with a label such as *disruptive behavior* or *defiant behavior*. Then as a group, the staff members brainstormed, discussed, and agreed on what observable behaviors represented disruptive behavior, for example. They used visual methods to list behaviors and gain consensus. From this point, the PBIS Leadership Team needed to have these same discussions with the entire staff to revise definitions and gain consensus. In Char's experience, this is a process that occurs over time and is not complete after the initial discussion. Anyone who works in a school knows how aware staff are of inconsistencies in discipline practices. It is important to get this consensus, because all your ODR reports rely on that consistency for planning. These definitions and consistency in discipline practices can reduce the risk of subjective decisions leading to disproportionate referrals (see chapter 11 for details).

During this process you will also decide which behaviors are "major behaviors" (office-referred) and which are "minor behaviors" (classroom- or teacher-managed). As we all know, behavior occurs on a continuum and varies in intensity, duration, and severity. Consequently, this process can take

some time. Creating these distinctions can help reduce potential bias in referrals. In Char's experience, these discussions are rich and useful and help build consensus. This leads to more accurate and consistent data for planning systemwide. The context of these discussions can provide an opportunity to understand and address implicit bias. This process will also help a school make appropriate revisions to its school discipline policy.

If your school does not already have an effective ODR form in place, we recommend designing the form to require very little writing. Checkboxes are ideal—quick and easy. Also include a few lines for teachers and other staff to give a brief summation of what happened. They can describe the behavior trigger (students were asked to complete a worksheet) as well as the behavior (student crumpled worksheet, swearing). If administrators need more information, they can ask the staff member who filled out the form.

Some schools design the referral form without much thought. They simply ask who did what to whom and maybe for the date and the teacher involved. They may also include a section about what consequence the office handed out (call home, apology, detention, suspension). The drawback to this approach is that it allows you to track only who did the behavior, what the behavior was, and who it affected. It doesn't provide enough information to determine if your schoolwide interventions are really working or to identify potential weak spots in your practices.

The ODR form is a key piece of data collection for your school, and staff must be able to complete the form accurately, uniformly, and quickly. The data collected from the form need to be available in a timely fashion. We recommend including the following items on your form:

- student name
- date
- time of the incident
- student's classroom or advisory teacher (optional)
- student grade level
- referring staff member

- location of the incident
- problem behavior (major or minor)
- possible motivation
- others involved
- administrative decision and signature

If your school has signed up for SWIS (see below), you will find all these items are covered. The SWIS data fields lead to graphs and reports that support effective problem-solving. These specific fields also allow your team to perform "drill-down" analyses for specific planning. Predefined fields ensure standardization of your process schoolwide. Even if you aren't using SWIS, the preceding list provides good information to have if your data entry system can support it. On page 79 is a reproducible "Office Discipline Referral (ODR) Form."

Figure 4.10 on page 72 shows a sample filled-out ODR form.

Develop a Data System

ODRs should be gathered, summarized, and reported consistently. This information should be regularly available to the PBIS Leadership Team, at least monthly, in a format and depth that enables the team to solve problems. The information should also be shared with the entire staff at least quarterly so they fully understand the school's progress. The data collection system that your school uses should allow this sharing of information to happen easily.

Schoolwide Information System (SWIS)

Although numerous information systems are available to schools, we use the web-based data collection system called SWIS to illustrate how the ODR is used in measuring progress and outcomes and in daily, active data-based problem-solving. We are not pushing SWIS over other programs, but schools have ready access to it and SWIS generates many reports that enable us to present thorough examples. This section is introductory; more detailed use and illustration with data-driven problem-solving is covered in chapter 5.

Rob Horner, one of the founders of PBIS, recognized the need to create a system that makes ODR data accessible and useful to staff. Based on experience and sound theory, Horner and University of Oregon staff developed SWIS in 1999 as a systems-change strategy to ensure that staff have easy access to the right data at the right time and in the right format to make the best decisions. Today, SWIS is used from coast to coast in thousands of schools and worldwide. Schools pay an annual subscription fee to use SWIS. In order to get SWIS, schools work with a SWIS facilitator to meet specific readiness requirements and to participate in formal training.

When Char first started her position as the state PBIS coordinator for Minnesota in 2005, she had the opportunity to become a SWIS facilitator in order to train schools in using the SWIS data system. She helped all the new PBIS schools learn the program. One of her first schools was in a small rural district. This was the first school where she trained the PBIS Leadership Team in using SWIS. The administrator showed her the shoebox in which he securely kept their current ODRs. After adopting SWIS, the principal commented on how much easier it was to go to the school board meetings with charts and graphs, rather than paper referrals, in that box. The shoebox may surprise you, but since then Char has trained many schools and worked with many SWIS facilitators and still she hears things like, "This school doesn't have a referral form; they just send kids to the office. Or we think that's where they go."

Beth consulted with a school that didn't even have a referral system—meaning no documentation of any kind regarding behaviors. Students were sent out of the room, mostly to an administrator and sometimes to the school social worker. The school had no data to track what behavior was causing the greatest challenge in the school or how many times students had been referred out and for what behaviors. Administrators were basing their needs on assumptions about what was happening in their school. The tradition was just to send students out as the teachers deemed necessary. Beth gave the school a sample referral form and asked them to start collecting data about behaviors. Staff were enthusiastic to learn more about their school.

Figure 4.10: Sample Office Discipline Referral (ODR) Form

Student: Johnny Jones   **Grade:** 6   **Date:** 10/12/17   **Referred by:** Ms. Nelson
Time: 9:45   **Others involved:** x Peer   ☐Staff   ☐Teacher   ☐Guest teacher   ☐None

Location:
☐Playground   ☐Cafeteria   x Hallway   ☐Classroom   ☐Media center   ☐Bathroom
☐Arrival/dismissal   ☐Bus   ☐Office   ☐Nurse's office   ☐Assembly   ☐Other _____

Problem Behavior	Redirections	Possible Motivation	Administrative Decision

Minor: Kept w/teacher; three minors of the same behavior = Major
 1. Inappropriate language
 2. Defiance/disruption
 3. Property misuse
 4. Other
 	
 Major: Requires immediate administrative attention
 5. Abusive language
 6. Fight/physical aggression
 7. **X** Defiance/ disrespect/ noncompliance
 8. Harassment/bullying
 9. Property damage/ vandalism
 10. Other
	X Take a break
	
	 X Proximity conference
	
	 Parent phone call
	
	 Move seat
	
	 Assignment modification
	
	 Other
		1. **X** Obtain peer attention
		
		 2. Obtain adult attention
		
		 3. Obtain item or activity
		
		 4. Avoid peer attention
		
		 5. Avoid adult attention
		
		 6. Avoid task or activity
		
		 7. Other
			Loss of privilege
			
			 Time in office
			
			 X Conference with student
			
			 X Parent phone call
			
			 Act of apology
			
			 Behavior room
			
			 In-school suspension
			
			 Out-of-school suspension
			
			 Other
			
			 Referral to:
			    School psychologist
			    School social worker
			    Nurse
			    Other

Comments: In the classroom, Johnny said "who cares?" when I asked him to name the capital of Canada. I asked him to take a break in class. These two things got the class laughing.

Student response: "Yes I said it. I was bored in class."

Administrative signature and date: Mrs. Gustavson   10/12/17

One PBIS portal provides all PBIS-related tools, including the SWIS Suite, PBIS Assessment, PBIS Evaluation, and SAMI (SWIS Account Management Interface). Visit www.pbisapps.org and select "Applications"; this will take you to a list of applications. On the pbisapps.org website, you can also find a list of resources, watch a demo or video, find user's manuals, and get more information about SWIS subscription, setup, and fees.

Now when implementing PBIS, we recommend that schools and districts thoroughly review their ODR process. It is sometimes more efficient to create a new ODR form and process rather than competing with a current referral form. It can be disheartening to recycle 3,000 printed Rediforms, but if your ODR system does not provide useful information, there is a bigger loss of staff time. We strongly encourage schools to use technology as holder of and processing tool for the data, which allows for immediate and active use of ODR data for decision-making.

As an information system, SWIS is designed to be a user-friendly tool for decision-making about student behavior. It is one of the best and most efficient tools we have seen. Char is a SWIS facilitator, and she has worked with coaches and building administrators who use it daily. She also works with many schools that are using other student information systems. Some of these alternatives do not seem as clearly defined and accessible for the type of decision-making done at the school level. SWIS has a very different purpose than districtwide student information systems because it is designed to monitor student behavior and was created for school-based decisions. Recent changes in the SWIS system now make data integration easier.

We both like using SWIS because it allows for easy data entry and easy monitoring of behavioral data. If your school is going to use another data system, make sure you can quickly find the core reports for behavioral data and ensure that you can drill down with custom reports to develop precision statements about the behavior in your school. Another key feature of SWIS, and embedded within

its training, is an in-depth, effective problem-solving model. The basic components of this model are derived from a multiyear research project conducted by the University of Oregon and produced under the title Team-Initiated Problem-Solving, or TIPS. (See chapter 5 for details on TIPS.)

What Are the SWIS Core Data Reports?
The University of Oregon developed and launched SWIS. This sophisticated system has evolved over the years based on feedback from practitioners and ongoing research. The dashboard automatically brings up seven core reports that are immediately useful to school teams (see **figure 4.11** on page 74):
1. Average Referrals Per Day Per Month
2. Referrals by Time
3. Referrals by Location
4. Referrals by Day of the Week
5. Referrals by Problem Behavior
6. Referrals by Grade
7. Referrals by Student

When you log into SWIS, you see the dashboard with up-to-date data on all seven areas, plus a chronological listing of referrals. This provides a picture of what has happened in your building. These are the most common data that teams use, but this system also allows you to do in-depth analyses of problems, called drill-down reports. You can create custom report templates that answer your school's particular questions for problem-solving. We will talk more about SWIS in the context of problem-solving in chapter 5, including how to use ethnicity reports to reduce disproportionate discipline practices.

As good as it is, SWIS is not the universal system in many states. Some states say their use is about fifty-fifty SWIS versus local systems. One of the barriers to some schools readily adopting SWIS is that they have to double-enter some of the information: once into SWIS and a second time into their district's student information system. There are some data integration mechanisms that help schools work through this. Also, districts have large student information systems that manage a lot of student data at the district level. Over the years, many of these providers have tried to modify their systems to produce similar access and reports for school teams. Sometimes schools have contacted us after using their district system asking how to

get started with SWIS because it allows them to get the data they need more easily and quickly. SWIS developers are well aware of these concerns and strive for ways to integrate data without losing fidelity. Each school and district can weigh the advantages of using SWIS.

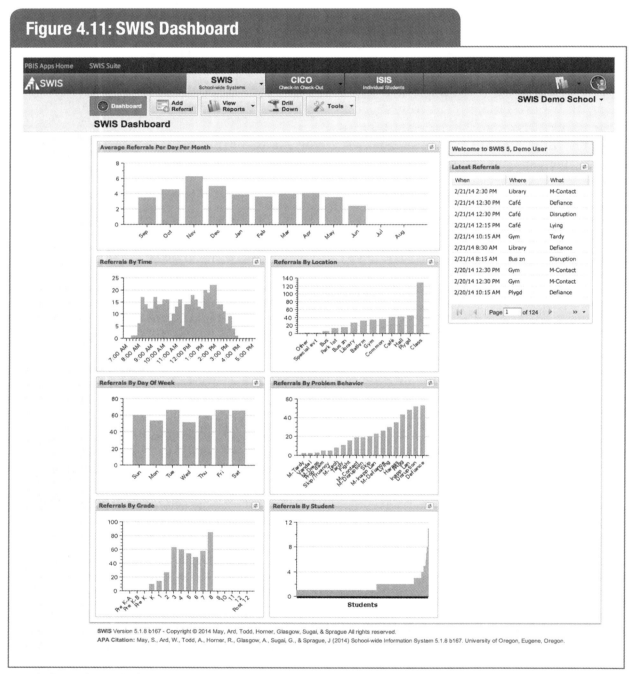

Figure 4.11: SWIS Dashboard

Using a Spreadsheet to Track ODR Data

If your school does not use a behavior monitoring system (such as SWIS or another formal data-based program), you can use a spreadsheet. Doing so will allow you to arrange and sort the data in many different ways. **Figure 4.12** presents a sample spreadsheet with all the necessary parts of data collection. Several states have created ODR templates and spreadsheets for schools and districts that don't use SWIS. A few examples can be found at pbismissouri.org under "Tier 1 Data Tools."

When all the referrals are recorded on the spreadsheet, they can be sorted by date (how many referrals on average per day?), by student (which students have the most referrals?), by behavior (which behaviors should we target?), by time, by location, and by action taken. You can also calculate the total number of referrals to monitor whether the total number of ODRs is going up or down. Multiply the total number of referrals by twenty minutes (the average length of time spent dealing with each referral) to see just how much academic time is lost to behaviors and how much administrative time is spent dealing with them. Visit the PBIS Maryland website (www.pbismaryland.org) for a cost-benefit analysis worksheet that will do this calculation for you.

As a framework to change systems, PBIS requires schools to collect baseline data about student behaviors. But remember, it can take two to three years to set up a solid foundation with PBIS Tier 1. *Patience is key.* Begin collecting some data as your school prepares to implement PBIS, and then continue the practice. Over time, as you follow the data trail, you will start to notice trends and patterns in your school.

Figure 4.12: Sample ODR Spreadsheet

Date	Student Name	Behavior	Time	Location	Outcome
9/11/18	Mark	Disrespect—minor	12:30	Art room Ms. Hanon	Reflection sheet
9/12/18	Abdul	Tech. violation	9:45	Comp lab Mr. Rubin	No computer for a week
9/13/18	Mia	Dress code	8:30	Front entry Mrs. Pena	Changed clothes
9/13/18	Juan	Inappropriate language—minor	12:15	Math class Mrs. Green	Reflection sheet
9/14/18	Kierra	Inappropriate language—minor	9:50	Office Mr. George	Reflection sheet
9/14/18	Fred	Fighting	1:30	Gym class Ms. Lopez	Suspension—2 days
9/14/18	John	Fighting	1:30	Gym class Ms. Lopez	Suspension—2 days

Annual Evaluation Schedule

Districts and schools will benefit from having an established evaluation plan for all schools that provides a basis for seeing where they are on the continuum of PBIS implementation. Go to www .pbis.org and find the *Evaluation Blueprint for School-Wide Positive Behavior Support*.

For your convenience, following is an example of an annual schedule for schools in training (years one and two). See **figure 4.13** on page 77.

For schools that are in sustaining and improving status, a slightly different schedule applies. Because some of these schools may have used other measures, the schedule in **figure 4.14** on page 78 offers choices for which tools to use and how often.

If your school or district is part of a formal state-led PBIS effort, you will find your schedule on your state's website or will receive it from the state coordinator. If you are not connected to a formal state or regional initiative, search the resources at www.pbis.org for best practice in evaluation. There are many resources available. Our home state of Minnesota also posts a recommended schedule for schools/districts that are implementing PBIS independently. You can find it online at www.pbismn.org.

Remember, your evaluation plan helps your team answer two simple questions:

1. Are we implementing PBIS as it was defined? This is what we call *fidelity*.

2. If we are implementing PBIS, is it making a difference? Collect and report progress, fidelity, and outcome data. Select your tools so that you can effectively and efficiently action plan and report to stakeholders.

Figure 4.13: Sample Annual Evaluation Schedule for New Schools
Minnesota PBIS

Data Calendar At-A-Glance

Schools in Training

Schedule
Note: Those items completed at training are identified. Other items are completed by school teams independently.

Purpose	Measure	Function	Year 1 Training				Year 2 Training			
			Fall	Winter	Spring	End of year	Fall	Winter	Spring	End of year
School information database	School profile/contact form	Provides a database for communication, statewide planning, and support	Aug. training	Confirm at training			Aug. training			
Progress monitoring: staff/building level	Self-Assessment Survey (SAS)	Used by school staff for initial and annual assessment of SWPBIS systems in their school and to guide action planning	Sept.–Oct.		Apr.–May				Apr.–May	
Fidelity of implementation	Tiered Fidelity Inventory (TFI)	Assesses the critical features of SWPBIS across each academic year	Aug. training	Nov. training	Mar. training	May	Aug. training	Nov. training	Mar. training	May
Student outcomes	Office discipline referrals (ODR) (SWIS/core reports)	ODRs provide data for monthly team reviews and decision-making by teachers, administrators, and other staff to guide prevention efforts and action planning	Monthly	Monthly	Monthly	Monthly	Monthly	Monthly	Monthly	Monthly

Figure 4.14: Sample Annual Evaluation Schedule for Sustaining and Improving Schools
Minnesota PBIS

Sustaining and Improving Schools

For schools that have completed the team training, including the evaluation elements required in the recognition system
https://www.pbisapps.org/Resources/Pages/Developing-District-PBIS-Evaluation-Plans.aspx

Purpose	Measure	Function	Schedule
School information database	School profile/contact form	Provides a database for communication, statewide planning, and support	Updated in September Contact evaluator to have your school information added to this database
Progress monitoring: team level	Team Implementation Checklist (TIC)	A self-assessment tool that serves as a multilevel guide for creating schoolwide PBIS action plans and evaluating the status of implementation activities	Completed annually
	Tiered Fidelity Inventory (TFI)	Gives teams a single, efficient, valid, reliable survey to guide implementation and sustained use of SWPBIS; teams measure the extent to which school personnel apply the core features of SWPBIS at all 3 tiers	3 times per year External facilitator recommended Annual walk-through recommended
Progress monitoring: staff/building level	Self-Assessment Survey (SAS)	Used by school staff for initial and annual assessment of effective behavior support systems in their school and to guide action planning	Completed annually
Student outcomes	Office discipline referrals (ODR) (SWIS/core reports)	ODRs provide data for monthly team reviews and decision-making by teachers, administrators, and other staff to guide prevention efforts and action planning	Monthly, based on school calendar
Fidelity of implementation	School-Wide Evaluation Tool (SET)	External evaluation to assess the critical features of schoolwide behavior support across each academic school year	Completed annually to provide an external evaluation of fidelity of implementation (benchmark 80%)
	Benchmarks of Quality (BoQ)	Used by teams to identify the level of implementation of critical components, as well as note areas of success and areas for improvement for the sustained implementation of SWPBIS	Completed annually after completion of training schedule (benchmark 70%)
	Tiered Fidelity Inventory (TFI)	Gives teams a single, efficient, valid, reliable survey to guide implementation and sustained use of SWPBIS; teams measure the extent to which school personnel apply the core features of SWPBIS at all 3 tiers	Once fidelity on a tier is met (70%), the team may choose to shift from 3 times per year to annually for the purpose of evaluating sustained implementation

Reprinted with permission from the Minnesota Department of Education.

Office Discipline Referral (ODR) Form

Student _____ Grade _____ Date _____ Referred by _____

Time _____ Others involved: ☐ Peer ☐ Staff ☐ Teacher ☐ Guest teacher ☐ None

Location:
☐ Playground ☐ Cafeteria ☐ Hallway ☐ Classroom ☐ Media center ☐ Bathroom ☐ Arrival/dismissal
☐ Bus ☐ Office ☐ Nurse's office ☐ Assembly ☐ Other _____

Problem Behavior	Redirections	Possible Motivation	Administrative Decision

Minor: *Kept w/teacher; three minors of the same behavior = Major*
1. Inappropriate language
2. Defiance/disruption
3. Property misuse
4. Other
 	
Major: *Requires immediate administrative attention*
5. Abusive language
6. Fight/physical aggression
7. Defiance/disrespect/ noncompliance
8. Harassment/bullying
9. Property damage/ vandalism
10. Other
	Take a break
	
	Proximity conference
	
	Parent phone call
	
	Move seat
	
	Assignment modification
	
	Other
		1. Obtain peer attention
		2. Obtain adult attention
		3. Obtain item or activity
		4. Avoid peer attention
		5. Avoid adult attention
		6. Avoid task or activity
		7. Other
			Loss of privilege
			
			Time in office
			
			Conference with student
			
			Parent phone call
			
			Act of apology
			
			Behavior room
			
			In-school suspension
			
			Out-of-school suspension
			
			Other
			
			Referral to:
			  School psychologist
			  School social worker
			  Nurse
			  Other

Comments: _____

_____

_____

Student response: _____

_____

Administrative signature and date: _____

Effective Data-Based Decision-Making

In chapter 4, we talked in detail about the various assessment tools for measuring progress, fidelity, and outcomes in PBIS implementation. These tools include ways to assess the presence of PBIS features and also student outcomes. In this chapter, we discuss data-based decision-making using these tools. This step relies on a solid foundation and fluency with the tools that your team uses. We offer the following advice to new PBIS Leadership Teams:

- **Learn the data tools right from the beginning.** Learn the name of the tool, the purpose, the source, the content, what the tool measures, and how to interpret it and use it in planning. In Minnesota, new teams complete the Tiered Fidelity Inventory (TFI) at the beginning of training. In some states, teams may begin with the Team Implementation Checklist (TIC). We advise teams to review the tool and its user manual so members are familiar with what aspects of PBIS implementation it measures and what the results mean for planning.

- **Read through each tool and ask questions about any item or scoring that you do not understand.** If your team is using the TFI, read through the questions for each tier as well as the recommended evidence for scoring. Because the TFI comes with additional components, such as the TFI Walk-Through Tool, it's important to know when and how

to use these features. If your school is using the TIC, it helps for the leadership team to be familiar with the wording on the tool. One item on the TIC (item 5) refers to conducting an audit of school committees. Without some clarification, teams don't know that this refers to the Working Smarter Matrix activity that helps schools identify and integrate or disband current activities and committees that have outlived their usefulness to the school.

- **Make sure that the PBIS Leadership Team is fluent with the tools.** Everyone on the team needs to spend time to become as fluent as possible with what the tools are, what they measure, and how to interpret them and use the results for action planning. If only one person such as the principal or the coach has access to or understands the tools, then the team may get stalled, not buy in, or not have the knowledge to effectively use the information when that person is gone.

- **Have a clear practice for ensuring transmission of information to team members.** You don't want information to get lost with turnover of team members and staff. The PBIS Assessment app has three user levels: coordinator, team member, and read-only. Typically, the school or district PBIS assessment coordinator logs in to set up surveys. An assigned team member may generate reports. It's important to define these roles and choose the coordinator of information. Also, have a plan for transferring this role to a new coordinator when the original person leaves. And be sure not to share or use others' log-in credentials.

- **Learn the tools and translate them to outcomes, goals, and action plans.** Each of the tools we discussed in chapter 4 has multiple reports available that provide details about the scores. Understand these reports so that you can use the information to plan actions and to answer questions from team or staff members. Once during a district PBIS planning day during which several school PBIS Leadership Teams presented all their data, one team member asked how two subscales compared on different instruments. No one knew the answer, or even what content was included on each instrument. If your team doesn't understand the content and how to translate and compare the tools, how will team members be able to present data to the staff and others?

- **Adopt an action-planning routine.** We give examples of these routines in this chapter. Some schools don't use data either because the data are not available or because the team doesn't know how to translate data into an action plan. This requires new skills and a broad base of buy-in. Without action-planning skills and consensus, it can be easier and more fun to focus on posters, T-shirts, tickets, celebrations, and other visible pieces of PBIS implementation *without* having the data to support these efforts.

- **Have the ability to "drill down" into data.** In Minnesota, for example, we promote systematic use of office discipline referral (ODR) data right away. When you have established the eight PBIS features and are problem-solving with the student data, you will need to be able to refine that data. This is very challenging for many schools, even if they are using SWIS (Schoolwide Information System). Some PBIS coaches do not have access to student data, or some alternative data systems cannot easily provide the information needed. This can be a huge barrier, but it can be overcome with practice, coaching, support, and patience. Many district data systems have improved greatly. SWIS has continually evolved and improved its utility, accessibility, and value. SWIS has a drill-down report process that makes detailed analysis immediately available. See the SWIS Drill-Down Worksheet at www.pbisapps.org.

With these thoughts in mind, chapter 5 focuses on specific routines for engaging your team in data-based decision-making or problem-solving. We will talk about some simple problem-solving approaches and then briefly review the SWIS model. There are straightforward problem-solving steps for basic PBIS implementation, as well as some detail about SWIS problem-solving as it pertains specifically to the use of ODR data. In reality, schools will be able to integrate these concepts, and we will highlight ways to do this. We also provide a brief overview of the Team-Initiated Problem-Solving (TIPS) model for team process and decision-making.

What Are Data-Based Decision-Making and Problem-Solving?

The concept of problem-solving is very common in fields such as education, business, and health care. The most basic approach suggests that you identify the problem, develop and implement solutions, and then evaluate the results. It sounds easy and straightforward, and it is—yet studies show that teams often do not follow a structured process. In any group process, there is always the human factor, and the group can be hijacked and taken off course by group dynamics. Perhaps the facilitator or leader is less experienced in facilitating a group or conflict develops as strong personalities among group members clash. Carrying out effective problem-solving is definitely a skill, and having a specific routine and structure is a huge benefit.

Along with the skills required, it helps to have a model that clearly delineates the problem-solving process. In the course of implementing PBIS as a team-led model, you will be problem-solving with data both to do basic planning and implementation and to develop detailed solutions for schoolwide interventions. This problem-solving relies heavily on all the data sources and methods discussed in chapter 4.

If you look at different state and regional PBIS websites, you will find numerous examples of problem-solving. Having a straightforward data-based decision-making model for action planning is really effective throughout PBIS implementation. In the initial stages, the leadership team focuses the action planning to establish the eight key features of the PBIS framework. The assessment tools we discussed in chapter 4 are the possible data measures you will use to evaluate your implementation progress and fidelity in Tier 1. Again, we want to remind you that you won't be using all the tools, but they represent the Tier 1 tools available to districts and schools. In addition, ODR data will also help you assess progress and student outcomes in order to make decisions about next steps.

Teams will use data from the very beginning. The problem-solving process works best when steps are precise and measurable. We highly recommend using SWIS for monitoring ODRs, but we recognize that many districts and schools will need to use an existing alternative. The steps to follow should work effectively regardless of whether or not you use SWIS.

Problem-Solving Using Student Behavior Data

The SWIS system was launched in 1999 with the intention of making ODR data systematic and easily available to school staff in order to improve the efficiency of problem-solving. Each school that adopts this data system meets clear readiness requirements and receives specific training in using SWIS and in data-based problem-solving. See www.pbisapps.org and click on "Applications," then on "SWIS Suite," and then on "Get SWIS" to read the SWIS readiness requirements. One of these requirements is evidence of an office referral form that is consistent with SWIS and that clearly and operationally defines all components and student behaviors and distinguishes between major and minor behaviors as well as classroom-managed behaviors and office referrals. A second major requirement is to establish a coherent and clearly documented discipline policy for all students and staff.

The SWIS approach to problem-solving can work with almost any ODR system, as long as the leadership team can gather the level of data needed. The steps described here illustrate problem-solving with ODR data. However, these same steps can apply to the progress, or effort, data you collect. For example, you can write precision statements that reflect implementation goals based on the TFI.

SWIS uses a continuous quality improvement cycle. Six steps comprise this approach, shown in **figure 5.1** on page 83.

In SWIS training, the facilitators do an excellent job of defining and describing what each of these steps means and looks like. Using real examples, the trainers demonstrate each step based on school data. Before concluding, the trainers provide case studies and simulations so that participants can build fluency through practice with active coaching. The materials are excellent and the delivery of the training provides effective teaching and learning outcomes. We define the six steps next.

> The steps described here illustrate problem-solving with ODR data. However, these same steps can apply to the progress, or effort, data you collect.

Figure 5.1: Continuous Quality Improvement Cycle

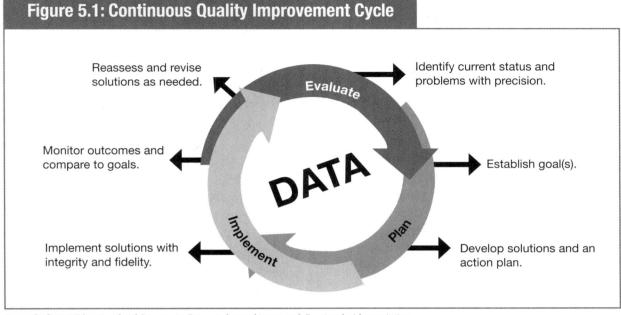

Reassess and revise solutions as needed.

Identify current status and problems with precision.

Monitor outcomes and compare to goals.

Establish goal(s).

Implement solutions with integrity and fidelity.

Develop solutions and an action plan.

Step 1: Identify Current Status and Problems with Precision

A requirement for good problem-solving is clearly reviewing your school's current status and precisely defining the problem based on current data. The SWIS model uses the term *precision statement*, meaning to articulate a problem in a very specific and concrete way so that the team can focus its efforts on a solvable problem. Many groups start working with a problem description that is too primary (or general) and, consequently, find it difficult to develop an appropriate solution. Precision statements are built on the *who, what, where, when, how,* and *why* questions. You'll develop your precision statements using the core data reports. SWIS has seven core data reports:

1. Average Referrals Per Day Per Month
2. Referrals by Time
3. Referrals by Location
4. Referrals by Day of the Week
5. Referrals by Problem Behavior
6. Referrals by Grade
7. Referrals by Student

SWIS also includes eight additional reports: Average Referrals Per Day Per Month Multiyear, Location Multiyear, Problem Behavior Multiyear, Referrals by Staff, Suspension/Expulsion, Ethnicity, Triangle Data, and Year-End. All these reports are immediately available when you log into your account. These data reports help you determine if you have a problem and help you answer specific questions. For example, looking at the average referrals per day and per month helps you determine if your referrals are stable or if you have trends across the year. SWIS also publishes an annual data summary showing data and trends in ODRs comprised of data from all schools using SWIS. The comparison may not be exact with data systems other than SWIS, but it provides a comparison of your school type to other similar schools to see where you stand.

We'd like to highlight the SWIS ethnicity reports, which now include four separate reports: Referral Risk Index, Referral Risk Ratio, Students with Referrals by Ethnicity, and Referrals by Ethnicity. Combined, these reports provide a readily available and strong base from which your team can identify and examine potential disproportionate disciplinary actions. See chapter 11 for more details.

We believe that one of the strongest components SWIS offers users is the Drill-Down Tool, which allows your team to dig deeper into problems to help you define them with precision. You can find the SWIS Drill-Down Worksheet at www.pbisapps .org. Do a simple search for the worksheet, and you will also find a filled-out example to show you how to drill down into your data. See also the reproducible form "Data Drill Down for Creating Precision Statements" on page 174 of the appendix.

The basic overview includes looking at ODR data to identify the number of students who receive zero to one, two to five, and six plus referrals. If you find large numbers of students with two or more referrals over many settings, dig deeper to analyze the who, what, where, when, and why and run the ethnicity reports. This suggests that Tier 1 is not in place.

Use SWIS (or your local alternative) and the materials from the OSEP Technical Assistance Center on PBIS to find strategies to identify discipline disproportionality and reduce potential bias in referrals by examining the components that are at risk of bias (see chapter 11 for details). The example below assumes your school has screened for disproportionate referrals and made appropriate adaptations in the advisory period.

Following is a chunk of data from which a problem can be defined with precision:

The total number of ODRs from last year was 243. The most frequent referral was "disruption to class" (65 percent, or 159), which breaks down like this: 15 percent during advisory from 8:15–8:45 a.m. and 35 percent were from ninth graders, 30 percent from tenth graders, 20 percent from eleventh graders, and 15 percent from twelfth graders. Regarding the remaining referrals, 40 percent occurred after advisory and before lunch, 10 percent were during lunch, and 35 percent were after lunch.

The chart in **figure 5.2** below shows how this data can be framed in general, or primary, statements or phrased in precise, evidence-based language that clearly defines the problem.

The PBIS Leadership Team for this school has chosen to focus on the advisory period for teaching the new skills, with a focus on ninth-grade students. The team will look for an overall reduction in disruptive behaviors as students transfer new skills to other classes.

Precision statements are based on refined, current data, which reduces the guesswork involved with a specific problem and focuses instead on finding a solution. This puts resources where they are most needed. Each problem identified by the PBIS Leadership Team should have a precision statement created by a data drill down and an action plan to correct the problem.

Step 2: Establish Goals

How many times have you been in a meeting in which everyone was really eager to brainstorm solutions and strategies but little data was used when presenting the problem? Use your data. Once

Figure 5.2: Primary Versus Precision Statements

Primary Statements	Precision Statements
Too many referrals. September has more suspensions than last year. The advisory period isn't working. There are too many referrals for disruptions.	The most frequent referral from last year was disruption to class (65 percent, or 159) [answers what]. 15 percent [answers how many] of referrals for disruption occurred during advisory [answers where] from 8:15–8:45 a.m. [answers when], 35 percent were from 9th graders [answers who] to gain peer attention [answers why].

you have precisely defined the problem, you can then define an outcome, or SMART goal.[*]

Keeping in mind the data sample for disruptive behavior presented in step 1, which indicates that the highest number of referrals occur in the ninth-grade advisory, the leadership team for this school identified the following SMART goal:

There will be less than 5 percent of referrals among ninth graders from morning advisories for disruptive behavior by the end of the school year.

The team further defined this goal by clarifying how each of the factors in SMART related to the goal:

Specific: The PBIS team wanted to decrease the total number of ODRs from morning advisories by ninth graders to 5 percent or less.

Measurable: The team will track and count referrals toward this goal level.

Attainable: The PBIS team has the data tools to track ODRs and institute prevention strategies to decrease the number of behavioral referrals.

Relevant: The goal is important because reducing ODRs, particularly disproportionate ODRs, is one of the top three goals in the school improvement plan.

Timely: This is the current data that show the need throughout the ninth-grade class, and the team has four months to implement the plan.

Step 3: Develop Solutions and an Action Plan

Once a SMART goal has been defined, the PBIS Leadership Team can then develop a solution to the problem. Solutions offer steps for action. Precision statements guide this process by enabling the team to focus on very specific areas where the problem occurs, rather than make broad, unnecessary interventions. For the precision statements shown in figure 5.2, the leadership team might recommend

strategies that prevent, teach, acknowledge, extinguish, provide consequences for, and specify data collection strategies for problem behaviors. For example, the administration can assign more staff to monitor the hallways to encourage students to get to advisory on time, or the leadership team might recommend that students serve on the advisory planning committee to make the activities more relevant and interesting to the students, thus encouraging more engagement.

Without precision statements, leadership team members might make general statements about what they are seeing; for example, "So many of our students are talking during my class and disrupting my teaching!" or, "Advisory is a waste of time. No one wants to be there." These statements do not lead to functional solutions. With the limited resources available to schools, PBIS Leadership Teams can't afford to try to guess where the hot spot areas are in their schools. Teams need to get it right the first time whenever possible. Using precision statements not only helps them get it right but also enables them to build functional solutions.

The Solutions Development Worksheet presented in **figure 5.3** on page 86 shows how six simple components can help determine a solution for the example of classroom disruptions in a ninth-grade class.

Step 4: Implement Solutions with Integrity and Fidelity

Once you have identified the solution components and the accompanying action steps, you are ready to develop a comprehensive action plan that includes the solution components as well as action items, persons responsible, timelines, and how you will measure the outcome. **Figure 5.4** on page 87 shows a sample action plan to address disruptive

---

[*] SMART goals were developed by George Doran in 1981 for the business world. SMART serves as a mnemonic device to remember the factors to incorporate into a goal: **S**pecific, **M**easurable, **A**ttainable, **R**elevant, **T**imely.

Figure 5.3: Solutions Development Worksheet

Prevention	How can we change the environment to keep the problem from occurring?
Teaching	What can we do to clarify behavior expectations and specifically teach prosocial behavior?
Recognition	What are the ways we can acknowledge students for achieving expected behaviors
Extinction*	How do we keep from rewarding problem behavior?
Consequences	What are the consistent and effective consequences for problem behavior?
Data collection	How do we monitor our interventions and their effects?

* Some readers may be unfamiliar with the term *extinction*, taken from behavioral psychology. It means removing the reinforcement for a behavior. Think of removing oxygen from a fire in order to extinguish it. Sometimes we unintentionally reinforce students' behavior.

behavior. Arrange the conditions and context to enact the plan. Make sure you have the resources needed.

Step 5: Monitor Outcomes and Compare to Goals

A major part of any successful action plan is evaluation. This process is straightforward; it requires you to monitor outcomes. Ask questions in two areas.

First: Did we do what we said we would do? Did we implement the plan? Yes? No? Partially? These are questions about implementation fidelity. They don't have to be complicated, but a simple follow-up with those assigned different action steps. You can ask, you can observe, and you can look at data. Whatever way you choose, just make sure you check that you have actually carried out the plan as you designed it.

Second: Did our efforts have an impact? This is the reason you put time, effort, and resources into an action plan. You designed your measures right at the outset so that you could determine whether you achieved the defined outcome. All the data you collect on fidelity of implementation and impact will help you if you need to make adaptations.

Step 6: Reassess and Revise Solutions as Needed

This is an important step in any continuous improvement process. Again, this step is based on the data you have gathered in defining the problem as well as in designing the solution and action plan. Your decisions rest on valid data as well as on professional knowledge and skills. If you implemented the plan with fidelity, then review your data and compare it with your solution. If you find gaps in fidelity, examine the areas and seek specific explanations for what impeded fidelity. Share and discuss this with faculty. Whatever the outcome, data informs all your future actions and adaptations.

You may want to take advantage of SWIS and TIPS. The best way to find SWIS materials and information is to go to www.pbis apps.org and click on "SWIS Suite" from the "Applications" tab. You can also select "Find a Facilitator or Coordinator" from the home page to locate a facilitator in your state. You may also contact your local or state SWPBIS entity. Visit www.pbis.org/pbis-network to find contact information for your state. *Note:*

Figure 5.4: Sample Action-Planning Document

Solution Component	Action Steps	Who Is Responsible?	By When?	How Will Fidelity Be Measured?
Prevention	1. Professional development for staff on handling disruptive behavior	William	October 2014	Check schedule and staff feedback
	2. Reteach expectations to students	Advisory teachers	October 2014	Email staff and ask
	3. Student council assist in making posters for hallways/classrooms to promote Expectation for October: Respect	Susan and Marty (student council supervisor)	October 2014	Observe posters
Teaching	1. Teach students to respond to teacher hand signal as cue for expectations	Advisory teachers	November 2014	Review lesson plans and teacher feedback
	2. 9th-grade team incorporates lessons on respect in their curriculum	Indira and 9th-grade team	November 2014	Review and observe lessons
Recognition	1. Increase Caught in the Act reward tickets during advisories	Fred	November and ongoing	Record number of tickets turned in
	2. School will have quarterly assemblies to recognize students who are demonstrating school expectations	Susan		Document assembly
Extinction	1. Create a structure and routine for advisories with student input to increase engagement	Advisory teachers	October	Review and gather ODR data from revised Advisory structure
	2. Upon early completion of routine students gain 10 minutes of social time			
Corrective consequence	1. Review with staff how to have a short student conference for disruptive behavior	PBIS Leadership Team at faculty meetings	October February April	Observe and gather staff feedback at meetings
Data collection	1. Staff accurately complete ODR forms	PBIS Leadership Team	Weekly	Summarize and report data at PBIS team meeting and faculty meetings
	2. PBIS team reviews data weekly			Compare trends and levels to 9th-grade baseline

SWIS is now available worldwide using local servers and language translations of materials. See the SWIS Suite Global Edition at www.pbisapps.org.

Team-Initiated Problem-Solving (TIPS)

Research has shown that even though teams use problem-solving approaches, they often do not meet their goals. As more schools adopted SWIS, it became clear that PBIS Leadership Teams wanted further assistance in how to effectively problem-solve. Leadership teams were gathering data but not using it in effective ways to create meaningful solutions. This led to research begun in 2008. The researchers studied leadership teams and determined that the process of a team moving from a problem to a solution required more careful and specific problem-solving and solution development as well as subsequent action planning. Specifically, the researchers determined that schools needed "a clear model with steps for problem-solving, access to the right information at the right time in the right format, and a formal process that a group could use to build and implement solutions."[1] To address this need, the researchers developed a specific, comprehensive model for problem-solving at the team level. Named Team-Initiated Problem-Solving, or TIPS, the model includes two major components:

1. A model for establishing effective teams

2. A model of effective problem-solving with data

TIPS is a formal, evidence-based model that is available to schools, regions, and states. The TIPS model works for teams at various stages of implementation that are charged with problem-solving with data. What TIPS adds to the PBIS implementation process is the integration of a systematic team/meeting process with a comprehensive data-based problem-solving approach. TIPS is a comprehensive approach that produces positive outcomes. We cannot adequately represent it in this short description. Our purpose here is to introduce you to the value and potential of TIPS and to point you to further resources for your school, district, or state. As you read the description of TIPS you will notice that it overlaps with the six problem-solving steps in SWIS. That is because TIPS incorporates the successful components of SWIS while also adding new emphasis on what research shows is needed to make problem-solving effective in real school settings.

Effective Teams

The first components of TIPS involve creating an effective leadership team and using a meeting process that is rooted in the foundations of problem-solving. These foundations enable teams to establish effective team functioning in which the roles, responsibilities, tasks, data, plans, and follow-up are understood and implemented by all team members. The goal of this process is to ensure that meetings have predictability, participation, accountability, and communication. Although a lot of it would seem like common sense, as Mark Twain once said, "Common sense ain't all that common." And common sense doesn't necessarily translate to common practice. To facilitate creating an effective team, TIPS defines the essential roles and tasks for meetings, shown in **figure 5.5** on page 89.

Teams use an established agenda, review data at the outset, review progress from previous meetings, document decisions and changes, and start and end on time. Participation requires 75 percent of the team members present. Team members develop and adhere to agreed-upon norms, and meeting minutes, including the time and location of the next meeting, are available to all team members within twenty-four hours. Having a predictable meeting routine, including the time, day, and location, supports effective group work and outcomes.

---

1. Todd, A.W. et al., 2013.

Figure 5.5: Roles and Tasks for Meetings

Roles	Tasks
1. Meeting facilitator	Ask questions Implement norms Keep to agenda Progress through agenda Start and end on time
2. Data analyst	Likes data Fluent in navigating dataset to generate reports Discriminate features/labels for creating custom reports Create a story from data summary (for both old and new problems) Generate data summaries and summary statements 15–20 minutes before meeting
3. Minute-taker	Use computer during meeting to take notes Listen to discussion and paraphrase critical information in written form Fluent with meeting summary forms Keep chronological records of meetings and accomplishments
4. Timekeeper	Keep track of time on agenda items Communicate time used as meeting progresses
5. Participants	Attend at least 75 percent of meetings Listen to and consider all perspectives Maintain a sense of humor Show mutual respect Cooperate and support the group

Effective Problem-Solving with Data

Figure 5.6 on page 90 illustrates the TIPS foundations for PBIS Leadership Teams to have effective meetings in which problems are solved. With this foundation, the TIPS model provides teams with a structure for using data in problem-solving. The structure enables teams to develop the knowledge and skills needed to define problems in a manner that leads to solutions. This includes learning how to define problems with precision using precision statements, as we discussed in the first SWIS problem-solving step (see pages 83–84). It also includes the creation of SMART goals: goals that are specific, measurable, attainable, relevant, and timely (discussed in the second SWIS problem-solving

step, pages 84–85). From the SMART goal, teams adopt a focus on solutions that includes six parts, as presented in figure 5.3 on page 86.

> The goal of this process is to ensure that meetings have predictability, participation, accountability, and communication.

In summary, one of the major benefits that TIPS offers is its model for meeting foundations, which facilitates team development toward an effective, high-functioning group. The content of this model is not typically available, but so essential to teach success. A second major benefit of TIPS

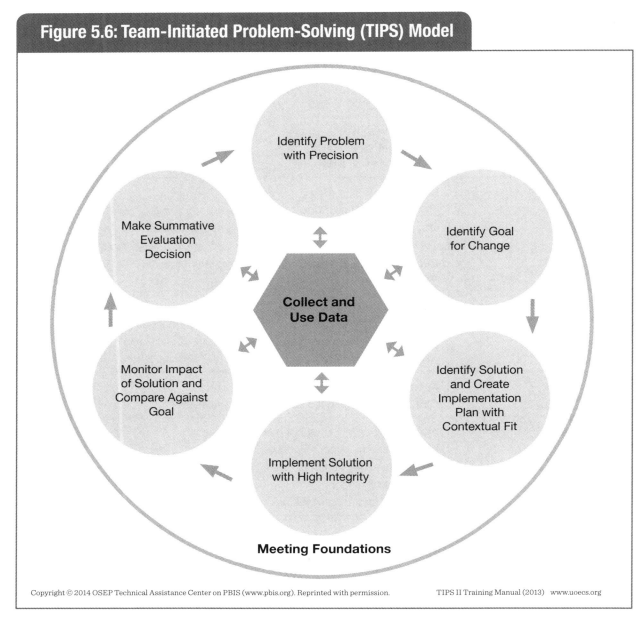

Figure 5.6: Team-Initiated Problem-Solving (TIPS) Model

Identify Problem with Precision

Identify Goal for Change

Make Summative Evaluation Decision

Collect and Use Data

Identify Solution and Create Implementation Plan with Contextual Fit

Monitor Impact of Solution and Compare Against Goal

Implement Solution with High Integrity

Meeting Foundations

TIPS II Training Manual (2013)   www.uoecs.org

is that teams receive detailed training and ongoing support in problem-solving. This includes the steps of problem-solving: how to identify behavioral problems with precision, define a goal for change, build a solution with action steps to achieve the goal, implement a comprehensive action plan, monitor outcomes, and evaluate and adapt the solution. The TIPS resources are available for free at the PBIS website and include overviews, training slides and videos, and multiple resources. See www.pbis.org/training/tips.

This chapter has presented examples of problem-solving frameworks using data within a PBIS system. You can use these approaches with implementation data from the Tiered Fidelity Inventory, School-Wide Evaluation Tool, Team Implementation Checklist, Self-Assessment Survey, and Benchmarks of Quality (measuring progress) and office discipline referral (ODR) data (measuring outcomes). Although using SWIS is not essential to monitoring ODR data, select a system that allows you to easily access very specific data in order to develop precise problem statements. We have included a "Data Drill Down for Creating Precision Statements" in the appendix (see page 174). This sheet is designed so that PBIS teams can use it to determine if they can access the specific data needed to create precision statements with their own ODR system. Some of these examples are simple and logical approaches. We have referenced a specific model, TIPS, which contains a general problem-solving approach that incorporates steps to ensure effective team functioning. Schools that successfully sustain PBIS must have effective PBIS Leadership Teams. It is essential for coaches and

teams to review and select the problem-solving framework that will ensure their school achieves its important outcomes. At the end of the day, schools want to be able to say, "We did what we said we would do and we achieved the important outcomes. We made a difference for kids and our school."

Chapter 11 on equity demonstrates ways your team can analyze ODR data to identify potential disproportionate referral practices and problem-solve to end them.

PART TWO

Implementing PBIS Tier 1

The chapters in part 2 of this book detail all the actions and desired outcomes of each stage of PBIS Tier 1 implementation. Be sure to complete all the checklist items and assessments noted in each section. It may seem like too much information at first, but eventually you will see how everything flows together.

The word *implementation* means to put something into action. In PBIS, implementation refers to putting in place a framework schoolwide that is defined by the eight key features outlined in chapter 1 (see page 11). Studies on implementation across various fields help us understand that putting new behaviors into practice is a process that occurs over time rather than a singular event that happens all at once.[1]

> The more you understand the big picture and the process, the more likely you are to achieve full implementation and long-term sustainability.

In 2005, the National Implementation Research Network (NIRN) published a cross-disciplinary review of research on implementation that also identified a progression of stages in the process of implementation. PBIS has adapted and incorporated this stage-based concept to guide efforts toward facilitating and sustaining full implementation.[2] **Figure 6.1** on page 95 offers a conceptual view of these stages in PBIS.

As you can probably surmise from looking at figure 6.1, the stages of PBIS implementation require a full-scale effort. In part 2 of this book, we devote a whole chapter to each stage. Before we delve into these chapters, however, let's consider three overarching messages that are implied in figure 6.1's outline of stages.

First, the time estimated from initial adoption to achieving PBIS as "business as usual" with a continuous improvement process fully in place is between three and five years. Everyone involved needs to remember this time frame. It means that you are committing to a long-term relationship with the process and outcomes and that PBIS is not something that will be accomplished within a single or even two academic years. Support and resources need to be available for a long time. Temporary funding with grants may be helpful initially but needs to be replaced with stable funding that matches the real time frame. Roles and functions need to be incorporated within existing positions to ensure stability and continuity of support.

Second, as you get started with implementation, you need to pace yourself, your leadership team, your staff, the district, and the community. Embrace realistic expectations for progress and outcomes. This outlook will affect your communications, assessments, and reporting to everyone concerned. Understanding how much time and effort is involved helps you better understand and respect the process that leads to important outcomes. We frequently see the great enthusiasm that new PBIS schools embrace and the ensuing disappointment when they cannot demonstrate outcomes after a short period of implementation.

Finally, your understanding of the process will empower you to plan for the frequent changes and challenges that are inevitable in any kind of system involving humans. Expect staffing and funding changes and build in the capacity to accommodate these so that you support continuity from day one. Stage-based approaches suggest a linear progression that is generally accurate. Yet in PBIS, you may at times feel like you are stepping backward even as you try to move forward. Rather than interpreting this as negative, view your implementation performance level as an indicator that informs your actions. Progress in any stage necessarily includes infrastructure maintenance as well as staff buy-in. The more you understand the big picture and the process, the more likely you are to achieve full implementation and long-term sustainability.

---

1. Sugai, 2013.
2. Goodman, 2013; Fixsen et al., 2005; Horner and Sugai, 2006.

Figure 6.1: Stages of PBIS Implementation

Stage	Description	Implications
Stage 1: Exploration and Adoption	Deciding to commit to adoption and implementation of PBIS	• Determine if your school has any need for behavioral intervention. • Become informed about the PBIS framework. • Discuss how PBIS might meet the need in your context. • Discuss whether or not to adopt it. • Secure support and sufficient staff buy-in.
Stage 2: Getting Ready—Installing the Infrastructure	Establishing necessary infrastructure to support the implementation	• Secure the support of administration in both your district and school. • Demonstrate priority. • Build leadership team. • Review existing resources that support proactive discipline policies and student support. • Develop action plan.
Stage 3: Getting Going—Initial Implementation	Putting key features of PBIS actively in place	• Carry out action plan. • Evaluate and compare plan to PBIS 8 key features. • Problem-solve. • Move toward achieving all 8 features with fidelity.
Stage 4: Up and Running—Full Implementation	Expanding the framework across people and settings	• Expand from a few to many: • across staff, families, and community • across schools in district
Stage 5: Sustaining and Continuous Improvement	Maintaining and improving	• Evaluate implementation fidelity and outcomes. • Revise based on implementation data. • Improve efficiency. • Adapt to change. • Embed within school or district routines.

Adapted from the work of Fixsen and Blase (NIRN) and Sugai and Horner (OSEP Technical Assistance Center on PBIS). Copyright © 2010. Reprinted with permission from Michigan's Integrated Behavior and Learning Support Initiative (MIBLSI).

PBIS Stage 1: Exploration and Adoption

Prior to adopting and implementing PBIS, most schools spend a period of time exploring the practice and considering the process for developing school readiness. The decision to implement PBIS in your school should not be taken lightly. It requires dedication and risk-taking. PBIS asks educators to let go of old ideas (for example, that suspension will change a student's behavior) and grab on to new ideas (that we need to teach the expected school behaviors while keeping an eye on our biases toward certain groups). Resources to gain PBIS awareness and readiness vary across districts and states; nevertheless, an intentional approach to this beginning stage is beneficial for coaches and school staff.

Tasks

Core objectives of stage 1:

1. Determine if your school has a need to address issues regarding student behavior and school climate; review all existing data and consider the concerns voiced by staff, students and their families, and the community. It's not just about problem behavior; it's about your vision for the school.

2. Gather information about options; research PBIS and decide whether this is a good fit for your school.

3. Review information with staff and get a sense of buy-in and commitment to move ahead.

4. Decide whether or not to proceed.

Determining Need
Consider Learning Outcomes and School Climate

How do you know whether PBIS is needed in your school? The school leadership and staff need to determine whether or not they have a problem or concern with the social behavior or safety in the school.

Begin by honestly answering these two questions:

1. Are at least 80 percent of your students fully engaged in the learning process?

   To answer this question, do a little data research: How many students have office discipline referrals (ODRs), and what percentage is that of your total student population? What should ODRs ideally look like for your population?

2. Are at least 80 percent of your students progressing on the learning continuum?

   To find this answer, dig a little deeper into your data: How many students are on target with their reading and math skills to meet school, district, and state academic goals?

If you answered "No," or "I'm not sure," or possibly "I don't think so" to either of these questions, then your school would definitely benefit from PBIS. This data-driven approach will help you answer these questions with ease. Schools that use PBIS benefit by becoming more aware of where their students stand academically; most also report significant drops in the number of ODRs, suspensions, and expulsions. With all those students back in the classroom, you can bet that academics are improving, teachers are teaching more, and administrators have time to do other administrative duties besides disciplining students.

What's more, the overall health of the school learning environment and culture improves once the entire school encourages the same set of positive student behaviors and discourages disruptive behaviors. Educational researcher Kathleen Cotton, in her journal article "Schoolwide and Classroom Discipline," shares her findings from reviewing numerous articles and criteria on what it means to be a safe school. She found the following characteristics showed up consistently in safe schools:[1]

- The **staff** is committed to creating and maintaining an environment that is, above all, conducive to learning and that does not tolerate inappropriate student behavior.

- High **behavioral expectations** are communicated to all students and staff.

- **Rules and procedures** for dealing with discipline problems are clearly conveyed and known to everyone in the school, students and staff.

- A warm **school climate** makes students and staff feel welcome and cared for as individuals.

- The **principal** is visible to students and staff daily and is generally supportive; the principal is not just a disciplinarian.

- **Teachers** are trained and authorized to handle minor behavioral problems in the classroom, with referrals being made to the principal or other administrator for serious behavioral infractions.

- Close ties with the **community** keep parents involved with the school and the wider community updated on school goals and activities.

The PBIS framework incorporates all these characteristics. They develop through the implementation process—your school doesn't need to have these pieces in place when you start to implement PBIS. Prior to participating in state cohort training, however, some states require an agreement from 80 percent of staff that they are willing to commit to creating a safe school that engages students in learning and that encourages staff to raise their standards of effective teaching.

Coaching During Stage 1

Ideally, your school's PBIS coach is selected even before the school has formally decided to adopt PBIS. This allows for continuity in leadership throughout the entire process of system change. (For more details on selecting a PBIS coach, see chapter 3.)

In this first stage, coaches can:

1. Gather data about your school's needs. For example, look at attendance, behavior incidents and disciplinary procedures, exclusionary practices, staff and student perceptions of safety, achievement, and any racial disproportionality.

2. Gather data on current perceptions of satisfaction among parents, staff, community, and students.

3. Gather and present information about PBIS—what it is, what implementation looks like (for example, from model schools), what outcomes have been demonstrated, and how PBIS would meet your school's identified need. Research shows that when staff have a good understanding of PBIS, they are more likely to buy in to the program.[2]

4. Gather information on necessary supports for PBIS implementation; for example, administrators, staff, funding, district-level commitment, and time commitment for building readiness and infrastructure. There are great resources at www.pbis.org

---

1. Cotton, 1990.
2. Filter and Sytsma, 2013.

that can assist in explaining the benefits of using the PBIS framework. The PBIS evaluation brief on economic costs specifically identifies the costs per school year ($12,400), as well as the costs per student ($12.40–$62.00), to implement PBIS. The brief remarkably also compares these costs to those of suspensions and school dropouts per student across their lifetime ($163,340). See www.pbis.org/blueprint briefstools.

5. Assist administrators and others to achieve buy-in from school staff. For example, gather and present local examples, visit other schools using PBIS, or talk to other school or district PBIS coordinators. Let staff know research has shown that schools implementing PBIS have less teacher burnout and that this is often more pronounced in schools with lower socioeconomic status.

6. Assist your school in adopting a process for decision-making—that is, determine how your school will decide whether or not to adopt PBIS.

Collect and Review Baseline Data

Another step in the decision-making process involves collecting some baseline data. The easiest way to do this is to look at your ODRs. Count the total number of referrals for a set period and then start breaking them down. For example, look at how many referrals have been written for certain behaviors and how many referrals per month, by grade, by boys versus girls, by race and ethnicity, and so on. Discuss what you think your pattern of referrals should look like. What is the difference between where you are now and where you want to be? Doing this will help you move from seeing the data as just a number—perhaps one that is big and scary even—to seeing the students who are behind those numbers and beginning to examine the underlying issues and circumstances that may be involved with the problem behavior.

> Are there too many referrals? Do students feel unsafe? Do adults feel unsafe? Do staff need more classroom management skills?

Once you have taken a look at your discipline data, consider your school's practices regarding behavioral problems and how those practices affect the problem and the students involved. Then, answer the questions on the worksheet titled "Current Practices for Behavioral Problems" on pages 106–107 to think about whether your school is working up to its potential.

The bottom line of whether your school will ultimately decide to adopt PBIS likely comes down to a perception of need: Are there too many referrals? Do students feel unsafe? Do adults feel unsafe? Do staff need more classroom management skills? Another way to look at this is to consider whether the top three priorities in your school improvement plan address student behavior, school culture, or other related issues. If none of these are a priority in your improvement plan, then staff may not perceive PBIS as a priority for your school to adopt.

Learning About PBIS

As a framework for improving school climate and reducing behavioral problems, PBIS offers both structure and flexibility. Part of deciding whether to organize your school efforts toward creating a safer environment that promotes learning involves examining the possibilities of using this approach. At this point, it is often helpful to review the ways that other schools have implemented PBIS. For example, if your district has implemented PBIS in other schools, it should be easy to visit them. Look at your state's PBIS website to find examples of other schools at the same grade level that have implemented PBIS and that might be able to share ideas with you. Inviting PBIS Leadership Teams and administrators to come talk to staff is a great idea. When Char was a state coordinator, she invited principals to PBIS information meetings to "tell the real truth" to prospective administrators and staff so they hear what PBIS is really like and not just her passion for PBIS.

Coach's Tip from Beth

I scoured the internet looking for examples of PBIS implementation before my school adopted it. The PBIS website (www.pbis.org) offers slide presentations, research articles written by academics in the field, and videos created by schools and school districts that explain how and why they decided to use PBIS and what outcomes they experienced.

Early Commitment and Buy-In

When schools decide to adopt PBIS, they need to understand the long-term commitment required to implement the framework. PBIS coaches, exploration committees, and leadership teams—once they are developed—are agents of change. You will face the challenge of staff buy-in not only before your school decides to adopt PBIS, but also as a constant factor throughout implementation. Don't assume that initial buy-in to an initiative means that level of commitment will remain constant. Anticipate this issue and pre-correct before buy-in lags. This topic is addressed in all the chapters in part 2, to consider what type of buy-in is required at each stage of the implementation process.

Understanding Reluctance

System change is difficult. Unfortunately, many teachers and other school staff have had the experience of starting many new initiatives and then watching them disappear slowly or quickly after changes in leadership or other new circumstances at the school. This creates a sense of revolving-door initiatives, which can leave many feeling cynical.

For example, have you ever attended a training, taken notes all day and maybe done some role-playing, all the while knowing in your heart that it wouldn't last beyond next Monday morning? Such experiences naturally leave staff questioning whether to invest at all, or at least wondering when they should get on board the next time something new comes along.

It's very helpful for PBIS coaches, exploration committees, and leadership teams to be familiar with the history of a school, especially how many initiatives have started and failed in years past. Knowing at the outset what you're up against in your efforts to gain buy-in will help you develop strategies and realistic expectations for convincing staff that this time will be different. When Beth worked on staff at public schools and new behavior or discipline models were introduced, the prevailing message from veteran teachers was that if you didn't like what they were doing, just hold on—because it would be something else in about three years. And they were right!

Char has encountered teachers who don't want to invest themselves in the model for numerous reasons. Frequently, both coaches and staff talk about colleagues who just don't buy in. This happens in nearly all schools, regardless of the situation. There are always team or community members who hesitate. Some teachers even refuse to participate in PBIS, arguing, "Kids should already know what to do in school—sit down, be quiet, and do their work." PBIS acknowledges that some students simply don't know what they are supposed to do, for various reasons, or they need help managing their feelings. Within the PBIS framework, it is our responsibility to teach students expected school behaviors, including ways to manage feelings and cope with stress and frustration in an appropriate way. Research supporting social-emotional learning in all schools, across all grade levels, continues to grow.

If after sharing your vision and explaining the fundamentals of the framework as well as the plans for implementation, you encounter anyone unwilling to budge from their viewpoint, it's often best to simply extend the invitation for them to join the effort if they change their mind. We typically encourage exploration committees and leadership teams to focus on those staff members who have already bought in and are working with the process. Still, it's helpful to gain a general understanding of the psychological aspects of learning and change and how this affects buy-in.[3]

- **Change means uncertainty.** That uncertainty may be about the specifics—or the lack of specifics—of what and how things are changing and who is directing or facilitating the change. Uncertainty may also be a reflection of whether the direction of change is viewed as positive. Some people may lack confidence that they can successfully implement the change. Good coaching and support help here.

- **Uncertainty is a powerful trigger for anxiety.** This reaction is natural and people vary in their response to uncertainty. Some may thrive and others may experience a lot of fear.

- **Anxiety may lead to avoidance.** Some people will go to great lengths to avoid feeling anxious. Anxiety is an unpleasant emotion. Sometimes we label this avoidance behavior as willful resistance and respond negatively to those who exhibit it. However, it might be more useful to recognize that adults, like kids, might be trying to protect themselves by responding this way. This perspective allows you to work toward easing the natural discomfort rather than blaming the person.

- **Lack of information and understanding can lead to a negative outlook.** This is really important, because you want to start off building positive expectations among staff and families. The good news is that this is something you can work to change—namely, by offering a clear vision of the outcome and by providing good information early and often.

- **Resistance is a natural human response to uncertainty.** Framing resistance in this way allows you to be proactive and positive in your interactions with others rather than blaming or focusing negative attention on people who are slow to buy in.

How to Achieve Buy-In

One of the questions that repeatedly surfaces across the stages of implementation is how to get and maintain buy-in. We approach buy-in with prevention logic and good teaching and planning. Attention to buy-in should occur early and often and include specific tasks.

During the five stages of PBIS implementation, there are seven possible audiences from whom you need buy-in:

1. Administrators/principals
2. PBIS Leadership Team
3. School staff
4. District staff
5. Students
6. Families
7. Community

First, let's talk about what we mean by staff buy-in, which is necessary even before the decision to officially commit to PBIS has been made. Staff buy-in, sometimes called staff investment, means that teachers and other school employees engage in decision-making and planning, behave consistently with decisions, and continue to follow through with and support all aspects of the initiative. They understand what PBIS is, how it will fit the school context, and what it will mean in terms of their time and effort.

Often when a school is considering adopting PBIS, there is usually a presentation to all school staff about the initiative and then some type of vote. A supportive vote more than likely represents the staff's understanding and sense of need at that point in time. In other words, it's a snapshot. What unfolds during implementation is the realization that the adults in the environment have to change the way they do business. And change translates to time and effort.

---

3. Bandura, 1977.

Indeed, the implementation period of change begins to take more time, effort, and commitment from staff. That's where coaches and leadership teams begin to see more issues with buy-in. For example, staff members who initially voted for PBIS may now be slow to make changes in the way they handle classroom behavioral problems.

Leading people through change requires a vision, road map, good leadership, and coaching. PBIS implementation means changing the system and relies heavily on changing adult beliefs. Coaches and leadership teams take on the role of guiding their colleagues through the process so that staff are part of and understand the direction, the outcomes, and the specific steps they'll need to take along the way.

It's important to demonstrate confidence in people's ability to change. This means conveying belief and support for the staff's ability to adopt the actions necessary to reach full implementation.[4] Coaches, exploration committees, and leadership teams have the job of helping staff see this possibility. This is done by modeling, sharing examples, and visiting and networking with other schools further along in the process.

Positive acknowledgment of each step is also helpful. New and changing behaviors need a lot of reinforcement. When we teach kids, we increase the ratio of reinforcement. Typically educators hear that classrooms should have a 4:1 ratio of positive comments to negative comments. When teaching new skills to students, however, educators are encouraged to reinforce a lot more—7:1 or even 8:1 in the beginning—because kids need to be praised when they are learning something new and they tend to increase use of the new behavior to get the positive attention from adults. The same applies when teaching adults—we have to increase the ratio of reinforcement and acknowledgment.

Steps Toward Gaining Staff Buy-In

The following steps can help you gain staff buy-in while you are exploring PBIS.

Involve staff from the beginning. Invite several staff members to be on the PBIS exploration committee and, later, the leadership team. Create a vision for your school. Communicate decisions. Make the process of implementing the features of PBIS transparent and shared. Consciously and frequently solicit staff input. This can be done in formal ways, such as staff surveys, as well as through informal conversations that occur naturally in the school setting.

Create and maintain ongoing communication. Build a communication plan and share the story of PBIS implementation. Use multiple methods for sharing news about PBIS with all key stakeholders, including face-to-face communication, presentations to small and large groups, bulletin boards in the staff lounge, blog posts, websites, and newsletters. Work to create a sense of community around this initiative. Share action plans and decision-making with staff and show them the data that demonstrate progress and outcomes.

Build trust. Listen to staff and work to build rapport with all, regardless of their position. Keep planning and teamwork transparent. Avoid any in-group/out-group dynamics. Demonstrate to staff how their input is used. Char spoke with an educator who said that in her setting the PBIS Leadership Team seemed to be a tight clique and not open to other staff. These dynamics are common, but good group skills help avoid or reduce these effects.

Regularly and authentically acknowledge all staff. Plan and show appreciation for staff efforts with notes, awards, drawings, preferred parking, errands, breakfasts, and so on. Develop a plan to acknowledge staff members who are working to implement PBIS; you can do this daily, weekly, or on an ad hoc schedule. Communicate confidence in all staff and in their ability to contribute toward the desired outcomes. Provide supports to staff quickly when needed.

---

4. Bandura, 1977.

Provide visible leadership support. Ensure that your administrator publicly supports the PBIS vision and initiative with verbal, written, and visual statements. It is helpful when administrators are present and participating at trainings and meetings and are open to visiting classrooms. The administrator plays a key role in communicating success to the district as well as to the community. We have heard administrators presenting their outcome data at PBIS conferences and thought: If that principal is willing to stand in front of a crowd and talk about PBIS at his school, then that's a school where we would want to work!

Celebrate successes regularly. If you are a member of the PBIS Leadership Team, be sure to acknowledge and celebrate success in achieving and advancing implementation. Though success is gratifying, it is still a lot of work. Share successes with the whole school, staff, and students at planned celebrations. For example, when the number of discipline referrals drops, congratulate students on their success in following school expectations and celebrate with a fun school activity. We've heard of such crazy activities as inviting kids to the auditorium to throw a pie in the principal's face because the number of referrals dropped by 10 percent. Char worked with a principal who agreed to sleep on the school roof if students achieved a specific behavior goal. The students won, and the principal slept on the roof on a cold January night in Minnesota.

Remember, buy-in doesn't come automatically and doesn't continue without conscious effort. If you had some staff buy-in during the fall, that doesn't mean it will still be there in the spring. Buy-in is not a single event but an ongoing process. It may feel a bit like herding cats; support ebbs and flows, and not everyone is going to champion this effort. Even so, most staff members will support practices that make their jobs more effective and efficient. As a PBIS coach or leadership team member, you have the job of enabling your colleagues to experience such outcomes.

> Remember, buy-in doesn't come automatically and doesn't continue without conscious effort.

Buy-In During Stage 1

While buy-in continues throughout PBIS, during the exploration process, it may include these specific steps:

1. The administrator clearly articulates a vision for the school and commits to adopting, implementing, and supporting PBIS with all the implications for staff time, resources, and so on.

2. Staff members demonstrate initial buy-in, or commitment, to implement PBIS. This buy-in may be established through a vote following a presentation about PBIS, a school visit from staff already using PBIS, and so on. Most often, an informal vote will be taken, but some schools use staff surveys or ballots. With good explanations from administrators up front, staff will see the need for initial buy-in; they have lived through the negative consequences of starting an important initiative without full buy-in.

3. District support is established. When a school is the first, or only, school in a large district to adopt PBIS, gaining strong support from the district is key. Often when other schools see support from the district, they come on board too. The district structure helps ensure continuity and sustainability, so staff won't view PBIS as an initiative that will last a year or so until the next newest, latest, greatest one comes along.

Figure 6.2 on page 103 charts a way to break down these tasks into specific measures and delegate responsibility for them.

Deciding to Adopt PBIS

There are many ways a school or district can come to the decision to use the PBIS framework.

Figure 6.2: Exploration and Adoption—Buy-In Roles and Measures During Stage 1

Person/Group Responsible	Buy-In Tasks	Measures
Building administrator/ principal	• Share vision for school • Identify school leaders and committee members to explore PBIS • Support exploration and adoption efforts	Allocate funding—paying for subs so committee members can attend trainings, providing money for posters, hiring reinforcements Grant time—for exploration committee to meet and attend trainings Provide resources—posters, lesson plans, large poster paper, community-building curriculum, various other supplies
Exploration committee	• Share knowledge of PBIS with school and district staff	Research PBIS Present and promote knowledge with school and district staff
School staff	• Decide if PBIS is right for their school	Majority of staff agree to implement PBIS
District administration	• Identify school leaders and committee members to explore PBIS	Agree to support implementation of PBIS—funding, time, resources
Families and community	• Decide if PBIS is right for the school	Agree to support PBIS in the school as part of the school community

A principal or administrator might read some research about it and decide it's just the thing she's looking for to improve the school. A teacher in graduate school may decide to research PBIS and passionately discuss it with anyone in the district who will listen. District administration could be looking for ways to improve the safety of the school to make it more enticing to prospective students and their families. Some teachers have brought PBIS to their schools after seeing it in action in their own child's school in a different district. Parents may see examples of PBIS in other schools and approach their child's school about pursuing similar strategies.

Part of making the decision to formally adopt PBIS includes being sure that your school is prepared to take on the implementation process. There are resources available to help you determine your school's readiness. Check to see if your state department of education has a readiness checklist

on its website. If not, take a look on www.pbis.org to find a readiness checklist that schools can use as they prepare for PBIS. Some items on the list are:

• district leadership and support

• a school improvement plan that includes schoolwide discipline

• commitment from principal to provide support and make discipline decisions

• commitment from a majority of staff and administration to implement PBIS knowing that full implementation may take three to five years

• a PBIS Leadership Team that agrees to meet at least two times per month and includes members who have a background in behavior (such as a school psychologist, school social worker, counselor, or special education teacher)

• faculty has received an overview presentation of PBIS

- the district agrees to provide funding to support PBIS initiatives
- an internal school coach has been identified by the principal or district administration
- an ODR form and behavioral definitions compatible with Schoolwide Information System (SWIS)

It is also possible to use the Tiered Fidelity Inventory (TFI) as a baseline needs assessment to see how many features or partial features your school has in place. Some states use a specific tool related to readiness. One example is the Hexagon Tool, which was developed by the National Implementation Research Network (NIRN). California provides this tool for schools considering PBIS implementation. See nirn.fpg.unc.edu and click on "The Hexagon Tool—Exploring Context."

Telling Your School's Story

A helpful activity as you adopt and prepare to implement PBIS is to articulate what we call your school's story. This activity means thinking about how you will communicate the changes your school is making to your staff, your families, your district administration, your community, and any other stakeholders.

We recommend that you develop a narrative based on your data (which you update regularly as you progress)—a narrative that you can share during each stage of implementation. In this and the following chapters on the stages of implementation, we include an example to help you tell your story. Use your own creativity to add details that make it your school's story. Reviewing your school's story periodically can also help you learn more about what's working and what may need to be fine-tuned. For example, when Beth was a school PBIS coach, she kept a three-ring binder that stored everything created around PBIS—the purpose statement and expectations, assessment scores, an informal survey done with students, photos of Student of the Month celebrations, photos of students collecting trinkets at the school prize box, emails the principal sent to staff regarding the implementation of PBIS, and team meeting minutes. This binder contained all the elements of her school's journey with PBIS. When Beth looked back at this binder as the implementation continued, she could see things she might have done differently, like *not* trying to start everything at once!

One way to tell your story is with data on a spreadsheet or a graph. This might become a poster hung in the teachers' lounge, a report to your school board, or a presentation to your community members at open house night. Some schools hang graphs in the hallway so the kids can keep an eye on referral numbers. Others make funny videos with staff and students to share with the school, the school board, the community, and maybe even at the national PBIS conference.

Whatever method of storytelling you decide to use, be honest about your starting point. Sometimes when you see how many ODRs your school has written in a year, you may want to shave off a few points so you don't look so bad. Resist this urge—it's unethical and a bad idea! Start exactly where you are starting. Talk about what is typical and where you want to be. Consider also any disproportionality of referrals for all groups in your school. Keep a running record of the data to demonstrate ups and downs that occur. Don't be surprised if the number of ODRs actually goes up during the second year—this seems to be a common occurrence. That may simply indicate that you are counting behaviors better, that teachers are following the behavior flowchart better, or that more students are being referred. That could be a part of your school's story, in a section called "The Year Our Referrals Doubled." Embrace and accept what is happening in your data and your school.

However you choose to do it, it's important that you tell your story. You have regular, valid measures of progress, implementation, and fidelity with PBIS. Let your audiences and stakeholders know that implementation occurs across stages and years. To tell your story at this stage in the process, work through questions similar to those in the sidebar "Our School's Story—PBIS Stage 1" on page 105.

Resources

If your school is considering using PBIS, or if you are planning to propose it to your school or district, there are many tools and resources available to help you get started. First, look at and make use of the PDF presentation included in the digital content for this book. (See page 201 in the index for details on how to download.) Also, check with your state for an organized system of training and support for schools and districts using PBIS. Many states have related information on their department of education website. Go to www.pbis.org/pbis-network to find your state coordinator or website. If your state does not have an organized system for training schools, visit the PBIS website (www.pbis.org) for resources. There are regional technical assistance centers located around the country. The OSEP Technical Assistance Center on PBIS offers an annual PBIS Leadership Forum in Chicago each fall. Check the website for details and dates. Another option is the Association for Positive Behavior Support (APBS) at www.apbs.org. They have listings for state networks and can help you get PBIS established in your school or district. APBS sponsors a yearly national conference, typically in early spring, showcasing terrific resources.

Our School's Story— PBIS Stage 1

In this stage of our story, we focus on why our school began exploring PBIS.

Why did our school get involved in PBIS?

Note: Include the reasons that your school decided to move ahead: *School climate was perceived by staff and students as unsafe . . . (elaborate); ODRs were rising significantly over the previous two years . . . ; Students of color were disproportionally referred out of the classroom compared to their white peers . . . ; Students with special needs were more often referred to self-contained settings before evidence-based interventions were implemented . . . ; Student achievement was below district/state/national norms . . . (elaborate with number from your state's department of education website).*

Example: During the school year, our school saw an increase in disruptive student behavior in the classroom, with a significant rise in ODRs for serious student behavior problems, which we think led to declines in perceptions of safety and academic achievement by our students. Therefore our school adopted a school improvement goal of reducing major behavior referrals. We chose to accomplish this by implementing a daily advisory period for all students and by starting a peer mentoring group.

Current Practices for Behavioral Problems: Staff Systems, Student Behavior, and Data Practices

Staff Systems

1. What insights about our students do we gain from looking at behavioral data?

   _____

   _____

2. How are teachers handling disruptive behaviors in the classroom? Do we have a consistent procedure for this? For example, does one teacher allow gum chewing and another refer the student out for having gum?

   _____

   _____

3. Where do the students go once they get referred out of the classroom? What does the referral process look like in our school?

   _____

   _____

4. Who tends to the students in the office or the behavior room, and what happens once they arrive? What kind of training has that person received in handling disruptive students?

   _____

   _____

5. What happens when a student returns to the classroom?

   _____

   _____

6. Where does the paper referral go once the student returns to class? How are we tracking behaviors and interventions?

   _____

   _____

7. What type of training does our school provide to teachers in positive classroom management procedures?

   _____

   _____

continued >

Current Practices for Behavioral Problems: Staff Systems, Student Behavior, and Data Practices, continued

Student Behavior

1. How are students learning the skills they need to stay in class? Are students being taught prosocial behavior? Calming strategies?

   _____

   _____

2. How is our school promoting positive behaviors between students and staff?

   _____

   _____

3. How are positive behaviors being reinforced and acknowledged in our school?

   _____

   _____

4. What kind of interventions are in place for students who have three or more referrals?

   _____

   _____

Data Practices

1. How is our school tracking behavior problems?

   _____

   _____

2. Who is looking at the data?

   _____

   _____

3. Who is actively monitoring the school improvement plan?

   _____

   _____

4. How does our referral data correlate to the racial makeup of our school?

   _____

   _____

5. Who are receiving most of the ODRs in our building? Look at grade, gender, race, ethnicity, and special education status.

   _____

   _____

PBIS Stage 2: Getting Ready—Installing the Infrastructure

Once you have formally decided to implement PBIS, the next step is to get ready by installing the groundwork for implementation. This includes some of the eight key features of PBIS that were noted in chapter 1. During stage 2, you will identify initial tasks and take some first steps. These tasks involve creating the basic infrastructure that will build capacity to support further actions. This intentional planning and prioritizing of tasks to fit the particular needs of your school—rather than jumping into all the elements at once—will go far in setting the tone and pace of implementation. What's more, it will help you achieve early successes and thus build momentum and gain additional buy-in for PBIS.

Tasks

Core objectives of stage 2:

1. Establish a leadership team that will guide implementation.
2. Develop a process to communicate at all levels.
3. Establish a system of technical assistance that will support the leadership team, staff, and community in accomplishing the tasks related to the practice of PBIS.

Key Features at Stage 2

As you prepare to begin PBIS during the installation stage, you'll start to assemble and develop items from the eight key PBIS features. The three boldfaced items in the following list highlight those features that are part of the process at the installation stage.

1. **Establish the PBIS Leadership Team.**
2. **Develop a statement of vision or purpose.**
3. **Identify three to five schoolwide positive behavioral expectations.**
4. Develop teaching procedures.
5. Develop lesson plans.
6. Develop procedures for acknowledging positive student behavior.
7. Develop procedures for discouraging rule violations.
8. Develop data systems for monitoring implementation, fidelity, and outcomes.

Establishing a PBIS Leadership Team

An important first step during the installation stage is for the coach and administrator to work together to identify potential members for the PBIS Leadership Team, including staff at various grade levels and with various academic expertise along with families and students. This diverse group of people from your school will be instrumental in every facet of implementation. The team should be representative of your student body, as well, in terms of racial and ethnic background, culture and religion, gender, ability, socioeconomic status, and sexual orientation. They will gain support and buy-in from other school staff, help with PBIS training, collect and use data to ensure that PBIS is being implemented with fidelity, and ensure that policies and procedures are being implemented equitably for all students. Ultimately, leadership team members help ensure that PBIS reaches its potential to promote a safe school and a positive learning environment while decreasing behavioral problems. (See chapter 2 for step-by-step information on forming a leadership team.)

Once all members of the leadership team have been chosen, consider attending PBIS trainings as a team. This not only helps you guide your school through the PBIS implementation process, but also allows the team members to become cohesive, learning about each other as they become a unit.

Once the leadership team is established and initial roles have been assigned, the team can begin developing plans and procedures that will become the backbone of PBIS in your school. But first, it's important to get a feel for how teachers and other staff see the current state of behavior at your school.

Coaching During Stage 2
Coaches can:
1. Talk with the principal about establishing a working and representative team.
2. Identify and clarify your role as a coach so that you and your principal can communicate this to staff and the wider school community.
3. Assist the administrator and the leadership team in the assignment of team roles (team leader/facilitator, notetaker, data manager, timekeeper, and archivist).

4. Identify the PBIS assessment tools and data monitoring system the school will use. Connect your school or district with your local PBIS coordinator for help in getting started with the PBIS assessment tools. (See chapter 4 for more on assessment tools.)
5. Assist the administrator in providing clear, tangible directions to guide the PBIS Leadership Team in making action plans that include data collection and progress monitoring.
6. Become fluent in using, analyzing, and reporting data that tracks implementation progress, fidelity, and outcomes.
7. Become fluent in understanding and using the school's (or district's) office discipline referral (ODR) system.
8. Acquire technical assistance to build personal fluency in using data tools. (See chapter 4.)
9. Build personal fluency in the team problem-solving process. (See chapter 5.)
10. Establish a regular meeting time and place for the leadership team.
11. Ask for a regular time slot on the faculty meeting agenda across the year.
12. Determine your process for communicating and sharing your school's story about PBIS. Every decision, accomplishment, and change should be shared with staff to encourage their engagement and buy-in.

Remember, your job is to oversee these areas, not to do it all! Work with your principal to select a strong leadership team and then divide the jobs. Know your strength and pull others onto the team who can dedicate their skills and expertise in implementing PBIS.

Coach's Tip from Beth

Be sure to involve all members of your PBIS Leadership Team right away. Ask team members if they have particular areas of interest and assign them related tasks when possible. Team members want to feel that they are contributing, so make use of their skills and talents. To do this, you can:

- rotate note-taking (use a consistent form and process)
- invite team members to submit agenda items for meetings (always follow up on previous agenda and action items before tackling new topics)
- rotate data presenters at faculty meetings
- create subgroups that might include staff not on the PBIS Leadership Team (for example, form a reinforcement committee to plan an award system, gather prizes or rewards, and set up how they will be distributed)

PBIS Team Training Tip from Char

My experience at the regional and state levels has been in a state that provides an opportunity to engage in training cohorts. The schools selected for this program received two years of very structured support with training and infrastructure building around data, systems, and practices. Formal training and coaching support offered a scope and sequence of training and practice. The training model will look different in each state, but the training content is consistent and faithful to the PBIS model suggested by the national OSEP Technical Assistance Center on

PBIS. Training is modified to include new tools and research that affect practice. In my personal experience, the most effective and efficient training approach is through an organized and systematic structure. I recognize that some districts and schools may find such centralized training difficult to accommodate. I encourage them to reach out to these state and regional entities for possible customization.

In recent years, regional PBIS technical assistance centers have been created as a means to build capacity around the country. Districts and schools can certainly choose to move ahead with adoption and implementation without participating in any external formal training system. My caution with this approach is that the district team must develop the capacity for this and become extremely fluent in their understanding of the entire system of PBIS and its components. When districts or schools hire an outside trainer who comes just once or twice, the staff hear about the eight primary features of PBIS much like they would in other conferences. They often don't receive the frequent assistance that ensures the availability and accuracy of coaching, evaluation, training, and behavioral support. As a result, some people adopt some features, but often there is no data system used to assist in measuring implementation and fidelity. In other words, although it can be less expensive or more convenient to hire a trainer and limit the amount of time teachers and others are out of the classroom or building, I suggest that districts or cooperatives and other entities follow the recommendations for a solid implementation, which includes the major components and especially the adoption of data and evaluation systems to measure progress and fidelity.

It's very difficult to change a complete system without a good road map and feedback mechanisms to keep you on track. Even when schools and districts go through prolonged and systematic training and coaching, there are enough naturally occurring challenges that sustainability often fails. After completion of formal training and support, sustaining districts and schools often face the same challenge: building and maintaining local capacity.

Collecting and Examining Baseline Data

One of the first tasks of the PBIS Leadership Team is to review the behavioral practices currently being used in the school. They ask all staff members—including office support, paraprofessionals, custodians, and cafeteria workers—to complete the Self-Assessment Survey (see chapter 4). This survey includes a section called the "Classroom System," which will help you assess current behavioral practices. This will give you a snapshot of staff perceptions. Additionally, the PBIS Leadership Team could opt to complete the Tiered Fidelity Inventory (TFI) as a needs assessment, which will provide a picture of what features may already be in place.

During this installation stage, the team can also look at behavioral data currently being collected to get an objective view of how the school handles disruptive behaviors. It's important to have this type of baseline data in hand and to use it as a starting point before fully implementing PBIS. This information is frequently found on ODR reports (see chapter 4). Use the data to guide your team to determine areas of strength and concern.

As your team sifts through the staff survey results and behavioral data, keep the following questions in mind:
- Who are your students?
- What is working well for students and staff?
- Where are the trouble spots in the building?
- What do your students need to achieve greater academic success?

- What do staff members need to achieve more successful teaching experiences?
- How does what you are doing now align with your school improvement plan?
- Are there groups of students who are overrepresented, or even underrepresented, when looking at student ODRs, suspensions, or expulsions?
- Are your ODRs at a number that you judge to be acceptable? Are they too high? What is your standard for comparison?

Developing an Action Plan

All the data collected can be used to develop an action plan, which is a more detailed, ongoing list of what the PBIS Leadership Team is working on. Teams can update the action plan as they go, checking off items as they are completed and then adding new tasks. **Figure 7.1** on page 112 presents a sample action plan.

Coach's Tip from Beth

When I started coaching, my action plan was long and complicated. I tried to implement everything that was missing all at once. This is a huge mistake, not to mention an exhausting and impossible endeavor! It's better to focus on implementing a few things really well. As things get done, add something else to your action plan. Remember, it usually takes three to five years to fully implement Tier 1.

Also, from the beginning, be sure to delegate various jobs and tasks on the action plan to all PBIS Leadership Team members. This keeps your to-do list from overflowing and builds the capacity of the whole team. It is really important to reinforce that PBIS is a team-guided process at all levels and is not person dependent.

Figure 7.1: Sample PBIS Action Plan

Key PBIS Feature	Action/Activity	Person Responsible	Start Date	End Date	When/How It Will Be Evaluated
#1	Establish the PBIS Leadership Team	Administrator and coach	5/8/18	6/12/18	Team will represent each grade level and include 2 paraprofessionals, 2 specialists, and 2 from other areas (e.g.,families, students)
#2	Develop the purpose or vision statement	PBIS Leadership Team	5/22/18	5/25/18	PBIS team will draft a purpose or vision statement for review at final staff meeting
#3	Develop five or fewer behavioral expectations	PBIS Leadership Team	5/22/18	5/25/18	PBIS team will draft behavioral expectations for review at final staff meeting

Establishing Schoolwide Behavioral Expectations

Using the data collected thus far, and focusing especially on the areas of need identified by staff, your next step is to define three to five school-wide behavioral expectations. These will be the expectations that all students are held to and will be followed in both classroom and nonclassroom settings. Often a first step in this task is to write a purpose or vision statement.

Write a Purpose or Vision Statement

The purpose or vision statement lays your school's foundation for the PBIS framework; the statement should support the academic and behavioral goals of your school. It guides all the work of the team; it says why you do what you do. The statement should be:

- positively stated
- two to three sentences in length
- supportive of behavioral and academic achievement

- contextually and culturally appropriate (for age, race, ethnicity, language, community)
- agreed upon by at least 80 percent of school staff
- communicated to families, community members, and district administrators

Include the statement on newsletters, websites, posters, referral forms, and anything else your school prints or publishes. This keeps it clearly in focus and puts it out into the community. When you talk about the purpose or vision, use this as a means to inspire and build enthusiasm among your audience for what is possible. See page 172 of the appendix for a brainstorming form.

Sample Purpose/Vision Statement
The following statement is from a hypothetical school named Evergreen School:

The Evergreen School is a community of learners. With school staff supporting us, we come to school to become our best selves by studying hard and becoming good citizens in a safe and friendly school environment.

Write the Schoolwide Expectations

Teams adopt or revise expectations that are reflective of the cultural values of the surrounding community. Expectations and specific rules are identified based on a legitimate purpose within the setting, as opposed to simply school tradition or maintaining the status quo. Within a culturally responsive framework, behavioral expectations should focus on high standards for all students, be able to be taught and learned, and be respectful of the students' cultures.[1]

Now, use your purpose or vision statement as a guide to write schoolwide expectations. The expectations should reflect the values of your school community. *Note:* We recommend using the word *expectations* instead of *rules* because *rules* seems stiff and threatening. *Rules* seems to say, "You will do . . ." and "You will not do . . ." Using the word *expectations* puts the onus back on the students. It says, "This is what we expect from you and we know you can live up to these expectations." Some schools like to have students assist in the process of writing the expectations. This may increase the representation of different student voices and students' ownership of the schoolwide expectations. One way to do this is to invite each homeroom to write three things that are important to school and that support the purpose or vision. Each homeroom can send a representative to a meeting, much like the founding fathers writing the Constitution, to share, vote, and agree on the expectations for the school. The representatives then bring the final expectations back to homeroom and explain how the group came up with the expectations. The adult facilitating the large group of representatives can guide the conversation and may set meeting ground rules, such as use positive statements, use expected school language, and every idea is considered. See the appendix on page 173 for a brainstorming form.

Sample Schoolwide Expectations
Using the Evergreen School as an example again, here is how their schoolwide expectations might look:

At Evergreen School:

We come to school to learn.
We respect ourselves and others.
We are responsible for our actions.

Writing open-ended expectations allows them to be used in numerous settings (hallways, gym, lunchroom, and so on) and tailored to different grades. These expectations should be displayed all over the school—in classrooms, hallways, entrances, the cafeteria, and so on. This allows a staff member who encounters a student running in the hallways to simply point to the expectations and ask the student, "Where in our expectations do you see that running in the hallways is okay?" These expectations will have been taught and retaught and reinforced to students, so the student knows that running in the hallways doesn't fit into your expectations. She can quickly make amends and, as long as no one was harmed and she was running to avoid being late to class, can go off to class walking. It's likely that the student will receive a tardy note and thus still be held responsible for her actions.

When implementing schoolwide expectations, keep in mind the culture of your students and the communities they come from, their traditions and rituals.

When implementing schoolwide expectations, keep in mind the culture of your students and the communities they come from, their traditions and rituals. A school in Minneapolis with a predominately American Indian student population writes their schoolwide expectations in Dakota as

---

1. Leverson et al., 2016.

well as in English. Another school has a predominately Hmong student population. Their posters of schoolwide expectations incorporate a design common in Hmong embroidery. We also know schools whose students made their schoolwide expectations into a rap and filmed a video to go along with it. What's important is that you involve your students, parents, and community members in creating the expectations for your school and in helping teach the expectations. This creates ownership and buy-in for students, making your PBIS program relevant to them and diverse in representation, and will increase involvement from families and the greater community.

Implementing the PBIS framework with fidelity, using tools such as the ethnicity reports or the Drill-Down Tool in Schoolwide Information System (SWIS) or something similar, can also help schools identify patterns and decision points in discipline practices that are prone to subjectivity and possible bias. Having the data can decrease racial disparity in behavioral referrals and suspensions by opening conversations about how teachers perceive and handle behaviors in their classrooms and by implementing solutions to prevent the behavior from happening again. You can also use data to compare the referrals among racial and ethnic groups in your school. For example, how many Black and Latino students are being referred out of class compared to white students? What behaviors are those referrals for? How did the teacher respond to the behaviors prior to referring the students out of the classroom?

In conversation with a white teacher, Beth mentioned her frustration with the disproportionate number of Black students who had ODRs. He responded, "I don't refer students out because they are Black; I refer them out because they are disruptive." This opened a discussion about implicit bias that teachers bring to the classroom. To that teacher, the kids who talked in class or couldn't sit still for the class period received the punishment he thought they deserved: referrals to the office for disrupting his class. As teachers, we have a responsibility to use teaching practices that are inclusive of all students, all the time. Perhaps this teacher

could have handled the blurting differently by using reminders to refocus, a visual signal to quiet down, or referring back to the classroom expectations. He could also have implemented a classwide positive reinforcement system that would have given positive attention to the desired classroom behaviors.

Of course, many teachers build wonderful relationships with students and their families. Beth has been privileged to watch amazing teachers who allow call-and-response, can quiet down students who blurt out with just a glance, and are glad to see students come to their classes even if the students are a few minutes late. These teachers celebrate successes with their students. They create classrooms that feel safe for students. We know good teaching includes high expectations for all students and multiple ways to respond. Students do well in these classes because the teacher accepts them, listens to them, corrects them, and honors them. And these are the teachers who typically refer very few students out of their classrooms.

Staff should have conversations about the data and discuss why racial disparity is happening in their schools. These will probably be very difficult conversations to have. They can lead to soul-searching for some teachers, while others may dig their heels in deeper, resisting the idea that they should have to teach students how to behave in their classrooms. Perhaps some professional development around cultural diversity that includes coaching in the classroom would benefit schools struggling with racial disparity in their referral process. View practice guides and briefs at www.pbis.org/school/equity-pbis.

Char recalls, in her early years in PBIS, working with an urban elementary school that was really struggling. The school was in a large metropolitan district in which student demographics had changed significantly. What hadn't changed were the teacher demographics. Teachers were almost exclusively white and had been at the school for much of their careers. When they started, the school was small and comprised of working- or middle-class families. Now it was mostly students of color, with many families living in poverty; however, the expectations at school remained the same. There were huge challenges to overcome the cultural mismatch in the expectations in order for students and staff to be successful. This scenario is common throughout the country and underscores how all staff and schools need to prepare for changes and adjust practices to support high expectations for all.

See chapter 11 for a deeper discussion of equity in schools.

Develop and Publicly Post a Schoolwide Behavioral Matrix

A behavioral matrix is based on your schoolwide expectations and is distributed to all staff. **Figure 7.2** shows a sample matrix that continues the example of the Evergreen School. Notice how this matrix uses Evergreen's purpose statement and expectations to guide the work. This matrix provides the basis for increasing consistency

throughout school settings and classrooms because it is taught to all students, and all staff are responsible for implementing the matrix. On page 118 is a reproducible "Behavioral Matrix Template" that your team can use to create your own matrix.

Developing a Process to Communicate at All Levels

As you get everything ready for PBIS implementation, think about how you will communicate the implementation plans with staff at your school and at the district level as well as with school families and the larger community. For example, how will you share with staff the purpose or vision statement and the expectations? How about the new referral system? The PBIS implementation plans

Figure 7.2: Sample Behavioral Matrix—Evergreen School

Expectation	Classroom	Hallways	Cafeteria	Office	Bathrooms
We come to school to learn.	Be on time. Have materials. Pay attention to the teacher.	Quiet in the hallways—voice level 1. Wait patiently for your teacher to open the door.	Go to class when dismissed. Bring class materials with you to lunch so you will be on time to class.	Get a pass from your teacher if you need to go to the office.	Do your business and get back to class.
We respect ourselves and others.	Ask for help if you don't understand something. Pay attention to the assignment.	Use respectful words with custodians. Greet others in a friendly way. Use walking feet for safety.	Use respectful words with cafeteria workers. Eat your fruits and vegetables.	Respect others' privacy. Be polite to office staff.	Respect others' privacy.
We are responsible for our actions.	Complete and turn in assignments.	Throw trash in trash cans. Walk on the right side.	Take only what you will eat. Throw away trash.	Quietly wait your turn in line.	Flush and throw away paper towels.

would be a good topic for a professional development day led by your principal or possibly your district. The schedule could look like this:

1. Present the vision and purpose of PBIS: 20 minutes

2. PBIS overview for staff: 1 hour

3. Behavior basics (what are behaviors?): 30 minutes

4. Present the behavioral expectations and lesson plans: 1.5 hours

5. The referral process, including the flowchart for handling behaviors and the behavioral matrix, minor and major behaviors: 1.5–2 hours

6. Reward system, natural and logical consequences: 1 hour

How will you let parents and families know that the school is making a major systems shift from a punitive approach to a prosocial learning-skills approach? Many schools host an open house near the beginning of the school year. Perhaps you can set up a table with various resources for

families and distribute a pamphlet about PBIS that introduces your purpose and vision statement, behavioral expectations, and how you plan to implement the framework. If possible, have someone from your PBIS team at the table who can share information with families and answer questions about it. The principal could also give a short talk to families about the changes for the coming school year to inspire confidence in the direction the school is headed. Many schools have great examples of multimedia approaches to showcasing and communicating their PBIS progress and other initiatives and accomplishments.

Buy-In and Support

At each stage of implementation, revisit the ongoing concern of how to keep support for PBIS strong and what steps need to be taken to continually sustain buy-in. Until recently, the topic of buy-in had not been studied systematically. A 2013 report of research on this topic reveals two factors that appear to predict greater staff buy-in:

Figure 7.3: Getting Ready—Buy-In Roles and Measures During Stage 2

Person/Group Responsible	Buy-In Tasks	Examples and Measures
Administrator	• Maintain focus on the vision or purpose • Invite staff to be on PBIS Leadership Team	Ensure professional development time for the PBIS team and staff TFI
PBIS Leadership Team	• Set the team meeting schedule for the year • Establish operating procedures • Define team roles • Meet with entire staff monthly	Team members agree to participate for at least 3 years TFI
School staff	• Review schoolwide behavioral matrix and vote for approval • Teach expectations	Produce evidence of reviewing behavioral matrix and documenting vote
District	• Agree to provide funding for PBIS Leadership Team	District leadership team is identified

(1) an opportunity to have input into PBIS-related activities and (2) an understanding of what PBIS is.[2] Keeping these preliminary findings in mind, we suggest that at team meetings you discuss which team members are going to take which actions and add those to your action plan. Consider every meeting and interaction as an opportunity to explain, demonstrate, answer questions, and ask for input. Also consider how school staff and the district can contribute to PBIS as a way to increase their buy-in. **Figure 7.3** on page 116 outlines buy-in tasks for the installation stage by person or group responsible.

Telling Your School's Story

In chapter 6, we introduced the idea of beginning to tell your school's PBIS story once you have decided to adopt PBIS. Now you have taken the steps to install PBIS infrastructure in your school, having put in place the first three of the eight key PBIS features: You've formed a leadership team and developed both a vision or purpose statement and behavioral expectations. In addition, you've started an action plan and established a process for communication. Your story has expanded.

Take some time now to share this part of your story, or experience, with your staff, your families, your district administration, and your community. Once again, you can develop a narrative based on your current data as you prepare to implement PBIS in your school. This update to your story can be shared in a poster, a report, a newsletter or newspaper article, a presentation, or some other method of communication. Remember to use your own creativity. Following are some questions to consider as you work to develop your continuing story.

Our School's Story— PBIS Stage 2

In this stage of our story, we focus on sharing how our school is doing with the installation of PBIS.

Where did we start?

Here's an example:
In August, we met during team training and completed the Team Implementation Checklist (TIC). Our first TIC looked like this: Of the ten subscales, our two highest were Commitment and Support. We achieved 75 percent on the Commitment subscale, which measures administrative and staff support.

A narrative for this school might be:
Our principal is fully supportive of this PBIS effort in our school. She attended meetings describing PBIS, met with principals in other schools using PBIS, and invited a PBIS Leadership Team from another school to our faculty meeting to describe their experiences and results. She has stated her commitment to this effort for the next five years. Our staff voted, and 90 percent of staff are in favor of this initiative. Our other high score was on the Support subscale, which measures the behavioral support we have in our school. We have several staff members, including a leadership team member, with special training and skills in conducting functional behavioral assessments and developing behavioral support plans. This will be a great asset as we move further along on the implementation of PBIS.

2. Filter and Sytsma, 2013.

Behavioral Matrix Template

Expectation	Classroom	Hallways	Cafeteria	Office	Bathrooms	(other area)	(other area)

PBIS Stage 3: Getting Going—Initial Implementation

The initial implementation stage involves putting the remaining features of the PBIS framework in place and then measuring their implementation progress. As your school gets going on PBIS, the leadership team needs to ensure that all eight PBIS features are described clearly to the entire school staff. Then as implementation continues, your school should exhibit tangible evidence of the presence and practice of the eight features. Using PBIS assessment tools, the leadership team confirms that each feature is in place with fidelity.

Tasks

Core objectives of stage 3:

1. Help the school staff understand the eight key features of PBIS.

2. Maintain and encourage staff involvement and input throughout initial implementation.

3. Understand the leadership team process as the core of PBIS implementation.

4. Understand and conduct action planning based on progress, fidelity, and outcome data.

Key Features at Stage 3

During stage 2, you installed the first three features of PBIS. Now, as you get going on the initial implementation in stage 3, you'll put in place the remaining five features of the framework. The boldfaced items in the following features list highlight the five features that are part of the initial implementation process.

1. Establish the PBIS Leadership Team.

2. Develop a statement of vision or purpose.

3. Identify three to five schoolwide positive behavioral expectations.

4. **Develop teaching procedures.**

5. **Develop lesson plans.**

6. **Develop procedures for acknowledging positive student behavior.**

7. **Develop procedures for discouraging rule violations.**

8. **Develop data systems for monitoring implementation.**

Training School Staff in the Features of PBIS

Training staff members on the PBIS framework includes helping them understand the eight key

119

features of implementation. This is a process that is not accomplished all at once. It typically begins with a presentation of PBIS basics that occurs before the staff vote on whether or not to adopt the behavioral framework in the school. Then it continues in formal and informal ways throughout the school year; indeed, it continues on as part of the long-term operating system of the school.

It's also important that all staff members are trained, coached, and supported to teach the schoolwide behavioral expectations identified in the matrix in chapter 7 (see page 118 and figure 7.2). PBIS does have a training manual, but the staff development is designed to allow leadership teams and school staff to determine the content details and order of implementation to best fit their situation and community values. Consequently, the behavioral expectations that your school uses are developed and taught by school staff, and sometimes also the students, to reflect your school's culture and values.

Most schools using the PBIS framework create their own lessons to teach the expected school behaviors. Consider creating a subgroup of your PBIS Leadership Team plus other staff to develop formal lesson plans to be distributed to staff. We have found that consistency of teaching the expectations increases when a small subcommittee designs formal lesson plans for the whole staff. Lessons can address sections of the behavioral matrix (how to walk in the hallways, for example). These lessons can be incorporated into a morning meeting or advisory, where students greet one another and share or participate in a short activity. **Figure 8.1** on page 121 presents a sample lesson plan for teaching cafeteria behaviors. A reproducible "Lesson Plan Template" is on page 129. You can also find many great lesson plans on the internet. Visit www.pbis.org/training /student and scroll down to "Lesson Plans."

Some schools or districts might also use a published, research-based curriculum on social skills to assist in teaching general social skills to students. Examples include Second Step and Responsive Classroom. If you use a published curriculum, consider tailoring parts of the curriculum to support your behavioral matrix and school culture. For example, if the week's lesson is on making and being

a friend, bring that back to the cafeteria column on your behavioral matrix by encouraging students to invite other students to sit with them at lunch. We discourage using a published curriculum to teach your schoolwide expectations, however, because PBIS is most effective when interventions and instruction reflect your particular context and the needs specific to your school or educational site.

Whatever methods your school chooses to use to teach behavioral expectations to students, there must be opportunities for staff to demonstrate the information and for students to learn, practice, and receive feedback. Some schools teach the expectations during morning meetings for younger students or during advisory time for older students. Mondays could become "Remodel Mondays" where staff and students can practice skills on the behavioral matrix. The PBIS Leadership Team could set up a yearlong schedule for teaching and reviewing behavioral skills. Routine practices like these increase consistency among staff and provide opportunities for them to reinforce the expected school behaviors. Remind staff to model and demonstrate the positive behavioral skills and to acknowledge students using desired skills. Beth recruited the help of the school social worker to make a weekly presentation for teachers to show their advisory students. This way, all students and staff got the same message about the behavior of the week.

Coaching During Stage 3
Coaches can:

1. Review the eight key features of PBIS with the PBIS Leadership Team, with other teams in the school, and with staff. Ensure that all staff members understand what the features are and what they look like in your setting.

2. Identify and use a tool for assessing progress. (See chapter 4 and www.pbis apps.org.)

3. Select a process for making team decisions—including who, what, when, and how. For example, will your leadership team make decisions through consensus,

Figure 8.1: Sample Lesson Plan

Lesson Plan for: *Evergreen School*

Schoolwide Behavioral Expectations:
We come to school to learn.
We respect ourselves and others.
We are responsible for our actions.

Area: *Cafeteria*   **Date:** *October 1, 2018*

Behavioral Expectation	We come to school to learn.	We respect ourselves and others.	We are responsible for our actions.
What It Means	*Go to class when dismissed.*	*Invite others to sit with you.* *Eat your fruits and vegetables.*	*Keep the cafeteria clean.* *Throw away trash.*

Purpose of the Lesson:

1. *To teach, model, practice, and remind how we are expected to behave in the cafeteria.*
2. *We will teach the expected behaviors of the cafeteria.*
3. *Our data show that 8 referrals came from the cafeteria because students were running and not clearing their tables. Our lesson will model and provide practice to the students.*

Supplies and Resources:

Whiteboard

Markers

Y chart (looks like/sounds like/feels like) on large paper

Time in the cafeteria to teach and model expected behaviors

Student Activities:

Discuss with the students expectations for the cafeteria.

Discuss the need for the expectations (safety, enjoyable lunchtime, orderly—so everyone can eat, and so on).

Ask students to share their ideas about why we have the expectations; fill in the Y chart. (What does it look like, sound like, and feel like when we have lunch in the cafeteria?)

Display the chart in the classroom as a reminder of expected cafeteria behavior.

Take the students to the cafeteria during a quiet time with cafeteria staff present. Have staff demonstrate walking to get a lunch and a seat and throwing away trash. Have students practice walking, sitting, and throwing away trash.

Reinforcement Activities:

During the practice session, provide reminders of how to walk in the cafeteria and throw out trash. Provide instant and specific feedback and positive reinforcement comments to students.

During lunch periods, review the Y chart with students. Have the cafeteria staff provide specific reinforcement and feedback to students. Praise the students who are following the expectations with tickets and positive comments about specific behaviors. Students return the tickets to their teachers for a weekly drawing.

majority vote, fist-to-five consensus, or something else? The decision-making process should always start by reviewing the current data.

4. Assist the PBIS Leadership Team in adopting and using a process for action planning and implementing the plan. For example, how will you assign specific tasks and how will you document the who, what, when, and how?

5. Teach the leadership team about assessment tools that measure progress, fidelity, and outcomes. Build a team routine for assessing and for reviewing results and using them to update the action plan. Your data will provide the basis for staff development.

6. Develop a series of questions that your team can use to actively and effectively engage in problem-solving.

Typically, the school PBIS Leadership Team creates a general plan for school staff to introduce the expectations to students, which includes answers to *who*, *what*, *when*, and *where*. Expectations are taught to students at the beginning of the year, with multiple booster sessions throughout the year, before and after breaks, in large and small groups, as well as with individual students. Teach expectations in all settings: schoolwide, classroom, and nonclassroom. As you use your office discipline referral (ODR) data, you will also identify times, places, and topics for added booster instruction.

Coach's Tip from Beth:

Your school may decide to use published curriculum for Tier 1 to assist with teaching social skills or for character education lessons. Be sure to check out the publisher's website as it may offer tips, ideas, and lesson plans that can support the PBIS framework in your school. For example, Responsive Classroom uses CARES (cooperation, assertion, responsibility, empathy, and self-control) as the foundation of its social skills program. This approach supports the framework of PBIS very well. You can incorporate CARES into your schoolwide expectations and behavioral matrix. Indeed, CARES promotes consistency and eliminates the need for your PBIS Leadership Team to spend a lot of time creating something that already exists. You can adapt this to your specific school and cultural context.

Develop a System to Acknowledge and Reward Students for Meeting Expectations

When you teach students new academic skills, the pattern usually goes like this:

1. Teacher instructs, models, or demonstrates.

2. Student practices.

3. Teacher provides feedback.

4. Student tries again or corrects mistake.

5. Teacher praises student for learning a new academic skill with a star and sticker, a high five, or a grade.

Repeat these same steps to teach a new behavioral skill. When students have demonstrated a new skill, acknowledge it. Use behavior-specific praise to emphasize the accuracy of a new behavior. In the classroom, you can use high fives, verbal praise, or a thumbs-up. Monitor positive verbal comments versus negative comments made to students. In general, try to keep the ratio four positive comments to one negative comment. When teaching brand-new behavioral skills, increase reinforcement initially to as much as eight to one.

Many schools design a ticket program where teachers hand out tickets when students demonstrate use of a new skill. Sometimes these can be traded in for something the students find valuable—a free homework pass, time with a favorite teacher, small trinkets, or maybe even a pair of tickets to a school dance or sporting event. Some schools select a Student of the Month and tie the selection criteria to the behavioral matrix; students who exhibit outstanding behavior or new behavior identified on the matrix are recognized at a school assembly. This is a topic for which your PBIS Leadership Team may want to solicit ideas from the staff. The idea of rewarding good behavior can be a major turnoff to some people and they may require some gentle persuading. To others, they see rewards as a natural part of learning and will happily jump on board. Personally, we like intangible rewards. Not only are they free, but they can also provide some students with much desired social time with friends or favorite staff members. See pages 181–184 in the appendix for reward ideas. If you find yourself in a heated debate over the use of internal or external reinforcements, check out the references and resources for a great article by Judy Cameron and W. David Pierce that reviews research on this topic (page 187).

Develop Procedures That Discourage Rule Violations

PBIS implementation starts with Tier 1 interventions that will affect, encourage, and support all students. Being proactive rather than reactive in handling challenging behaviors takes some preparation. The following ideas may help you discourage rule violations:

- Be diligent and consistent in acknowledging and enforcing schoolwide expectations with all students.

- "Pre-correct" students, which means reminding them about school routines. For example, you might say to a class: "Who can tell me where we put completed homework?" or "What do we need to remember about using the computer lab?"

- Be prepared each day with an academic lesson plan and keep it moving. The more time students are on task, the less time they have to goof around.

- Provide many different opportunities for students to respond. Some kids like writing answers on whiteboards, while others may like group discussions to arrive at an answer. Be aware of different abilities too. Students with special needs may have a disability that favors one response method over another, such as writing over speaking.

- Demonstrate high expectations for all students regardless of race, ethnicity, gender, or ability.

- Give very clear instructions—say what you want the students to do, not what you *don't* want them to do. For example, say: "Remember to walk on the right side of the hallway."

- Redirect students for misbehavior. Use simple reminders rather than a lecture, such as: "Remember when we talked about expected school language yesterday? Can you say that in another way?"

- Use minor behavior infractions as teachable moments, such as a quick lesson on how to walk in the hallways or when to sharpen a pencil. Allow for redos; then praise the positive behavior.

Respond to behaviors in predictable ways; this reinforces the schoolwide expectations for students and may reduce the amount of time teachers spend responding to disruptive behaviors. Predictable environments are better for students and staff. The PBIS Leadership Team and the rest of the staff will decide when an infraction warrants an ODR. For example, if a student exhibits three minor behaviors with no behavioral change, this might be cause for a referral. If the student's behavior moves from a minor to a major behavior, it is probably time to write a referral. The flowchart in **figure 8.2** on page 124 includes a list of minor behaviors, which are managed in the classroom, and major behaviors, which incur a visit to the office.

Clear definitions of acceptable and unacceptable behaviors are critical for schoolwide expectations. For example, when Beth was a teacher of students with intensive behavioral concerns, what she considered inappropriate language may have been viewed as abusive language by other teachers. While developing these behavioral tools

Figure 8.2: Sample Behavioral Discipline Flowchart*

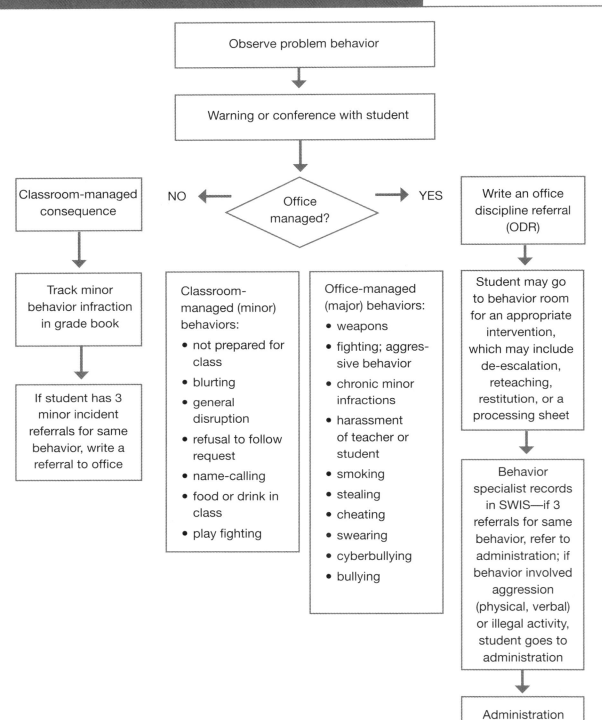

Observe problem behavior

↓

Warning or conference with student

↓

Office managed?

NO ← → YES

NO branch:
Classroom-managed consequence

↓

Track minor behavior infraction in grade book

↓

If student has 3 minor incident referrals for same behavior, write a referral to office

Classroom-managed (minor) behaviors:
- not prepared for class
- blurting
- general disruption
- refusal to follow request
- name-calling
- food or drink in class
- play fighting

Office-managed (major) behaviors:
- weapons
- fighting; aggressive behavior
- chronic minor infractions
- harassment of teacher or student
- smoking
- stealing
- cheating
- swearing
- cyberbullying
- bullying

YES branch:
Write an office discipline referral (ODR)

↓

Student may go to behavior room for an appropriate intervention, which may include de-escalation, reteaching, restitution, or a processing sheet

↓

Behavior specialist records in SWIS—if 3 referrals for same behavior, refer to administration; if behavior involved aggression (physical, verbal) or illegal activity, student goes to administration

↓

Administration considers consequences and contacts parent or guardian

*Teachers and staff should try at least three interventions to change minor behaviors before sending students out of the classroom or to the office. Administration is expected to relay consequences back to the referring teacher.

and definitions, keep in mind different teachers' classroom management styles and tolerance levels for classroom disruptions. In addition, we are well aware that staff may have different reactions to students based on race, gender, and special needs status. In chapter 11 on equity, we discuss the concept of implicit bias, as well as "vulnerable decision points" and how staff can avoid bias when handling challenging behaviors. The goal is to increase consistency in how adults deal with student behavior throughout the school.

If your school uses Schoolwide Information System (SWIS), then your behavior definitions must be compatible with SWIS definitions of behavior. Using the definitions from SWIS reduces discussions or arguments among staff over what is a major and minor offense. You can find a complete list of behaviors and definitions in the SWIS materials and resources at www.pbisapps.org. Schools that choose to opt out of using SWIS can create their own definitions. Some schools use this as an opportunity to unite staff and create buy-in because they have had the opportunity to contribute to the implementation of PBIS. When Char has worked with teams discussing behavior definitions, she has found it helpful to develop consensus for an operational definition of each behavior.

For students who are receiving special education services, be aware of what their Individual Education Plan (IEP) and Behavior Intervention Plan (BIP) say. Federal and state laws generally require schools to determine if certain behaviors are related to a child's disability before suspending or expelling the student. Due process requires schools to follow specific steps in intervening. The IEP, and sometimes more specifically the BIP, may outline responses, or it may need to be revised when interventions don't seem to be working. You may want to consult with your special education director or coordinator for more information. We want to note that despite protections for students with disabilities, they are still suspended at disproportionate rates.

Develop Data Systems That Monitor Progress

During stage 2, the installation of PBIS infrastructure, you developed an action plan, and you have been updating this plan continuously since then. Monitoring the completion of action plan steps is essential to fully implementing PBIS. You also want to ensure you are implementing these steps with fidelity—in short, that everyone is handling situations in the same way. For example, think back to stage 2, when you developed schoolwide behavioral expectations: How will your PBIS Leadership Team be sure that all teachers have a poster of the expectations displayed in their classroom that is consistent with the schoolwide expectations? The coach or a PBIS team member could go around and count, or staff could photograph the posters in the classrooms and other areas (save the photos for your archive book). You might also use the TFI Walk-Through Tool or something similar. If your school or district is using the School-Wide Evaluation Tool (SET) or Benchmarks of Quality (BoQ), this will also help your leadership team assess the progress and fidelity of implementation.

Other parts of your action plan may take longer to implement and the progress may not be immediately evident. Be patient. Set deadlines that are doable. If your initial deadlines appear to be unrealistic, move them out a bit and note the changes on your action plan. Keep track of your action plan items at each PBIS Leadership Team meeting.

Problem-Solving

As the PBIS Leadership Team develops an action plan and works to accomplish each item, problems will undoubtedly arise. Some of these may concern the timeline you have established, and you'll need to decide whether or not it can be adjusted. Other problems that occur may involve the actions of other people and, thus, may be more difficult to resolve. For example, in a perfect world, all teachers will willingly take a copy of the behavioral expectations poster and hang it in a prominent location in their classrooms. Yet experience tells us that some people may refuse or simply don't follow through with this. What to do? This is an issue for the coach or a PBIS team member to handle. Ask the teacher if there are barriers to using or making a classroom poster. It helps to be a good listener. Gracefully and tactfully, the coach can remind the teacher of his or her commitment to the initiative and ask that the teacher hang up the poster. Staff refusal to buy in to PBIS initiatives could be a topic for a PBIS Leadership Team meeting. Refusal may reflect a lack of buy-in, which can wax and wane. It may also be a training need, and you should respond to adults as you respond to students: teach, model, and reinforce. It's a good issue for team discussion. Ultimately, as a very last resort, this particular issue could be one for the principal to resolve.

Obstacles to successful problem-solving may spur your team to consider the Team-Initiated Problem-Solving (TIPS) model (see chapter 5).

Refining Your Action Plan

As chapter 7 explained, the PBIS Leadership Team formulates an action plan both to guide and to track PBIS implementation. Assessment results from the Tiered Fidelity Inventory (TFI), the Team Implementation Checklist (TIC), the Self-Assessment Survey (SAS), the Benchmarks of Quality (BoQ), or the School-Wide Evaluation Tool (SET) provide concrete items for action planning. The leadership team prioritizes action items and considers how to accomplish them, who will take charge of each item, and by when it will be completed.

> We know from research that it is imperative that the schoolwide expectations be replicated in individual classrooms.

As you move forward in the implementation process, be sure to update and refine the action plan continually. Also consider sharing the action plan with all school staff at a faculty meeting and explain how staff will be involved in completing action items. For example, if your team has determined that the three to five behavioral expectations need to be posted in every classroom and hallway and in the cafeteria, gymnasium, and office, what will the plan be to accomplish this? We know from research that it is imperative that the schoolwide expectations be replicated in individual classrooms.[1] Classroom teachers may adapt the behavioral matrix to the classroom setting, but the matrix still needs to mirror the schoolwide expectations. Some leadership teams decide to print the posters and hand them to teachers to hang in their classrooms; team members also ask school volunteers to display the posters in other areas of the school.

Buy-In and Support

Stage 3 is about putting the pieces in place. Teams often find, at this stage, that they need to take a step back and move at a slower pace. *Remember:* PBIS is a long-term commitment. The goal is to establish a solid Tier 1 with fidelity. Doing this can only occur with ongoing staff buy-in and schoolwide commitment. To sustain buy-in, it's best not to compare your process or progress with other schools'. Implementing PBIS means adapting it to your individual school culture. Take time to do it well. Consider how you'll keep support for PBIS strong during this stage. What steps need to be taken to sustain buy-in? How will you determine which team members need to take action to support buy-in? **Figure 8.3** on page 127 outlines the buy-in tasks for stage 3.

---

1. Mathews et al., 2013.

Figure 8.3: Getting Going—Buy-In Roles and Measures During Stage 3

Person/Group Responsible	Buy-In Tasks	Measures
Administrator	• Rally staff • Arrange for staff development time for training • Support capacity building to provide in-house staff development	TFI, SET, TIC
Coach	• Prompt team to complete data tasks • Engage staff in discussions • Prompt team to update and stay focused on the action plan	TFI, TIC, ODRs
PBIS Leadership Team	• Train and coach the staff in teaching behavioral expectations to students • Review with staff the schoolwide system for handling problem behaviors	SAS, TFI, SET, TIC
School staff	• Agree to follow behavioral matrix and schoolwide expectations • Agree to follow schoolwide system for handling behavioral problems • Agree to follow student acknowledgment system	TFI walk-through, SET, SAS
Students	• Participate in learning behavioral expectations and reinforcement systems • Able to describe schoolwide behavioral expectations	TFI, SET
District	• Visibly support the PBIS vision • Monitor implementation of PBIS • Build capacity for district-level coaching • Build capacity for staff development	Invite PBIS Leadership Team to present to school board
Community	• Behavioral systems and practices are explained to the families and community to assist with their buy-in	Newsletters, school and district websites

Telling Your School's Story

During the initial stage of implementation, your school's story will expand from sharing baseline data and information about PBIS infrastructure to reporting on how the implementation process is moving along. While you may still include baseline data in your narrative, you may also choose to add some of the reports and graphs that illustrate your progress in teaching the expectations and rewarding students. Following are some questions to consider as you develop your continuing story.

Our School's Story— PBIS Stage 3

In this stage of our story, we'll focus on sharing how our school is doing with the initial implementation of PBIS.

What is our midyear progress?

Here's an example:
We are two-thirds of the way through year one of initial implementation. We have twice measured our progress using the TIC or TFI, and we have surveyed staff with the SAS.

This might be demonstrated to others by sharing a report, shown in **figure 8.4** below.

Our second TIC shows that we have made progress in establishing the key features of PBIS. Under Define Expectations, we increased from 33 percent to 67 percent, and for Teach Expectations, we went from 0 percent to 50 percent.

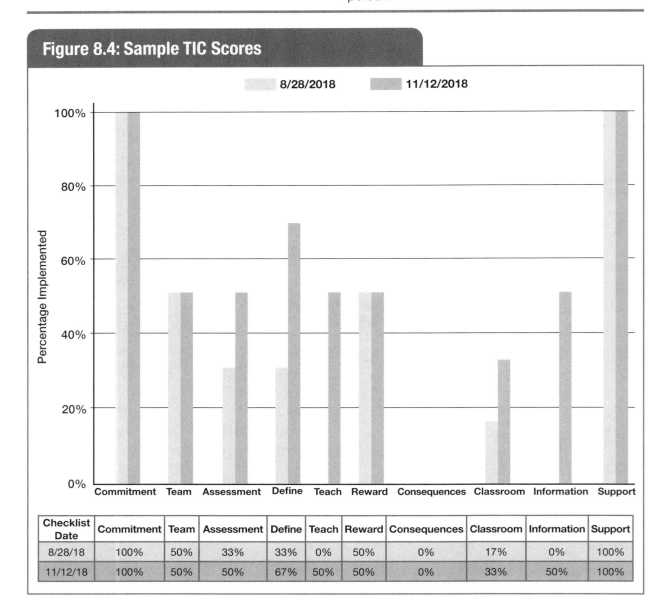

Figure 8.4: Sample TIC Scores

Checklist Date	Commitment	Team	Assessment	Define	Teach	Reward	Consequences	Classroom	Information	Support
8/28/18	100%	50%	33%	33%	0%	50%	0%	17%	0%	100%
11/12/18	100%	50%	50%	67%	50%	50%	0%	33%	50%	100%

Lesson Plan Template

Lesson Plan for:

Schoolwide Behavioral Expectations:

Area: _____   Date: _____

Behavioral Expectation			
What It Means			

Purpose of the Lesson:

Supplies and Resources:

Student Activities:

Reinforcement Activities:

PBIS Stage 4: Up and Running— Full Implementation

By the time you reach implementation stage 4, all eight PBIS features are fully in place and operational—meaning they are visible and used by all staff with all students, all of the time, across all settings within the school.[*] The eight features are visible in school reports, newsletters, videos, press releases, policy, and procedures, and this communication extends to the district as well. So while initial implementation means that schools and teams are selecting and adapting PBIS to their particular setting, full implementation means that your school's specific version of the PBIS features are used by all and that speed bumps, migrations, and adaptations during the initial implementation have improved the fit and fidelity of these practices. By stage 4, PBIS has become an established routine in your school.

Schools typically make great strides toward initial implementation during the first year with PBIS, but full implementation takes longer. It may be three to four years after the exploration and adoption stage before the school has fully implemented the PBIS framework. This is long enough for the honeymoon to pass and for several rounds of staff turnover and other political shifts to occur. During the course of

stage 4, schools should be seeing evidence of changes in student behavior and school culture. Staff confidence and enthusiasm for the PBIS initiative should also be evident. The PBIS Leadership Team continues to assess implementation fidelity and student outcomes reflecting the school and district routine. In general, PBIS features should be solidly in place and demonstrate measures of fidelity at designated criteria levels. If you are one of the first schools in your district to implement PBIS, you may become the demonstration site that others will visit before deciding if they will also implement PBIS. Telling your story and showing your data are priceless.

> **Tasks**
> Core objectives of stage 4:
> 1. Achieve and document implementation fidelity.
> 2. Expect fluctuations in fidelity and continue using all data to redirect staff actions.
> 3. Continue to measure support and buy-in from administration and staff.
> 4. Measure and communicate fidelity and outcomes to entire staff.

---

[*] This is the ideal, since fidelity scores have an expiration date. Best practice is to have at least 80 percent of staff committed prior to implementation; in most cases, some staff may not fully participate. The administrator and coach may work with these staff members and eventually get them on board. Additionally, staff and students change over time, highlighting an ongoing need for training and coaching.

Coaching During Stage 4
Coaches can:

1. Work with the PBIS data manager or subgroup to use the instruments that measure implementation fidelity (such as the TFI, TIC, SET, SAS, and BoQ; see chapter 4). Remember you will not use *all* of these, but rather one or two on a regular basis.

2. Remain connected with district, regional, state, and national technical assistance centers that offer support and guidance.

3. Facilitate continued regular communication with staff, administration, and community about implementation, fidelity, and outcomes.

4. Ensure that the PBIS Leadership Team continues to meet on a regular basis to monitor implementation fidelity, system changes, and so on.

5. Be prepared to quickly redirect any missteps that occur. Use your student data to quickly target interventions.

Full Implementation in Action

Let's follow one student, Johnny, on a typical morning to see how PBIS might look when it is fully implemented in his school:

Johnny is in fifth grade at Evergreen School. When Johnny arrives at school on the bus, the bus driver (who has been trained in PBIS) reminds Johnny to wait his turn to get off the bus and then thanks him for doing so. Johnny turns to the bus driver and says, "Thank you!" The bus driver smiles and says, "Have a good day, Johnny. I'll see you after school. I want to hear a good report!"

Johnny races his friend into the building, where the principal, Mrs. Garcia, asks the two students to slow down, reminding them of the school expectation to walk in the hallways. She also says, "Have a good breakfast! Johnny, come and see me after lunch and tell me how your day is going!" He agrees to stop and see Mrs. Garcia later in the day and then goes to the cafeteria with his friend.

The cafeteria worker greets the students. She gives Johnny an extra big smile as he takes the egg rollup and a carton of milk. When she is finished serving breakfast, she finds Johnny and compliments him on walking in the cafeteria and throwing away his trash. She also gives him a "Caught Ya" ticket that can be turned in for a prize at the end of the week. After a healthy breakfast, the students go to their classrooms.

Each classroom starts the day with twenty minutes of community-building strategies. Ms. Moe, Johnny's teacher, has the students gather in a circle on the floor. This month's theme is friendship, and the lesson includes an activity to help the students get to know each other better. Ms. Moe encourages the students to invite other students to join them at lunch today; she also refers to this item on the behavioral matrix. The lesson ends with a game of Silent Ball. Johnny wins and is feeling pretty proud. Ms. Moe congratulates him with a high five and words of praise: "Wow, Johnny, that was a great game of Silent Ball. You were awesome. Next time we play, you can start."

The students are dismissed from homeroom and Johnny heads with his class to the science lab. Posters in the hallways remind the students of the school's behavioral expectations: *We come to school to learn. We respect ourselves and others. We are responsible for our actions.* At Evergreen School, each school setting (such as the hallways) has a behavioral matrix that identifies the specific behaviors for each expectation for that setting. Teachers and other staff members monitor the hallways between classes and remind students to walk and bring down their voice levels. One staff member pats Johnny on the back for following the expectations and gives him another "Caught Ya" ticket (to reinforce his new and improved habit of walking in the hallways). The science teacher, Mr. Smith, is standing in the doorway greeting the students. When Johnny shows off the pencil he has remembered to bring to class (a rarity for Johnny), Mr. Smith gives Johnny a high five.

Mr. Smith has a solid lesson plan, with learning targets posted on the board. He also has the school-wide behavioral expectations posted in the front of the room to be visible at all times. In addition, Mr. Smith has a behavioral matrix posted on the wall that lists the specific student behaviors for each classroom expectation. Mr. Smith has built a routine: students come in, get their science notebooks, and try to figure out the brainteaser on the board. Johnny goes to the bin where the science notebooks are and grabs his as well as two other students' notebooks. Play fighting over the notebooks starts, and Mr. Smith directs Johnny to hand over the notebooks. Mr. Smith quietly reminds Johnny of the routine and asks him to take his seat. Johnny sits at a table with three other students. Johnny moves his chair right next to Omar, who pushes Johnny away while trying to solve the day's puzzle. Johnny laughs until Mr. Smith comes over and reminds Johnny of the "We respect ourselves and others" expectation. He also quickly quizzes Johnny about what that looks like in the science lab, using the behavioral matrix as a guide. He then requests that Johnny apologize to Omar, which Johnny does and Omar accepts. Mr. Smith thanks Johnny for showing his respect by apologizing to Omar.

Mr. Smith reads the learning targets for the day. Meanwhile, Johnny flips his pencil and hits Omar in the head. Johnny laughs out loud while Omar rubs his head. Mr. Smith asks Johnny to move to a seat near the front of the classroom and continues with the lesson. Johnny turns around in his seat trying to get Kia's attention. She ignores Johnny. Mr. Smith tells Johnny to face the front and be respectful to the other students by following the lesson. Johnny soon turns around again and makes faces at Kia. Realizing that he has redirected Johnny four times, Mr. Smith writes a referral for Johnny to go to the behavior room, per the discipline flowchart the faculty created. The ODR has blanks and checkboxes for the date, student, grade level, time of day, where the behavior occurred, who was involved, and what the behavior was. Mr. Smith signs it and sends Johnny out the door.

Johnny walks down the hallway to the behavior room. When he arrives, Mrs. Dillard greets Johnny warmly and firmly, and she takes the referral. She immediately enters the data into a SWIS spreadsheet for data collection. Then she talks to Johnny about the behaviors and he completes a processing sheet that asks what expectation he wasn't following, what he was supposed to be doing, and what

will happen when he gets back to class. She has him practice what he will say to Mr. Smith. She jots some notes on the referral form for him to bring back to Mr. Smith. Mrs. Dillard encourages Johnny to do well and reminds him that he likes science class. On the data spreadsheet, Mrs. Dillard marks that she processed the situation with Johnny and he returned to class. Upon returning to the classroom, Johnny sees Mr. Smith at the door. Mr. Smith glances at Mrs. Dillard's notes, and he and Johnny discuss Johnny's plan to take his seat as directed and complete his work. Mr. Smith keeps a close eye on Johnny while the class completes the lab project. He makes eye contact with Johnny a couple of times—once to remind him to work and once to let him know he was doing a good job.

After school, the PBIS Leadership Team gathers in the media center to review the monthly data. The team also discusses the auditorium program they will have next month to honor the successes of individual students (for which teachers from each grade submit the names of one boy and one girl to honor). They check the teachers' nominations against the ODR data and agree to give the names to the honoring committee so they can print up certificates for the students. It's the fourth grade's turn to perform a skit about the expectations. Ms. Snyder says they are already working on making a short video, which everyone is very excited about.

> Someone well versed in PBIS will likely be able to pick out the components of PBIS after spending a day in your school.

This is just one example of what PBIS might look like in an individual school. It might look quite different in your school, depending on factors such as the age range of students, the expectations your team has developed, and the cultures and values of your school. Because PBIS is a framework, the scenario above could vary from building to building. Even so, someone well versed in PBIS will likely be able to pick out the components of PBIS after spending a day in your school.

Achieving and Documenting the Fidelity of Implementation

Even when PBIS is fully implemented in your building, fidelity continues to be a priority. Research shows that fidelity can vary over time. Failure to watch fidelity and outcomes increases the risk that your school will drift, or lose the accuracy of implementation. You can use the Tiered Fidelity Inventory (TFI) as your fidelity measure. When conducted by an outside coach, the TFI cutoff score is 70 percent (on a Tier 1 scale). If your school, district, or state recommends use of a different or an additional annual tool for fidelity assessment, the School-Wide Evaluation Tool (SET) and the Benchmarks of Quality (BoQ) are also available.

> Even when PBIS is fully implemented in your building, fidelity continues to be a priority. Research shows that fidelity can vary over time.

Late spring is usually the best time for completing these evaluation tools. At this point in time, staff might also complete the Self-Assessment Survey (SAS), taking into account how well the school year went and what could be changed for the fall. The PBIS Leadership Team may be able to meet during the summer to do some action planning using this data. (For more information, see the *Evaluation Blueprint for School-Wide Positive Behavior Support* at www.pbis.org.)

The PBIS Leadership Team may also review school and student data (such as ODRs, attendance, grades, state test scores, and student surveys) along with the fidelity measures to get a well-rounded picture of implementation fidelity. Or the team could choose to review the data for areas in the school that are doing well (low ODR rates in specific settings) and other areas that are struggling (high ODR rates in specific settings). One of the areas that TFI walk-through and SET evaluators focus on is the visibility of schoolwide expectations (including a behavioral matrix) around the school. If the evaluator notes a lack of posters in the hallways and the data subgroup notices a lot of referrals coming from the hallways, then the hallways might be an area that the PBIS Leadership Team would want to improve. They might, for example, decide to hang up more expectations posters in the hallways, create lesson plans that teach students the expected behavior in the hallways, and provide additional training and coaching to staff.

Buy-In and Support

Even during full implementation, it's important to consider how to keep support for PBIS strong. What steps need to be taken to sustain and improve buy-in? Which leadership team members need to take action in this effort? **Figure 9.1** on page 134 outlines the buy-in tasks and responsible party during stage 4.

Communicating with the Local Community

> In the broadest sense, connecting with the community means understanding your own cultural identity, as well as those of your students and the surrounding community, in the most authentic way possible. This involves reaching out and listening. It may be easy or it may not be. Char met a white woman who is a librarian at an American Indian cultural center in Arizona and who has been working among the tribe for nearly ten years. Even now, she says it is difficult as an outsider to fully gain the tribe members' trust and acceptance. She said she has been humbled and sees small steps as big achievements.

Some people may find it odd to see community participation listed in a school behavioral plan. However, if your school is near local businesses (convenience stores, drugstores, restaurants), your principal may tire of phone calls detailing the students' antics in these businesses: "*Your* students are stealing candy!" "*Your* students are play fighting and making the other customers uncomfortable! Keep them out of my store!"

Yet we know that these aren't *your* students; they are *our* students. Students have a place in communities just as adults do. Many students have parents who work in, or even own, these establishments next door to your school. Students themselves may

eventually work in these very stores and restaurants. So wouldn't it be great if we could help students learn to transfer the behavioral skills they are learning in school to their actions in the larger community as well? Many businesses like to support their local schools. For example, Beth's car mechanic liked the local school so much that he would donate bikes every spring for a drawing for students who had perfect attendance. To involve your larger community in PBIS, you may choose to ask nearby businesses to hang the school's expectations near the cash register,

Figure 9.1: Up and Running—Buy-In Roles and Measures During Stage 4

Person/Group Responsible	Buy-In Tasks	Measures
Administrator	• Continually review the school's vision • Regularly attend PBIS Leadership Team meetings • Support ideas agreed upon by the PBIS team	TFI, SAS, SET, BoQ
PBIS Leadership Team	• Regularly attend PBIS meetings • Report and discuss data with staff • Invite staff input • Increase training and coaching as needed	TFI, TIC, SAS, SET, BoQ
School staff	• Teach and monitor schoolwide behavioral expectations • Acknowledge and reward use of appropriate behaviors	TFI, TIC, SAS, SET, BoQ
Students	• Learn and demonstrate behavioral expectations	TFI, ODRs, SET, SAS
District	• Invite PBIS Leadership Team to share data results at school board meetings • Send district representative to school PBIS meetings • Adopt PBIS districtwide • Expand internal capacity for training and coaching support	Rates for attendance, graduation, enrollment, suspensions, and expulsions Districtwide ODR data
Community	• Secure the support of nearby businesses by expanding the behavioral expectations into the community • Invite families to be a part of the PBIS Leadership Team • Invite families to share in celebrating school successes • Invite community partners to share in celebrating school successes	Participating in the reinforcement system, e.g., handing out the school's "Caught Ya" tickets when students follow the expectations in neighboring businesses Attendance at PBIS meetings, parent attendance rates at open houses

since "Be respectful," "Be safe," and "Be ready" also apply to the desired behavior of customers. Store owners can be given a pile of "Caught Ya" tickets and asked to hand them out to students behaving appropriately while in the stores.

Involving the families of your students in your PBIS efforts also includes communicating with them. Families play a huge role in the social and academic development of children. Invite families to attend open house nights to celebrate progress on a schoolwide behavioral goal. Include the behavioral matrix lesson plan themes in monthly newsletters so that parents can encourage the behaviors at home and in the community.

Another way to expand community involvement is to include a parent on your PBIS Leadership Team or to have the team give updates to the parent-teacher organization in your school. (Due to the confidential nature of some data, you'll need to refrain from sharing student and staff names when discussing the data.) This helps inform parents of the behavioral goals in your building and enables them to share the progress with other parents and community members.

Schools can use the school website to inform the public about improved academics and behaviors (lower ODR and suspension numbers, lower rates of disproportionate discipline, improved attendance, and so on) as a result of the PBIS initiative. This would be wonderful for prospective families to see when they are looking at schools for their children. With parent permission, any behavioral videos created by the students about following expectations or what they like about their school could also be posted on the school website to show the world your sense of humor and your commitment to creating a safe and calm school environment. Some schools create blogs. As technology advances, so do creative opportunities.

Telling Your School's Story

Once PBIS is fully implemented in your building, you may think that your school's story of the PBIS

implementation process is no longer unfolding. However, the work of creating and maintaining a safe school environment that supports learning is not over; it has simply become the norm. To keep the momentum going, it is vital to remind staff and others about the progress that has been achieved and the continual efforts required to keep the school on the right track with student behavior.

As in earlier stages, we recommend that you develop a narrative based on your data and present your story in a variety of creative ways. Following are some questions to consider as you work to develop your continuing story.

Our School's Story— PBIS Stage 4

In this stage, we'll focus on sharing how we are doing now that PBIS is fully implemented in our school.

1. What is our end-of-year progress?

Here's an example:
We completed our first two years of implementation. We have measured our progress using the TIC quarterly each year. We have also surveyed staff with the SAS, and we have completed a SET.

We used the TIC and the SET for this purpose. Our results demonstrate our success in words, pictures, and numbers as illustrated in **figures 9.2** and **9.3** on page 137.

Review the TIC scores over the two years. They fluctuate. This is not unusual but is a good reminder of how regular assessment is useful as a formative tool to see if some of the features are sliding. At the end of the two years of formal training, this school looks pretty good. It will be really helpful for the PBIS Leadership Team to review the TIC, SAS, and SET data in detail and be prepared to explain what some of the shifts mean. They will celebrate progress and continue to action plan.

Figure 9.3 shows this school's SET score at the end of two years of formal training. It is hard to argue with 100 percent across the board. Some team members may find it interesting to compare scores across measures. What we often hear is that the PBIS Leadership Team is more critical or strict than an outside evaluator when scoring their efforts. They know things at a level that might not be obvious to an outside evaluator.

2. What is our year-end summary and action plan? Our narrative might be:

At the end of the second year of implementation, our school made great strides in implementing PBIS. In reviewing our TIC, we achieved 100 percent for implementing the following: well-defined expectations, teaching the expectations, a reward system, and consequences for behavior problems. Two areas are below 80 percent: the team and the use of information. These issues require further examination and action planning. We will look at the TIC Item Report. At the next PBIS Leadership Team meeting, we will discuss the details presented in the TIC Item Report, which indicates that the PBIS Leadership Team is questioning how representative it is—for

example, who is not there who should be. The other items have to do with summarizing and using ODR data. The PBIS Leadership Team rated this partially in place. This is an important item to address soon.

Our action plan for beginning next year is to implement two planned buy-in activities with staff that address teaching the schoolwide expectations as well as implementing our student recognitions system. In addition, we have improved our ODR form and have planned an additional staff training in September to assist in consistency. We will revise our process for handling ODR data at the PBIS Leadership Team meetings so that we are effectively using data-based decision-making. Our team has met consistently and will meet twice a month beginning next September. We are seeking parent involvement on the team for next school year. We have planned lessons for the beginning of the school year for all staff and students. We will also develop a presentation that we will give to the school board in October demonstrating the goal, the progress, and student outcomes to date.

Figure 9.2: Sample TIC Scores

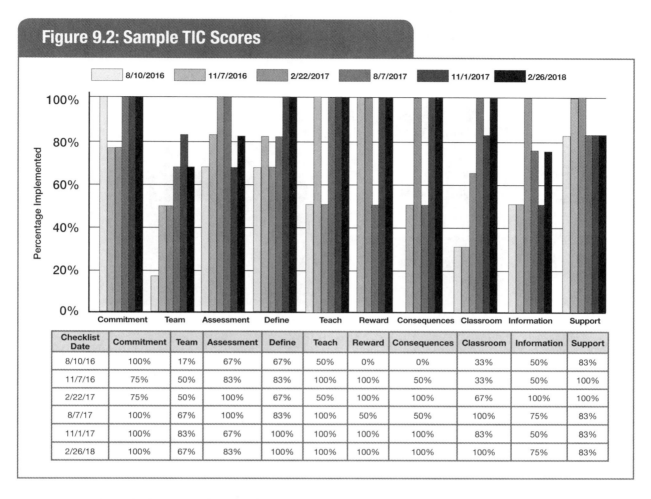

Checklist Date	Commitment	Team	Assessment	Define	Teach	Reward	Consequences	Classroom	Information	Support
8/10/16	100%	17%	67%	67%	50%	0%	0%	33%	50%	83%
11/7/16	75%	50%	83%	83%	100%	100%	50%	33%	50%	100%
2/22/17	75%	50%	100%	67%	50%	100%	100%	67%	100%	100%
8/7/17	100%	67%	100%	83%	100%	50%	50%	100%	75%	83%
11/1/17	100%	83%	67%	100%	100%	100%	100%	83%	50%	83%
2/26/18	100%	67%	83%	100%	100%	100%	100%	100%	75%	83%

Figure 9.3: Sample SET Scores

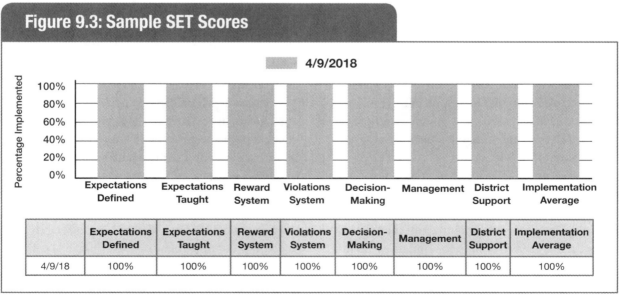

	Expectations Defined	Expectations Taught	Reward System	Violations System	Decision-Making	Management	District Support	Implementation Average
4/9/18	100%	100%	100%	100%	100%	100%	100%	100%

PBIS Stage 5: Sustaining and Continuous Improvement

Along the continuum of implementation, schools arrive at a point where PBIS practices are fully in place and stable, for all students, for all staff, in all settings. Staff has gained experience with all aspects of implementation and tackled predictable challenges. It is tempting at this point to rest and declare that the initiative is fully implemented and that the school can now simply coast and continue to reap the benefits of the previous work. But there is still another stage of implementation: sustaining and continuous improvement. Again guided by the PBIS Leadership Team, stage 5 offers opportunities to make further adaptations to fit your specific school and to address any changes that have occurred since the inception of PBIS. These adaptations may include new and more efficient ways to achieve goals and to maintain consistency and fidelity.

One of the key issues during stage 5 is to ensure that there is no drift, or movement away from fidelity of the eight core features of PBIS. Simple examples of drift include infrequent use of the acknowledgment and reward system for students who meet expectations, discontinuing the regular teaching of expectations, becoming inconsistent in discipline practices, or not providing enough training to staff and students. While posters, T-shirts, and mottos may provide visible reminders of expected

behaviors, they do not necessarily reflect a deeper, more consistent practice. Sustaining schools benefit from annual fidelity assessment. Studies show that schools that sustain PBIS demonstrate high criteria scores for fidelity on the continued teaching of expectations (80 percent on the School-Wide Evaluation Tool, or SET), and they maintain high levels of implementation (80 percent on the composite SET score). Another measure that is commonly used to assess fidelity is the Benchmarks of Quality (BoQ), which has a criterion of 70 percent. The Tiered Fidelity Inventory (TFI) measures the fidelity of all three tiers, and the required score for Tier 1 fidelity is 70 percent or greater.

So, the task for PBIS teams and coaches at stage 5 is to continue to regularly assess the school's outcome data and its fidelity to core PBIS features. Remember that social and academic outcomes are tied to full implementation with fidelity. Although we expect PBIS to be well integrated at this stage, reality reminds us that change is inevitable. Char worked with a school that made good progress implementing PBIS. Then another elementary school in the district closed, and half of the students and many staff transferred into this school. The changes far exceeded the typical enrollment bumps you might expect and required significant planning and adjustment.

At this stage, the PBIS team is using office discipline referral (ODR) data regularly to monitor outcomes and implement interventions when and where needed. Large increases in ODRs may signal a loss of fidelity. It may also signal a loss of buy-in. Adults will stay motivated when they are part of the process and continue to see the positive outcomes.

Tasks

Core objectives of stage 5:

1. Adapt to changing contextual factors, such as staff turnover, team member attrition, enrollment changes, demographic changes, or financial issues.
2. Create more efficient and effective ways to implement core PBIS features.
3. Ensure that new or existing practices continue to match all core features with fidelity.
4. Maintain support, buy-in, and acknowledgment of practices and regular assessment.

Coaching During Stage 5

Coaches can:

1. Continue using data actively in decision-making. For example, review your data at the beginning of each meeting to identify questions, gather more data as needed, write precision statements to describe problems, and create goals, solutions, and evaluation measures that ensure appropriate implementation of solutions.
2. Make sure that the PBIS Leadership Team administers and uses regular data checkpoints throughout the year. Use a tool like the TFI, BoQ, or Self-Assessment Survey (SAS) in Tier 1. Conduct regular self-assessment of implementation; use the SAS with staff and the TFI or the Team Implementation Checklist (TIC) with the PBIS Leadership Team.
3. Continue to assess implementation fidelity (TFI, SET, or BoQ).
4. Evaluate, report, and problem-solve with student data from ODRs.

5. Continue to communicate within the school and throughout the district, region, state, and local community about implementation progress, changes, and outcomes.
6. Celebrate and promote successful practices at all levels.

Sustainability

Most of us have probably had the experience of working on a project for a period of months or years and watching it disappear either suddenly when new conditions arise or gradually as staff and constituents change. Sadly, some initiatives are abandoned just when they are on the cusp of making a lasting impact and effecting real change. That is why PBIS is considered a long-term undertaking and why schools are advised about the level of commitment required and the timeline for full implementation before they decide to adopt the framework. Making a substantial commitment like this helps schools achieve buy-in from staff and key stakeholders and assures those involved that their time and efforts are being well spent.

Our purpose in this chapter is to explain what sustainability means within PBIS, talk about why it is important, discuss what researchers tell us about sustainability good practices, and, most important, identify steps that coaches and teams can take to achieve sustainability and protect their important accomplishments.

What Is Sustainability?

Generally, when people find something that works, they want to keep it going. Unfortunately in education and other fields, there is often turnover of initiatives and popular practices. Many challenges occur with changing priorities and practices. It takes years to fully implement PBIS, and sustainability assumes the ability to handle these challenges.

Sustainability, according to Kent McIntosh, refers to the "durable implementation of a practice at a level of fidelity that continues to produce important outcomes."[1] This definition is important because it stresses the key factors of fidelity and outcomes in sustaining PBIS.

It is possible to sustain ineffective practices. A good example of this is the high rate of school suspensions, which do not teach students appropriate behavior, and yet the practice continues. Our goal is to avoid this scenario by establishing the effective, proactive practices of PBIS with a high degree of fidelity and demonstrated and continued positive outcomes.

Why Is Sustainability Important?

Sustaining practices requires a commitment of time, money, support, and emotional investment over the long haul. If a practice fails, the financial and human costs can be huge. For example, formal team training for a team of eight can require off-site staff development for ten to twelve days over two years or more. Training costs can be as high as $10,000 to $15,000 for each team, which may not include the school costs for substitute teachers and lodging. If this training is paid by a state or regional entity, the expense for a district with twelve schools could be as much as $180,000. School and district costs may increase this number. If schools do not fully implement a practice or stop supporting it, this investment is lost. Besides the fiscal loss, there are human capital losses. People become discouraged and cynical about taking on new initiatives that disintegrate or no longer produce outcomes.

An important aspect of state, regional, and national PBIS practices is the commitment to "capacity building." This means that the school, district, region, or state develops internal leadership, supports, and structures to fully implement PBIS at fidelity and is no longer dependent on outside experts. As we've stated throughout this book, there are numerous tools available at the PBIS website (www.pbis.org) for measuring all aspects of PBIS implementation. And the support available to schools and other entities continues to evolve and includes online classes, courses, videos, handouts,

and innumerable resources. The website also constantly updates and posts trainings, technical assistance, current research, and easily accessible resources.

In spite of all these resources, schools sometimes still fail to sustain their PBIS initiatives. There has to be a conscious, intentional plan for sustainability with data and measurable action steps that precisely define the who, what, where, when, and how.

Implementation with Fidelity

Once the practices of PBIS are observable, the question is whether they are performed consistently in the manner in which they demonstrated success. You need to ensure that new or existing practices continue to match all core features with fidelity. Let's take an example. "Develop teaching procedures" is one of the eight key features of the PBIS framework. Once a school has identified its expectations, the leadership team and staff develop a behavioral matrix and lesson plans for teaching these expectations in various settings (classroom, hallways, cafeteria, library, and so on). Then all staff proceed to teach these expectations to all students. Typically, the PBIS Leadership Team develops a plan for doing this, which includes the who, what, when, and where involved. Expectations are taught at the beginning of the year with multiple booster sessions throughout the year, before and after breaks, in large and small groups as well as with individual students. The practice of teaching the school expectations is ongoing for all students and all staff.

What can happen with this practice (or any practice in any field) is that drift occurs—the practice is done less frequently and with less consistency to the original standard. So while the original standard requires teaching the behavioral expectations regularly and consistently, in time a school may teach the expectations at the beginning of the

---

1. McIntosh, Horner, and Sugai, 2009.

school year, gradually teach them less often, and stop doing boosters or teaching expectations to new staff or students. It may also discontinue acknowledgments, and expectations may become less clear and consistent. Such drift leads to a watered-down version of the practice—it is no longer being implemented with fidelity.

When fidelity declines, the associated benefits of PBIS may also decline. The most efficient way to avoid this gradual drift is to establish a routine pattern for assessing progress, for monitoring sustained practice with fidelity, and for responding to any shifts. Many PBIS experts describe the benefits of a strong coaching system. This directly relates to both fidelity and sustainability. A strong coaching system is important to assessing status and providing midcourse correction when fidelity is declining. Coaches can also increase their support when the need arises to boost sustainability.[2]

> When fidelity declines, the associated benefits of PBIS may also decline.

Barriers to Sustainability

What interferes with sustainability? Numerous challenges may arise. Sometimes the practices were never implemented to full fidelity standards in the first place, so it is impossible to sustain them with fidelity. Perhaps the implementation process stalled in the early stages and a deeper level of practice and change was never achieved. In this case, it is best to regroup and work on an action plan to get the implementation process going again.

Sometimes your own behavior can drift away from the initial high-level practice. For example, the staff and team at one school worked very hard to get the key features of PBIS in place during the first year. Then when they began their second year, they thought they no longer needed to acknowledge

students for following the behavioral expectations because they had done so much of that the first year. As a result, the key feature of regular acknowledgment decreased in frequency and was missing for new students and staff. Implementing with fidelity means that we put the practice fully in place and continue to perform it at the same level.

Think of an analogy with physical fitness. You may be excited when you work out to achieve a new level of competence, like being able to run a 10K, but are dismayed to discover that this optimal level of fitness quickly dissipates when you stop working out regularly. When your behavior drifts away from the level of effective practice, you simply cannot maintain the same fitness level. So it is with PBIS: When you stop putting in the time and effort, the benefits decline.

Other challenges to sustainability include the lack of resources to support the practice. Schools commonly use grant money or special funds to get started with PBIS. Yet without specific planning for transition, the loss of those funds can undermine ongoing implementation. The PBIS Leadership Team and administrators need to determine which funding needs will be ongoing from the start and include these items in the yearly budget.

Another common challenge is the turnover of staff and administrators. Schools that are able to build and sustain capacity across various teams, the school, and the district have planned for such turnover by sharing tasks within the PBIS Leadership Team. They also keep accurate records of action plans and other related documents and establish a staff training cycle that ensures new staff are initiated into the practices of PBIS and existing staff are reminded of proper protocol.

Sometimes school teams become overly reliant on a single individual "champion" to carry the enthusiasm and effort of the initiative. This can be the principal, the coach, or someone else who is strongly committed. When that person moves on and leaves the PBIS Leadership Team, it creates a huge void that disrupts the continuity of leadership team and

---

2. Barrett and Duda, 2011; Sugai, 2013.

school functioning. This underscores the need to develop fluency among all team members and to share responsibilities for implementation tasks.

> Proactive planning for expected events can help prevent loss of progress, time, and efficacy.

In other situations, the PBIS Leadership Team and action plan may lack structures, processes, or system pieces necessary to ensure implementation and fidelity. The failure to self-monitor can cause teams to miss important milestones and opportunities to self-correct. Some very general considerations to address these barriers include awareness and knowledge of sustainability and of the factors that impede implementation and fidelity. Proactive planning for expected events can help prevent loss of progress, time, and efficacy.

A Theoretical Model of Sustainability in PBIS

A model of sustainability is emerging based on research specifically related to schoolwide PBIS and its features. This theoretical model, its validation, and the science of implementation offer great promise for the study and achievement of sustainable practices and systems. Kent McIntosh, Rob Horner, George Sugai, and others propose that PBIS sustainability is based on the presence of four factors:

1. PBIS is a priority in the school and district.
2. PBIS is effective; it achieves important outcomes.
3. PBIS is efficient; its efforts target results.
4. PBIS implementers continuously use data to evaluate and adapt to the local context, which enables continuous regeneration.

In their efforts to validate this model, these researchers and others have studied schools implementing PBIS across the United States. Two important and practical findings are coming from this work. First, evidence suggests that certain specific actions predict long-term implementation of PBIS with fidelity. Second, they've developed a tool called the SUBSIST Checklist that practitioners can use to self-assess their school's degree of sustainability; the checklist includes an accompanying action plan for responding to identified needs.[3]

> **SUBSIST Checklist Tool**
> Kent McIntosh and others have been actively studying how schools can sustain PBIS once it has been fully implemented. They have developed and are testing a research tool called the SUBSIST. A variation of the research tool is the SUBSIST Checklist, a self-assessment for coaches, administrators, and leadership teams. This tool allows teams to rank sustainability features as fully, partially, or not yet in place in their schools. Teams can use the results of this assessment to identify strengths, needs, and priorities for action planning. A reproducible version of the checklist appears on pages 177–180 in the appendix.

Research on PBIS Sustainability: Four Key Factors

Research has identified four critical factors that correlate with high-sustaining schools. These include:[4]

1. A strong PBIS Leadership Team
2. Regular use of fidelity data
3. Regular use and sharing of discipline data
4. Implementation of PBIS in each classroom

---

3. McIntosh et al., 2013.
4. Barrett and Duda, 2011.

Factor 1: A Strong PBIS Leadership Team

In chapter 2, we talked about the PBIS Leadership Team with recommendations for how to organize the team, including team roles and responsibilities, operating procedures, and use of data. Studies further emphasize the importance of these factors. In our experience, we have met or talked with schools that, after years of implementing PBIS, have only one or two people who are actually providing leadership and trying to sustain efforts. Sometimes it's a coach and sometimes an enthusiastic teacher. Some schools call and tell us that they went through formal training five to ten years earlier and there is no longer anyone at the school who knows about PBIS and that the school doesn't know what its own status is and believes it needs to start from scratch.

A strong PBIS Leadership Team and the school will need to adapt to changing circumstances. One big concern is turnover on the leadership team. Change is a given, so a team must be vigilant and intentional about building its capacity so that all roles are covered. Several ideas include:

- clearly defining roles and responsibilities
- creating a plan for training new team members for roles
- systematically recruiting new members
- rotating staff through roles
- using consistent and clear operating procedures
- avoiding having a single person provide a disproportionate amount of leadership
- holding regular meetings
- keeping meeting minutes and archives

Factor 2: Regular Use of Fidelity Data

We talk a lot about data methods and sources as well as action planning. Now research shows even more how important this is, in particular the use of fidelity data. Remember that fidelity is *the extent to which your practice matches the PBIS core features with integrity.* This is crucial because student outcomes are tied to this fidelity. Improved student outcomes motivate staff commitment to the practice as well as community support.

One of the wonderful aspects of PBIS in Char's experience is that it provides schools, teams, states, and others with the tools necessary to measure this fidelity. Very few initiatives do this. These tools are discussed in chapter 4.

Factor 3: Regular Use and Sharing of Discipline Data

A school's office discipline referral (ODR) data are a convenient and available means to measure changes in the school's social culture. The Schoolwide Information System (SWIS, see chapters 4 and 5) is an extremely powerful tool for collecting, analyzing, and using these data for action planning and reporting. We also know that many districts have adapted other school information systems to produce similarly sophisticated data. The crucial function of such systems is to have a routine and practical process for using these data in decision-making and action planning.

In addition to planning and evaluating progress, it is important to use these data to report regularly to your staff, school board, families, and other stakeholders. People need to see and hear the results you are achieving. Successfully sustaining schools all do this.

Factor 4: Implementation of PBIS in Each Classroom

Considering that students spend more than 90 percent of their time in school in the classroom, it is no surprise that most discipline referrals come from classroom settings. Studies show that sustaining PBIS schools have strong implementation and fidelity in classroom settings. This means that all the schoolwide features are fully and consistently implemented in each classroom, including clear definitions of expected behaviors, teaching and acknowledgment of expected behaviors, and consistent consequences for problem behaviors.

Early on in PBIS implementation, teams often spend a lot of time on the schoolwide aspects of

PBIS. But it's equally important for individual classrooms' practices to closely match the school's practices as a whole.

See resources on schoolwide PBIS in the references and resources on pages 187–192.

Adapting to Changing Circumstances

Change is hard for many people. Often, just when a new project gets rolling along, someone in leadership leaves. For PBIS Leadership Teams, a change in school staffing can affect the makeup of the team. To adapt, teams need to recruit new members. (Perhaps you can entice them with snacks at the meeting, the best parking spaces, or reduced morning supervision duty.) If your PBIS coach leaves, you'll need to adapt by having someone else step into this role. If your school and team planned ahead for this possibility, then you likely already have someone on your PBIS Leadership Team who can easily take over the coaching responsibilities. Even if this change catches your team off guard, your documentation of archived notes, electronic records, and your three-ring binder of materials will help the next person take on this task. This documentation should include the titles of team roles as well as a description and time commitment for each. Part of planning may include a predictable succession plan and possibly term limits.

Students, too, can change as PBIS initiatives continue. For example, they can tire of the expectations and start to blindly repeat them without knowing what they really are. When staff and team members notice this, it may be time to freshen up the expectations, teaching, and acknowledgment systems.

Perhaps one of the biggest challenges to sustaining PBIS is when a supportive principal leaves and is replaced with a principal who does not believe in PBIS and would rather go back to the way things were.[5] To prevent such an awful scenario from occurring, the PBIS team and coach could proactively approach the new principal to schedule an appointment to discuss the benefits of the initiative; then bring along the three-ring binder of archives and go over the baseline data (before PBIS) and the current data (reflecting the continued emphasis on the key features of PBIS). A couple of useful and informative tools include the Cost-Benefit Analysis Worksheet created by PBIS Maryland, which allows you to calculate the amount of time reclaimed for student instruction as well as administration time (search "cost-benefit" at www.pbis.org). Also consider discussing the brief on www.pbis.org titled *What Are the Economic Costs of Implementing SWPBIS in Comparison to the Benefits from Reducing Suspensions?* Show photos of happy students being honored for being awesome and photos of staff enjoying teaching. Show the behavioral matrix with the lesson plans and share academic assessment scores (hopefully they've also improved), surveys, and TFI, SET, and SAS scores. We recommend getting sound bites from parents and the person who owns the convenience store next to the school. It would also make sense to remind the principal about the district commitment to PBIS and invite him or her to your next PBIS Leadership Team meeting. (*Note:* It is the district's responsibility to replace the principal with one who would commit to PBIS.) We know of schools that have lost funding and administrative support but have carried on with PBIS as best they can, knowing it is the best way to run a school. These teachers meet on their own time to sustain PBIS.

Buy-In and Support

At each stage of implementation, we recommend taking time to consider how to keep support for PBIS strong. Buy-in is just as crucial during ongoing sustainability as it is during the earlier stages of implementation. What steps need to be taken to continually achieve buy-in? Which team members need to

---

5. Strickland-Cohen, McIntosh, and Horner, 2014.

take action? **Figure 10.1** below outlines these tasks and responsibilities for stage 5, as you are working to sustain and improve PBIS in your school.

Telling Your School's Story

As your PBIS Leadership Team and school staff are working to sustain and improve how they use the PBIS framework, telling your school's PBIS story to others is especially important. Communicate what is going well and what aspects of the initiative you are working to improve. This may elicit ideas from others too. We recommend that you develop a narrative based on your data as you prepare to sustain and improve PBIS in your school (including ODRs, implementation, fidelity, and outcomes).

When schools prepare displays of their PBIS progress, they often use a format typically seen at science fairs: telling a story with data, images, and attention-grabbing headlines. Start by creating an outline of information you want to share, add graphic displays of progress, and outcomes, and include mottos, photos, and other examples to create human interest. Remember to tell your audience what you intended to do and what you have accomplished.

Figure 10.1: Sustaining and Continuous Improvement—Buy-In Roles and Measures During Stage 5

Person/Group Responsible	Buy-In Tasks	Measures
Administrator	• Continue to support openly at the school and district levels • Secure needed funds to support activities	TFI, TIC, SET, BoQ
PBIS Leadership Team	• Meet regularly • Use and report ODR data • Use data to monitor fidelity • Adapt and plan for changing contexts	TFI, TIC, SET, BoQ, ODRs
School staff	• Assist new staff with professional development and continued practice • Acknowledge, support, listen, clarify • Implement schoolwide expectations in classrooms	TFI, SAS, SET, BoQ
Students	• Continue to learn and demonstrate behavioral expectations, which are acknowledged appropriately by adults	ODRs, TFI, SET or BoQ scores, SAS scores Student surveys
District	• Provide district leadership with data and information about status and progress • Show commitment to PBIS by hiring PBIS-supportive administrators • Provide ongoing, readily available professional development	District evaluation plan Implementation blueprint
Community	• Keep a parent on the PBIS team • Support local businesses with PBIS products (expectations posters, "Caught Ya" tickets, etc.)	Parent satisfaction survey Increase in positive comments from area businesses and community members

Equity and Disproportionality: How PBIS Can Help

Much has been studied and written about disproportionality in disciplinary actions at schools, and rightfully so. The systems and policies of how schools and districts respond to behaviors must ensure a quality education for *all* students, regardless of race, ethnicity, special education needs, religion, gender, language, sexual orientation, and socioeconomic status. How can schools provide a quality education and a safe learning environment while meeting the needs of an increasingly diverse student body? While the majority of teaching staff continues to be white, female, and middle class, educators must be ready to teach all students and welcome them equally into our schools. This means taking a look, especially, at how systems and policies tend to favor white students over students of color. We believe that our greatest responsibility as educators is to increase equity among students across racial, social, and cultural lines.

The framework of PBIS applies to all students and all staff in all settings throughout the school. This consistency is important for many reasons and is especially critical when addressing and overcoming challenges to equity and reducing disproportionality in any domain. We believe the PBIS structure and practices are particularly suitable for these challenges.

> "In these days, it is doubtful that any child may reasonably be expected to succeed in life if he is denied the opportunity of an education. Such an opportunity, where the state has undertaken to provide it, is a right which must be made available to all on equal terms."
>
> —Chief Justice Earl Warren, *Brown v. Board of Education* (1954)

What Is Educational Equity?

Equity in education has been a concern for many decades. *Educational equity* means that all students have equal opportunities for a high-quality education and successful outcomes. The *Brown v. Board of Education* Supreme Court decision put into law that separate is *not* equal. Yet over seventy years later, equity remains a challenge regardless of how integrated schools are. There are, in fact, disparities in staffing and student populations. A report from the National Center for Education Statistics (NCES) states that roughly 80 percent of all public school teachers and administrators in the United States are white, while less than half of public school students are white. Projections for the school year beginning in 2018 indicated that the 50.7 million public school students entering preK through grade 12 would include 26.6 million students of color: 7.8 million Black students, 14.0 million Hispanic students, 2.6 million Asian students, 0.2 million Pacific Islander students, 0.5 million American Indian/Alaska Native students, and 1.6 million students of two or more races. Meanwhile, the percentage of white students enrolled in public schools is projected to continue to decline through at least fall 2027.[1] In this chapter, we try to address educational inequity among all students of color, while occasionally referring to data for a particular group addressed in a study or report.

Equity and Equality

Educational equity is often considered synonymous with equal access, yet there are subtle differences. Equity recognizes that students come to school with different needs, some of which prevent them from benefiting from the educational opportunities offered. To achieve equity, we must provide additional supports to ensure students have equal access to quality education. For example, when students come to school hungry, we feed them, because we know hungry kids don't study well. Some schools set up after-school clubs to ignite girls' interest in science and math. We use evidence-based reading interventions to help improve students' reading skills. Schools provide supports to raise the playing field of education to create equitable learning environments for all students.

Equal opportunity, on the other hand, ensures that students across schools and districts are offered the same educational opportunities to learn and succeed. As a singular focus, equal opportunity misses the barriers to student success that are based on individual students' needs.

To ensure that schools achieve *both* equity and equal opportunity for students, it's important to look at the student supports and their effects as well as at various outcomes. Multi-tiered systems of support for academic and social learning offer examples for how to screen and provide targeted supports for students. Additionally, a systemic approach helps schools identify differential student treatment, such as disparities in discipline or in participation in gifted and talented programs. Schools need a solid process for self-monitoring of supports for equity, access to and participation in opportunities, and student outcomes using accurate data in real time in order to make course corrections.

Eighty percent of all public school teachers and administrators in the United States are white, while less than half of public school students are white.

A Look at Racial and Ethnic Inequities Among Students

So what does inequity look like? It looks different depending upon the racial and ethnic groups discussed. For example, here are the most prominent disparities in schools involving Black students when compared with their white peers:

- a gap in academic achievement[2]
- lower involvement in gifted and talented programs[3]
- higher dropout rates[4]
- lower graduation rates[4]
- **more office discipline referrals (ODRs)[3]**
- **higher rates of suspension and expulsion[3]**
- **disproportionate placement in special education[3]**

---

1. National Center for Education Statistics, 2018.
2. Stanford Center for Education Policy Analysis, 2013.
3. Office for Civil Rights, 2016.
4. National Center for Education Statistics, 2018.

- **harsher punishments (including greater use of seclusion and restraint)[3]**
- **disproportionate placement in juvenile justice[3]**

While many of these disparities are related and positive school behavior systems seek to mitigate them all, the final five (bold) are the most closely related to our current PBIS efforts. The following sections provide a brief summary of the research on these five key disparities involving Black students and other racial/ethnic student groups.

More ODRs and Higher Rates of Suspension and Expulsion

Numerous studies have caused concern about the high number of Black students who receive ODRs and suspensions when compared to white students. The Office for Civil Rights Data Collection for the 2013–14 school year shares disturbing numbers: Across the US, 6 percent of all students in grades K–12 received at least one suspension, but for Black students the percentages were 18 percent for boys and 10 percent for girls; for white boys it was 5 percent, and 2 percent for white girls. Overall, Black students were *3.8 times as likely* as white students to receive at least one out-of-school suspension and nearly twice as likely to be expelled from school without further educational support. In addition, American Indian/Alaska Native, Latino, and Native Hawaiian or other Pacific Islander boys represented 15 percent of the K–12 population but 19 percent of students receiving out-of-school suspensions.[5]

ODRs and Black Preschool Children

A special note is warranted on the topic of school discipline of preschool-age children. The Office for Civil Rights report informs us of the high racial disproportionality of suspension and expulsion in this age group. For example, among children

in preschool programs with one or more suspensions, 47 percent—*nearly half*—of those suspended were Black children, although they made up only 19 percent of the total preschool population. Compare this to white preschool students who made up 41 percent of the total preschool population but only 28 percent of preschool children receiving one or more suspensions.[6] Black children in preschools and childcare centers are expelled at higher rates than Black students in K–12 programs. Furthermore, researchers Walter Gilliam and Golan Shahar found that large class size and greater teacher stress correlated with these findings.[7] The Yale Child Study Center published a brief exploring possible causes for disproportionate suspensions and expulsions of preschool children. Although the study was a simulation rather than actual behavior observations, it suggests that implicit bias might be a factor contributing to gender and racial disparities and offers suggestions for further research.[8]

Disproportionate Placement in Special Education

Educators have also studied and expressed concern about racial disproportion in special education. Although the disparity has been well documented for decades, the reasons vary from state to state and community to community. Some readers may remember the term "six-hour retarded child" from the late 1960s and early 1970s, which referred to certain racial groups who were labeled "mentally retarded" and placed in segregated school programs, yet were perfectly functional in their own communities, calling to question our system of identification.[9] The US Department of Education, Office for Civil Rights, tracks overrepresentation of racial groups in special education. Particular patterns show that Black students are most typically overrepresented in the categories of developmental cognitive disabilities (formerly mental retardation)

---

5. Office for Civil Rights, 2016.
6. Office for Civil Rights, 2016.
7. Gilliam and Shahar, 2006.
8. Gilliam et al., 2016.
9. Mercer, 1973.

and emotional-behavioral disorders (EBD). American Indian/Alaska Native students are also disproportionately represented in the category of learning disabilities.[10]

The causes of disproportionate special education placement are complex and beyond the scope of this chapter. However, the particular concerns we want to underscore are the factors that negatively affect equity and educational opportunity for students. For instance, students labeled with disabilities are disproportionately disciplined with exclusionary practices, in particular students with EBD.[11] And school exclusion disrupts learning and leads to student disengagement. Hence, mislabeling students of color as having disabilities, such as EBD, may contribute to their disproportionate exclusion and negative outcomes.

A Word from Beth About Special Education and Racial Inequity

When I was a special education teacher for students with EBD, the majority of my students were Black; I accepted this as how things were. However, as I became more aware of issues surrounding equity in education, I soon realized that this was *not* how things should be. I began to look at my own racial bias. I quickly recognized my bias against students of color being good students because they seemed uninterested in school and because they did not behave according to my expectations. I also found that I usually believed the stereotypes too often portrayed in the media of boys and men in the Black community being more dangerous, being prone to crime and violence, and having lower academic skills.

I began to realize and pick apart the racial biases I brought to the classroom once I understood that my students' behavior was often rooted in issues beyond their control and occurring in a school system set up for their failure (Black special education students were suspended far more often than white students were). I discouraged principals from suspending my students and looked for resources and strategies to help them stay in school while managing their complex emotions and reactions. I also began to think about the experiences from my own cultural background that I brought to my classroom. How was I contributing to the racial inequality in the classroom and the school? How did my white, middle-class upbringing compare to the backgrounds of my students of color who were raised in highly social urban environments and often in families struggling with poverty, unsafe housing, and a lack of resources for physical and emotional health? Finally, I began to question whether some of my students should even be in special education with IEP goals such as, "Student X will sit in his chair for 100 percent of the class period," and "Student Y will reduce blurting in class to zero incidents." Could *I* sit in a hard plastic chair for fifty minutes without squirming or talking, especially if I had attention issues and/or grew up in a culture that encouraged frequent animated dialogue?

My own bias needed confronting. Likewise, our special education placements and school behavior policies must respect and incorporate cultures that honor community over the individual. All educators need to look at their systems of belief and values in relation to the students who are in their classrooms every day.

Harsher Punishments

The use of physical restraint and seclusion are considered highly restrictive procedures and are closely regulated in US schools. In 2016, the Office for Civil Rights released a data report highlighting several issues related to these punishments and the implications for equity. During the 2013–14 school year, 100,000 students were placed in seclusion or physically restrained at school. Of those, 67 percent were students with disabilities, a group that was

---

10. Office for Civil Rights, 2016.
11. Skiba et al., 2008.

only 12 percent of the student population. Black males made up 18 percent of students subject to seclusion or restraint (many of them also in special education), while they comprised just 8 percent of the student population. Research confirms that harsh punishment does little to teach adaptive behavior, is more reactive than planful, and likely contributes to pushing students to drop out of school and into the "school-to-prison pipeline."[12]

Disproportionate Placement in Juvenile Justice

Black students are more likely to be referred to school resource officers or be subject to arrest at school. In fact, Black male students are more than three times as likely as white students to be arrested at school.[13] In September 2017, the Sentencing Project reported data from the US Department of Justice, which documented worsening disparities in incarceration. African American youth were *five times as likely* to be placed in detention centers as white youth. They represented 16 percent of all youth in the United States, but 44 percent of incarcerated youth.[14]

Zero Tolerance and the "School-to-Prison Pipeline"

A lot has been written about racial disparity and what is termed the "school-to-prison pipeline." According to the American Civil Liberties Union (ACLU), the zero tolerance policies that many schools adopted to increase safety criminalized minor infractions (nail clippers and scissors were considered weapons) and instead of making schools safer, ended up pushing many students of color out of schools and often into the juvenile justice system. The most striking numbers refer to Black males, Latino students, and those with disabilities. Additionally, zero tolerance policies have in some instances made schools seem more prisonlike than educational.[15]

In addition to implementing zero tolerance, many districts hired school resource officers (SROs), some of whom are connected to local police departments. Many SROs have little training in working with young people, people of color, or people with mental health needs. If a student is displaying behavior in school that could be considered "out of control," such as yelling, throwing objects, or refusing to leave an area or follow any directions from staff, schools may feel their only recourse is to call the SRO to move the student to another area of the school or to remove her or him from the building. School staff who stereotype Black students as violent, uncontrollable, or unmanageable often make decisions to escalate situations by quickly calling in SROs rather than utilizing de-escalation or diversion techniques that can help students identify the cause of the incident.

> PBIS first and foremost supports creating safe and efficient learning environments.

Schools are moving away from zero tolerance approaches to student behavior, which tend to remove students from access to instruction and alienate them from school. Best practice and federal guidelines guide schools to use more positive, instruction-based approaches as well as clear and consistent discipline systems to encourage positive behavioral change. However, as schools move away from zero tolerance and reliance on SROs, concerns about safety may return. In conversations with educators, families, and community members, Char fielded continual complaints about students whose behavior seriously disrupted the school environment. Before the PBIS framework began growing and schools changed, administrators would call her to ask what the legal mechanism was for permanently removing disruptive students from school. Sometimes legislators would argue that "these students" didn't belong in public schools, and some parents thought their children's

---

12. Office for Civil Rights, 2016; Elias, 2013.
13. Blad and Harwin, 2017.
14. The Sentencing Project, 2017.
15. Penn Wharton Public Policy Initiative, 2015.

education and safety was compromised by the students' disruptive behavior. Complex and difficult topics, for certain.

In response to these concerns, PBIS first and foremost supports creating safe and efficient learning environments; it does not condone violence or illegal behavior. The framework promotes change through a prevention-oriented approach that applies to the entire school: all students and all staff. It also stresses school preparedness. Besides day-to-day readiness, there are safety procedures for handling crises and major disruptions. Schools should be prepared with crisis teams who are trained to de-escalate behavior or secure areas and protect students and staff. It may be difficult for individual staff members not to step in during a crisis, but staff stepping in is often not the best option. Char recalls following after a student who was running off campus. When she reached the student, the young woman grabbed Char's hair and pulled out a handful of it. With some preplanning, this situation might never have occurred. This is a minor example, but many more serious examples exist where both students and staff sustain serious injuries. These are significant and troubling events that can polarize staff and community opinions. The best approach is to have a solid prevention framework established and a formal proactive response team.

Causes of Racial and Ethnic Disproportionality in School Discipline

The Equity Project at Indiana University offers a succinct summary of some causes for disproportionality in school discipline.[16] They discuss five possible, but not exclusive, causes:

1. **Poverty.** Poor families and underresourced communities tend to correlate with disproportionate effects on students of color, although socioeconomic status is not a single causative factor. It is well documented that students of lower socioeconomic status tend to be overrepresented in disciplinary exclusion.[17] Poverty can lead to factors that affect learning and behavior, such as inadequate food and sleep, exposure to unhealthy substances, parental stress, homelessness, and trauma. But even controlling for poverty, racial disparities are evident.

2. **Unequal educational opportunities.** Schools and districts serving primarily students of color often have undertrained staff, subpar facilities, and limited resources. The Office for Civil Rights reports that students of color are more likely to have inexperienced or inadequately licensed teachers and to be in schools with high rates of teacher absenteeism.[18] These disadvantages contribute to disproportionality because staff may not be trained to develop effective classroom management, engaging lesson plans, and skills in working with high-needs students. Char was shocked to learn about districts where teacher absenteeism was so high and no substitutes were available that students were assembled in the gym for the day.

3. **Special education eligibility process.** The Equity Project suggests that some state special education criteria may lead to higher failure rates, since students often have to fail before meeting eligibility requirements for services. Once students have fallen far behind, it is difficult for them to regain those academic losses. Because we know students often misbehave when confronted with tasks they do not comprehend (or are too easy), we can recognize the link between academic performance and behavior. With delays built into the eligibility

16. See http://www.indiana.edu/~equity/docs/Highlights011415.html.
17. Skiba et al., 2012.
18. Office for Civil Rights, 2016.

process, students may enter special education with huge academic deficits. As we've discussed, Black students and other students of color are overrepresented in special education, and special education status is associated with more exclusionary discipline and lower school completion.

4. **Cultural mismatch.** As noted early in this chapter, the teaching workforce in the US has been and remains primarily white, female, and middle class, while the student population continues to grow ever more diverse. This cultural and socioeconomic difference between teachers and students may negatively affect staff interpretations of student behavior and their subsequent responses to it.

5. **Educator bias and exclusionary practices.** There is clear evidence that Black, American Indian/Alaska Native, and Latino students are excluded in school more frequently than other students and that this exclusion begins in the classroom. Additionally, Black students, in particular, receive harsher punishments than other students for the same behavior.[19]

When you look at each of these causes, you can clearly see that they are interrelated and have multiple causes and effects. For the rest of this chapter, however, we will focus on the final cause, educator bias, and its role in the disproportionality of school discipline practices, including suspension and expulsion. We will discuss this topic and demonstrate the ways that PBIS and other behavior frameworks can address it.

Explicit and Implicit Bias

A person's bias consists of prejudices against certain groups of people, and it is the primary reason that our students of color continue to be disproportionately disciplined by a staff of educators who are primarily white.[20] Bias takes two forms: explicit and implicit. *Explicit bias* involves the attitudes and beliefs we knowingly have about a person or group. Some teachers wrongly believe that Black students are naturally more violent than other students, as Beth confessed to doing earlier in this chapter. And for many years, scientists (who were white and European) explicitly believed that people whose skin was darker were less intelligent. We know this is not true, of course, but there are people, including some educators, who still hold this belief today.

Implicit bias refers to the attitudes or stereotypes that affect our understanding, actions, and decisions in an unconscious manner. For example, teachers may have lower expectations for certain groups of students related to race and socioeconomic status, or they may assume all students know how to ask for help. The concept of implicit bias has been around since the mid-1990s. Social psychologists such as Hermann von Helmholtz identified it as a separate phenomenon from explicit bias. It was viewed as common, damaging, and beginning early in childhood. Originally, it seemed like implicit bias might be unchangeable, but studies since then offer more hope and specific ideas for actions that may correct it.[21] For resources on addressing bias, see the references and resources on page 187.

> ## We all have both explicit and implicit bias to some degree.

We all have both explicit and implicit bias to some degree. In establishing expectations for behavior, consider not only your students, but also your staff and the backgrounds and bias they bring to the classroom. Following is a story about a time when Beth examined her own implicit bias, outside of a school setting:

---

19. Office for Civil Rights, 2016.
20. United States Government Accountability Office, 2018.
21. Hardin and Banaji, 2013.

I was raised in a white, Catholic, German-Norwegian family. Every Sunday morning, we went to Mass, which started promptly at 10:30 and ended at 11:30. We were taught to be very punctual. This is also how I experienced school as a student and, later, as a teacher—be on time, in place, and quietly waiting for the next direction. These were the expectations I had for myself and my students.

Then one Sunday a dear friend invited me to attend her church, where most members were Black. The service started at 10:30, and I thought we should arrive on time and sit down so we would be prepared for the service to begin. My friend laughed when I said this and mentioned that the service had already started. "Can't you hear the music?" she asked. Finally, we went in to take our seats—five minutes late according to my watch. I noticed that more people drifted in during the service, while others seemed to be leaving. Throughout the service, some people walked across the aisle to socialize with friends and family. There were times when we were all standing and singing and clapping and other times when we were seated and listening, punctuated by shouts of "Amen!" and "That's right!" All in all, the service lasted about three hours.

Afterward, my friend, who also works in a school district, asked me what I thought. "I could have written 100 behavioral referrals!" I joked in shock. This church service was loud and joyous and full of love and energy. Although many people welcomed me, I still felt like this was a community that I didn't quite belong to. I didn't know the rules or the system; not too many people looked like me. I felt out of place. My friend then pointed out that this is the environment many Black students come from—participating in call-and-response with the pastor, arriving and departing when you choose, and frequently leaving your seat to socialize with friends a few rows over. And these are all the very things that drive many white teachers crazy. I realized that perhaps my Black students were bringing their church experiences to school, the same way I had brought mine when I was a student. But it was easier for me, because all the teachers looked like me and my quiet, studious behavior was deemed more socially acceptable. Our students of color don't often have that same advantage.

PBIS and Educator Bias

Just as Beth walked into her friend's church unaware, many students, and students of color in particular, may walk into schools or classrooms not knowing the school's system or expectations. PBIS addresses this by establishing a clear set of positively stated expectations that are taught to students and acknowledged by all students and staff. The framework emphasizes developing these expectations to match your specific school's culture, which reflects both staff and student diversity. The exemplary expectations will reflect these diverse values. The unexemplary ones will reflect the values of only a few—typically the few in charge.

The PBIS framework in your school must address the needs of *all* your students *all* the time. PBIS Leadership Teams need to look at the histories of their schools, including the teaching and disciplinary practices, to see if their schools have been engaging, recognizing, and validating students' diverse backgrounds and the values and traditions students bring to school. Be aware of explicit and implicit bias involving:

- race and ethnicity
- socioeconomic status
- religion
- gender identity
- language
- sexual orientation

- mental health
- cognitive disabilities
- physical disabilities
- family makeup
- homelessness

As Beth's story illustrates, shared behavior and beliefs of one group may seem difficult to understand by another group unfamiliar with its traditions—in this case, related to religion and racial/ethnic background. Behavior is learned and contextual. Some behaviors are learned in a specific setting for a reason. However, taken out of that context, the behavior could be seen as negative or disruptive.

As educators, we must respect and validate each culture's behavioral norms, while also teaching and modeling those behaviors shown to be more conducive to certain school contexts. For instance, in a math class while the teacher is explaining a lesson, it may not be helpful to have students calling out answers or walking around the room socializing. However, this behavior may be totally appropriate during group work, a quiz bowl, or various other more social activities. Teachers acting on their biases and labeling a specific student's or group's behavior "wrong" at all times and disciplining students for displaying it—particularly if they do not discipline white students for displaying similar behavior—is an example of how implicit and explicit biases are embedded in our school systems and why it is vitally important that we check our systems and practices for disproportionality and bias. The following sections provide strategies for doing so.

Strategies to Reduce Bias and Disproportionate Discipline

PBIS is a framework to change the systems and practices of your school to make them more efficient and effective for all students, across all school settings, all the time. To be sure that our efforts are equitable to all students (students of one group are not receiving preferential treatment over another group), school staff must be sure all students are truly treated fairly.

PBIS offers strategies to change the entire system: schools and the district as a whole. Disproportionate discipline is one problem amid many contributing to inequity. Approaching this issue with a view of the overall system will facilitate changes. A great resource is the publication *Key Elements of Policies to Address Discipline Disproportionality: A Guide for District and School Teams*, found at www.pbis.org. This guide identifies seven key elements of effective policy:[22]

1. Specific commitment to equity
2. Family partnerships in policy development
3. Focus on implementing positive, proactive behavior support practices
4. Clear, objective discipline procedures
5. Removal or reduction of exclusionary practices
6. Graduated discipline systems with instructional alternatives to exclusion
7. Procedures with accountability for equitable student outcomes

These elements provide a solid foundation for overall change.

Also available is a straightforward guide, *A 5-Point Intervention Approach for Enhancing Equity in School Discipline* (again, see www.pbis.org). The five steps are:[23]

1. Collect, use, and report disaggregated discipline data.
2. Implement a behavioral framework that is preventive, multi-tiered, and culturally responsive.
3. Use engaging instruction to reduce the opportunity (achievement) gap.
4. Develop policies with accountability for disciplinary equity.
5. Teach strategies for neutralizing implicit bias in discipline decisions.

---

22. Green et al., 2015.
23. McIntosh et al., 2018

In the next section, we have chosen to elaborate on the final step in this approach: teaching strategies for neutralizing implicit bias in discipline decisions. A critical way PBIS is trying to effect changes in disproportionate disciplinary practices is by careful analysis of discipline data, given the concept of implicit bias. By using a multidimensional view of ODR data, this approach illustrates the interaction among implicit bias, the specific situation, and the resulting disproportionate outcomes. Kent McIntosh and others have introduced a process for teams to identify situations and factors that create vulnerable decision points, which are more likely to result in disproportionate ODRs or other discipline practices. They propose an analytical approach to identifying such factors.

Vulnerable Decision Points

In the Schoolwide Information System (SWIS), teams can use the Drill-Down Tool for analyzing specific data. Your school information system may provide you with a similar tool. These data reveal situations that may involve vulnerable decision points, or VDPs. One factor that contributes to a VDP is a teacher's subjective interpretation of problem behavior. Teachers and students may have differing experiences with what is considered disruptive, disrespectful, and defiant. Lack of clarity and consistency in what is a major versus a minor behavior can be another factor. Then there are specific precipitating factors affecting staff at the time of the referral, which may include certain settings, internal factors like hunger or fatigue, and so on. In the absence of clarity and the presence of precipitating factors, quick decisions are often made that are vulnerable to implicit bias and hence are called vulnerable decision points.

For example, a white teacher who sees two Black students in the hallway and hears them rapping loudly, surrounded by a crowd, might assume that the students are arguing, being disruptive, or even inciting violence and may send them off with a referral. This snap judgment made at a vulnerable decision point, likely fueled by bias, has now sent two kids—who were harmlessly entertaining their peers—to the behavior room where they will miss out on instruction in the classroom.

Being aware of our biases can help us stop a snap judgment about a behavior and process it more thoughtfully. In addition, adding clarity to behavioral definitions for major and minor behaviors and evaluating setting factors help reduce the likelihood of poor decisions. In general, there are four factors to consider when deciding if a potential referral may be occurring at a vulnerable decision point:

1. **Ambiguous subject matter.** For behaviors labeled disrespectful, defiant, or insubordinate, have implicit and explicit biases been considered?

2. **Vague discipline system.** Has your PBIS team set clear definitions for major (ODR) and minor (classroom-managed) behaviors, especially when considering the behaviors listed in the first factor?

3. **Lack of contact or relationship with students.** Sometimes teachers or staff come upon a situation and assume that it is a major behavior and refer students to the office without understanding the context or even knowing the students' backgrounds or histories.

4. **Early morning or late afternoon.** Staff who are not morning people need to consider how they are feeling physically and emotionally before referring a student to the behavior room at 7:45 a.m. The same goes for the afternoon, when some teachers are fatigued from a long day or may be hungry and need an afternoon snack.

In order to be sure that you are going to write a referral for a "true" behavior and not because you are just reacting to a situation, pause a few seconds and ask yourself if you are at a VDP. Consider your personal state of mind at the moment. Consider your relationship (or lack of) with the students involved. Beth worked with a white teacher who referred her Black students for a suspension whenever they called her a "b—" because she was offended by that. What she didn't realize was that the boys were planning ahead to take off certain days from school, sometimes together. All they had to do was call her that name, and the next day they got to stay home from school. The teacher's decision to suspend the students came at a VDP, since she did not have relationships with the students and let her racial bias influence her decision. If she had known these students better, she might have handled this situation differently and prevented the boys from achieving their desired joint suspensions. By building a relationship with these students, she might have noticed a pattern (using the word toward her mainly in the afternoon) and could have set up a restorative justice circle to discuss with the boys why they used that word with her. She might have offered a "rewind" and said, "I get the feeling you are upset with me. It's okay to be mad, but not to use that language. So tell me what you are upset about and let's problem-solve together."

Defining Problem Behaviors

We see "defiant" and "disrespectful" behaviors, but how do we actually define them? In the PBIS implementation process, schools identify three to five positively stated expectations for school behavior. These are short phrases, such as "Be respectful." However, a crucial part of implementing PBIS requires operational definitions of each of these expectations within the social and cultural context of the school. These definitions are included in the behavioral matrices, which are displayed around the school and in classrooms. They are the basis of teaching students about behavior, and it is important that they reflect the values and culture of the school population as a whole. We are not fans of using generic "school expectations" that are not defined to reflect your particular school's values and culture. The previous example, "Be respectful," is a frequent schoolwide expectation, but what one person thinks is respectful, someone else might think is disrespectful. There are some great examples on YouTube and TeacherTube of students and schools demonstrating culturally relevant behavioral expectations.

Vulnerable decision points underscore the need for a systemic, holistic approach to data using a guide such as the one discussed in the previous section. Considering VDPs can help teachers slow down and examine their decisions about referrals and try to minimize the influence of their own bias in this decision-making.

Staff Development Addressing Implicit and Explicit Bias

Much has been studied, researched, and written on the topic of teacher bias in the classroom. We encourage your PBIS team to look around your area to find workshops or trainers who are willing to come to your school or district to help school staff identify areas of concern. We also encourage teams to look to local PBIS training centers for workshops or trainings available in your area. Until school and district staff are willing to look at and identify systemic issues and their own biases, equity will not exist in your school systems and practices. Admitting there are problems is the first step toward rectifying unjust beliefs and judgments.

Coaching is another strategy to help address bias. The MyTeachingPartner-Secondary (MTP-S) program is an evidence-based example of how coaching teachers on educational practice can reduce disparate disciplinary actions. The underlying research demonstrated that teachers who were coached for up to two years on the dimensions of emotional support, classroom organization, and instructional support achieved discipline rates for Black students equal to those for white students. Even more interesting is that these effects lasted throughout the year after coaching ended, when teachers engaged a new group of students.[24]

As discussed previously, the guide *A 5-Point Intervention Approach for Enhancing Equity in School Discipline* on www.pbis.org contains steps your PBIS team can take to be sure discipline practices are fair and just to all students—from examining how teams look at and report data to having teachers consider their implicit bias before handing out a discipline judgment. Following are descriptions of more specific tools on the PBIS website that you may consider using.

---

24. Mikami et al., 2011; Gregory et al., 2017.

Tools to Help Schools Reduce Disproportionality

We suggest that you retrieve the following tools from www.pbis.org and share them with your team. Each of the tools explains concepts in detail and provides school examples, which are helpful to see in practice.

PBIS Disproportionality Data Guidebook

Char has directly encountered issues of racial and ethnic disproportionality throughout her career, first as a teacher and later as a specialist for the Minnesota Department of Education (MDE). Working as a teacher of students with emotional-behavioral disorders, Char could not deny the fact that 99 percent of her students were Black and were primarily boys. Later at MDE, Char was on a team examining disproportionate identification of Black and Latino students for special education and developing materials on conducting unbiased assessments. The team also began to examine disciplinary practices. In this process, one of the facts they discovered was the difficulty of accessing the right data. For these reasons, the guidance that PBIS provides is particularly salient and promising.

PBIS is a framework that emphasizes the use of data at all levels of implementation. According to a report on www.pbis.org, *Using Discipline Data Within SWPBIS to Identify and Address Disproportionality: A Guide for School Teams*, the following data sources and features are recommended and some are required in addressing issues of disproportionality.[25]

Required Data Features:
1. Consistent entry of ODR data and student race/ethnicity
2. School enrollment by race/ethnicity
3. Immediate access to data for school PBIS teams

4. Ability to disaggregate ODR data by race/ethnicity
5. Capability to calculate risk indices and risk ratios

Recommended Data Features:
1. Standardized ODR forms and data entry
2. ODR forms that have multiple fields
3. Operational definitions of problem behaviors
4. Guidance and consistency in discipline procedures
5. Immediate graphing capability
6. Ability to disaggregate graphs by race/ethnicity
7. Automatic calculation of disproportionality graphs, risk indices, and risk ratios

These features are extremely important to begin the process and to engage in active problem-solving around inequity. SWIS has all these features, but so do many other student information systems. If yours does not, this is an opportunity to work with your district administration to achieve these features.

The first step is to determine if a problem exists in your school and district. The OSEP Technical Assistance Center on PBIS recommends using multiple measures including risk index, risk ratio (see the following section), and composition metrics. Probing disproportionality involves using data and drill-down methods to create precision statements, as we discussed in chapter 4. Problems may include six possible elements:

1. Inadequate PBIS implementation
2. Mismatch of schoolwide expectations
3. Academic achievement gap
4. Disproportionality across all settings
5. Disproportionality across specific settings
6. Lack of student engagement

A particularly interesting aspect is that disproportionality across all settings is considered an indicator of explicit bias, while disproportionality in specific settings may be an indicator of implicit bias.

---

25. OSEP Technical Assistance Center on PBIS, 2014.

Risk Ratios

The US federal government has issued rules that require a standard formula for calculating and reporting significant disproportionality. Currently, the proposed rules leave it up to states to establish their own thresholds, which means thresholds will differ across the country. *Risk ratio* refers to how much more or less likely a specific group is to receive a certain outcome, such as suspension. An equal risk ratio would be 1.0. Ratios higher than 1.0 reflect overrepresentation, and ratios less than 1.0 reflect underrepresentation. As it stands now, federal law would allow states to set their own risk ratios. Recent reports suggest that states have reported ratios between 3.0 and 5.0. This means that a particular racial group is three to five times more likely to receive a particular outcome. It is critical for such data to be transparent, accessible, and thoroughly examined.

PBIS Cultural Responsiveness Field Guide

We have repeatedly discussed the importance of using data. This means data that are accurate, valid, and available in a form that teams can use. One of the new tools being used, the Tiered Fidelity Inventory (TFI) described in chapter 4, has a companion piece related to cultural responsiveness. The document, *PBIS Cultural Responsiveness Field Guide: Resources for Trainers and Coaches*, can be found at www.pbis.org. Published in 2016, this document is a terrific resource. You can also find a video with Kent McIntosh, "Equity in School Discipline: Enhancing Commitment Through Teacher Training," online at www.pbis.org/school /equity-pbis. Section 2 of the field guide, "TFI Cultural Responsiveness Companion," focuses on using the TFI with a culturally responsive lens. Our purpose here is not to repeat all the great work done to enhance the TFI and culturally responsive practice in general, but to bring it to your attention and encourage you to follow up with your school and district.

PBIS Culturally Responsive Self-Assessment Tool

Also available is a team self-assessment to examine the cultural responsiveness of your PBIS Leadership Team. The tool, the Culturally Responsive Schoolwide PBIS Team Self-Assessment, is available at the Midwest PBIS Network website; visit www.midwestpbis.org and search "equity." This instrument has four sections: The first three assess cultural responsiveness at Tiers 1, 2, and 3, and the fourth section is a simple action-planning template.

You may be reading this and feel like you are in "tool overload." We caution teams not to get overloaded, meaning drowning in data that is not useful. Teams need the right data, in the right form, at the right time. For the most part, it is up to your team—be it at the school, district, county, or state level—to choose when you are ready and which tools best fit your needs at a specific point in time. The PBIS tools prompt us to check in with ourselves and our practice to ensure we uphold the goal of all students achieving the highest educational outcomes and success in life. Sometimes in communities where we are members of the dominant culture, we are not aware of what we don't know and may be maintaining the status quo. That is why we need to connect with the whole community, and not just a part.

In Summary

As she discussed at the start of this chapter, Beth has taught students receiving special education services for emotional-behavioral disorders. These middle and high school students had been placed in Beth's school by their home schools. The majority of her students were Black, several were American Indian, and just a few were white. The goal was to teach students how to manage their emotions and behaviors so they could return to their home schools. However, few students ever returned to their home schools or even graduated from that school centered on emotion and behavior management. Many students ended up in the juvenile justice system.

How different could things have been for those students if schools had used PBIS back then? Instead of schools rushing the paperwork through the district system, what if there were thoughtful systems and practices in place that supported students' needs? What if teachers and other staff had training in recognizing their biases toward students of color, especially those receiving special education services? Schools must be invested in positive outcomes for all students, both academic and behavioral. Many of Beth's students would have benefited from Tier 2 and 3 practices in their home schools before being referred out, only to end up incarcerated. We must create schools that are efficient and effective for all students, including those who are at risk for being swept up in the school-to-prison pipeline and who may need more intensive supports and interventions.

As a former behavior specialist at the Minnesota Department of Education, Char has had a long history with the evidence of disproportionality in special education, and in the category of EBD in particular, where Black boys were often overrepresented. A commonly quoted student remark was, "I'd rather be bad than mad." These students were frequently referred to and served in separate-site programs or detention centers where fewer mental health services were available and graduation rates were abysmal. PBIS has provided a tremendous model for helping to reverse these trends, integrating best practices from a variety of fields and perspectives to improve school environments and ensure the success and safety of all students, and of staff as well. Positive, safe, and more effective environments are best for all involved.

This chapter has focused on the data and concerns about equity and disproportionality in school disciplinary systems. It was necessarily brief; there is a long history of research and hundreds of books and articles on all aspects of this topic. It is a continual focus of policy reform and solution development. Our purpose was not to do an in-depth review, which has been done better by others, but rather to highlight the issues and introduce readers to some of the promising approaches emerging from the work of teams of professionals and the OSEP Technical Assistance Center on PBIS. There is much more to learn and put into practice to create change and realize the vision of what schools can—and should—be for all students.

PART THREE

Setting the Stage for PBIS Tiers 2 and 3

CHAPTER
12

Are You Ready for Advanced Tiers?

As we have stressed repeatedly throughout this book, it can take three to five years, sometimes even more, to fully implement all eight key features of PBIS Tier 1 with fidelity. Now that your implementation of this tier is fully in place, one thing you probably have noticed is that most students do quite well with these supports. They follow the expectations, participate in the acknowledgment systems, and strive to keep their school a safe and calm place to learn. And perhaps staff has redefined behaviors (major versus minor) and reflected on how they are choosing to respond to behavior. But you probably have also noticed that some students—often the same ones it seems—are being referred out of the classroom repeatedly for similar behaviors. You may also have noticed that a few of these same students lead the school in the number of referrals and suspensions, as if someone had told them it was a competition to get the highest numbers. How can the PBIS continuum of supports in your school reach these students? That is the purpose of PBIS Tiers 2 and 3.

PBIS follows a three-tiered model of prevention that comes from the field of public health. The tiers in this model represent a continuum of prevention strategies that depend on teaching and acknowledgment to improve students' engagement in school as well as their social competence. These tiers are called primary, secondary, and tertiary prevention, or Tier 1, Tier 2, and Tier 3. In general,

these intervention strategies are viewed on a continuum from least to most intensive:

- **Primary prevention** refers to those practices applied to the general population to avoid the development of social-behavioral problems in the first place.
- **Secondary prevention** refers to activities used with members of the population who experience risks for developing social-behavioral problems.
- **Tertiary prevention** encompasses activities designed to reduce the frequency or severity of social-behavioral problems among students who have already exhibited these problems.

The Three-Tiered Prevention Logic of PBIS

Prevention logic suggests that systematic use of effective practices at each of these tiers prevents and reduces the occurrence of social-behavioral problems and lessens the effects of those that do occur. At the end of the day, you have fewer new cases and better and more effectively handled existing cases. These outcomes benefit individuals, groups, and service systems. You may recall from chapter 1 the three-tiered PBIS triangle. It is shown again in **figure 12.1** on page 163.

Viewing the prevention model as a triangle makes sense and fits the three-tiered logic. In PBIS, the triangle is made up of evidence-based practices that are essential for the whole school (Tier 1), for a few students who need some additional support (Tier 2), and for those students who need intensive support (Tier 3). The big idea is to organize a school intervention system that prevents as many problems as possible so there are fewer severe problems requiring extensive services. The challenge facing educators is to create a school environment that effectively and collectively promotes the success and well-being of all students and all staff.

Tier 2, the middle tier, represents interventions for ideally about 15 percent of students—those who need more support beyond the schoolwide interventions. These students may have two to five referrals in a year. Tier 2 interventions may include small social-skills groups (such as a girls' group, friendship group, calming strategies group, or maybe a lunch bunch) that are typically led by the school social worker, counselor, or behavior specialist; or there may be other interventions to help at-risk students. Intervention strategies for

> **Students need to see how their behavior not only affects them, but also ripples out and has an impact on others.**

this tier utilize evidence-based, intensive teaching of prosocial behavior and can include the use of behavior contracts; Check-In Check-Out (CICO); behavior education programs; Check, Connect, and Expect; the HUG strategy; and cognitive behavioral therapy, to name a few. (See the references and resources for more information.)

Students need to see how their behavior not only affects them, but also ripples out and has an impact on others: teachers (whose teaching is interrupted), students (whose learning is put on hold while the teacher writes the referral), the behavior specialist (who has to process the behavior and do the data entry for the referral), the administrator (who has to call the student's parents), the parents (who may get interrupted at work because of the behavior), and so on.

Beth remembers one student's eyes growing as big as the clock on the wall when she was told that every time she called her teacher a so-and-so, at least five people were involved in handling the incident (student, teacher, behavior specialist, parent, behavior room staff, and sometimes the school social worker). The girl explained that she felt like her teacher didn't listen to her, so she yelled at her teacher. This student, her teacher, and Beth had a sit-down conference during which the student could be honest about how she felt being singled out by the teacher. The teacher accepted the feedback and acknowledged and apologized for the implicit bias she demonstrated during class. They reached an agreement to help each other out during a somewhat chaotic class period. Over a few weeks, the problem gently righted itself.

Tier 3, the top tier, represents specialized interventions for students with the highest level of need. At this level, the behavioral team can do a functional behavioral assessment and create

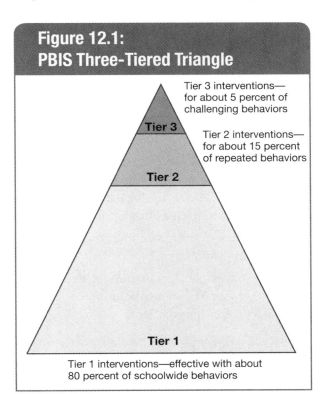

**Figure 12.1:
PBIS Three-Tiered Triangle**

Tier 3 interventions—for about 5 percent of challenging behaviors

Tier 3

Tier 2 interventions—for about 15 percent of repeated behaviors

Tier 2

Tier 1

Tier 1 interventions—effective with about 80 percent of schoolwide behaviors an individualized behavioral plan for the student. Some of these students may also be receiving special education services, or the data may show that an evaluation for special education may be in order. These students tend to be at high risk for challenging behaviors, which are the leading cause of expulsion. Generally, these interventions may be necessary for about 5 percent of the school population—students who may have six or more referrals. *Note:* Char has worked with schools that have as few as 1 percent of students receiving Tier 3 interventions and with others that have as many as 30 percent of students needing Tier 3 interventions. In fact, one school had only 40 percent of students succeeding with Tier 1 interventions and 60 percent needing Tier 2 and 3 interventions. Since this was a school of 700 students, that meant that *420 students* needed specialized services.

> Remember to use your data to make decisions. By this point you should have good data on implementation, fidelity, and student outcomes to guide your actions.

Is Your School Ready to Implement Tiers 2 and 3?

So when is it time to implement Tiers 2 and 3? Before your school considers taking this step, be sure that all components of Tier 1 are soundly in place. It's best to give your team at least a couple of years for full Tier 1 implementation. That isn't to say that students with high needs are being ignored while you focus on the universal tasks of Tier 1 PBIS. Some schools will already have groups in place or have a behavioral team discussing students who have challenging behaviors. If that is true for your school, continue those efforts while you focus primarily on completing Tier 1 implementation. If your school is beginning to adopt or has already adopted the Tiered Fidelity Inventory (TFI), this tool will assess the Tier 2 and 3 supports you have

in place in addition to Tier 1 fidelity. When your school believes it is ready for a formalized process to implement Tiers 2 and 3, consider your system readiness with these questions:

- Is Tier 1 implemented with fidelity across all settings and is it effective?

- What data sources document that Tier 1 is in place with fidelity? (For example, TFI = 70 percent, SET = 80 percent, BoQ = 70 percent.)

- Are Tier 1 schoolwide data consistently collected, reviewed, and used in decision-making?

- What are your current outcomes measured by office discipline referrals (ODRs)? Has the number of referrals decreased?

- How many major and minor ODRs will trigger Tier 2 or Tier 3 strategies for students in your school? (For example, two to five referrals for Tier 2.)

- Will your school weigh major ODRs against minor ODRs? (For example, will three minor referrals equal one major referral? Minor ODRs are often written for behaviors that could be managed in the classroom; teachers generally lose less instructional time when they handle these issues within the classroom.)

- How will you address students with internalized behaviors? (For example, sleeping in class, acting withdrawn, not participating in activities, experiencing failing grades, or visiting the nurse frequently—behaviors that are often ignored but could benefit from Tier 2 supports.) Research demonstrates that Tier 2 interventions and supports can change the trajectory of problem behavior, lost instructional time, or school exclusion.[1]

- Has the school principal committed to Tier 2 or Tier 3 implementation?

- Do you have a plan to make all staff aware of Tier 2 or Tier 3 implementation and integration with existing practices?

---

1. McIntosh, Frank, and Spaulding, 2010.

Big Idea: It is more efficient and effective to prevent problems from occurring or getting worse than it is to simply react to them. PBIS redesigns the school environment, not the students. In other words, PBIS changes adult behavior.[2]

For all three tiers, it is important to examine whether you have the existing resources, staff, funding, and commitment. Some schools and districts use the Hexagon Tool in order to determine if important system features are in place to support further action. (See page 104 in chapter 6.)

A discussion on how to implement Tiers 2 and 3 is beyond the scope of this book, but the preceding guidelines and questions can begin your exploration stage of implementation for Tiers 2 and 3. Don't rush your school into implementing strategies for all the tiers on the first day of school or let staff pressure you to do too much too soon. Give yourself and your staff time to make sure the features of Tier 1 are solidly in place with fidelity. You wouldn't build a house without a strong foundation. Hence, you shouldn't build up the PBIS triangle without a strong foundation in Tier 1. Take your time with the first tier. Build your foundation and build it well. That foundation will help you create a strong second tier, and then a third tier.

Some resources from the OSEP Technical Assistance Center on PBIS may be helpful to your team: the *Tier 2 Systems Readiness Guide* and "What Are the Organizational Systems for Tier 3?" (both can be found at www.pbis.org).

Coach's Tip from Beth

I remember trying to do all three tiers simultaneously when I didn't have a good handle on what Tier 1 was all about. With Char's suggestions, I took a step back and focused my energies on implementing Tier 1 strategies. There were still students participating in groups and teachers creating behavioral plans for the at-risk students, so there was support available for all students and staff. I took the necessary steps to implement Tier 1 with fidelity and in a way that would be sustainable. Besides the benefits that come with staying focused on one tier at a time, having the pieces of Tier 1 in place (the ODR procedure, teaching schoolwide expectations, a continuum of consequences, data collection and monitoring, and so on) will help you identify the students who are not responding to universal prevention strategies.

2. Sugai, 2013.

Conclusion

Positive behavioral support is a continually evolving initiative, and we've updated this edition to reflect current best practice in PBIS. We also chose to revise the book in order to include a special chapter on the important topic of disproportionality in suspension and expulsion of students of color. We believe PBIS offers solid strategies to identify implicit bias and reduce these troubling trends.

PBIS is a framework designed to improve the school learning environment through improved social and academic behavior. It is based on a three-tiered model of prevention, which is a difficult concept to sell because it's hard to attach a dollar benefit to the absence of a behavior.* However, if your school is one that suffers from uncontrolled student behaviors, and perhaps racially disproportionate disciplinary practices as well, you know you need help. The intense needs for Tiers 2 and 3 might suggest you are operating in a crisis-intervention framework. But more than anything, you need a solid Tier 1 prevention system that successfully reduces the demand for higher tiers. Perhaps you don't have enough resources to support a three-tiered system right away. Perhaps staff and students are burned out. We believe in the value of establishing a strong first-level prevention framework. That is why we chose, in this book, to explain the step-by-step process of Tier 1 implementation at fidelity. The process can be slow and not always complete, as Char explains from her experience as a coordinator and trainer:

> When I first began PBIS team training in Minnesota, PBIS cofounder George Sugai was our trainer. He did it all. Two days, all day. We gave every participant his or her own copy of a wonderful team-training manual. That was in 2005. Now we have

a whole team of homegrown trainers, and Minnesota PBIS (MNPBIS) has developed a new training manual that guides high-quality systematic training over the state's two-year team training period. When I was at MNPBIS, we started the first cohort with nine schools. This is year fourteen. The state's infrastructure has progressed tremendously and there are many supports for teams and coaches, Tier 2 and 3 training, evaluation, sustainability workshops, and an annual conference. Minnesota has worked hard to build capacity throughout the state and regions to support schools in their implementation and maintenance of PBIS. It is an adventure to observe. We wrote this book to provide a supplemental resource to schools, districts, and states that reflects current best practice and aligns with the state and national initiatives. We benefited greatly from the support of the national center, many other state PBIS initiatives, and the large national support network.

Just as prevention is a hard sell, so is change. As a PBIS coach, Beth was not sure what she was getting into, as she describes:

> I loved PBIS from the get-go and was sure everyone would love it as much as I did. However, that was not the case. As mentioned earlier, implementation of PBIS isn't so much about changing student behavior but about changing the way adults respond to behavior, and in some cases rethinking what we define as a "behavior." Some people were right there with me about PBIS, others weren't quite

---

* See chapter 10, page 144, for resources for conducting a cost-benefit analysis.

sure, and still others didn't want to go near it. I was lucky in that our principal was on board with PBIS and she knew that forcing people to get on board isn't the way to go. Start small and keep good data. People cannot argue with the data. As we went along, we implemented Tier 2 and 3 interventions because our school social worker saw they were necessary and was willing to do whatever was needed to help our students succeed. We also had a committed PBIS team.

So when you get frustrated with lack of buy-in, confused by all the assessment and data pieces, and bored with the slow pace of change, reach out to others who are successfully implementing PBIS in their schools and districts. They will understand. Take your time with implementation and enjoy the journey. There will be ups and downs along the way. But stay the course and eventually the logic of prevention will prevail and you will find your school to be a calmer, safer, more peaceful, and more equitable place to be. It is our hope that you find this book to be a useful companion on your personal PBIS journey and that you share your knowledge and experience with others.

Appendix

Contents

Coach's Self-Assessment

This self-assessment is designed to assist beginning coaches in identifying current strengths and professional development goals. It is organized to assess perceived knowledge and skills in the PBIS implementation areas of data, practices, and systems. The self-assessment may also serve as a data source schools and districts can use to identify the training and support a new coach might need.

Coach: _____ Date: _____

School system/district: _____ State: _____

Beginning Coach
Coaches at this level should have fluency with universal (Tier 1) PBIS items involving schoolwide, classroom, and nonclassroom settings. Coaches should be able to facilitate leadership team progress by guiding members through the PBIS implementation process.

3 = Fluent/mastered   2 = Building skills, but not yet fluent   1 = Still learning

Area	Skill	Self-Assessment
Data	1. Familiar with multiple data collection systems and their uses with PBIS Leadership Teams; e.g., Team Implementation Checklist (TIC), Self-Assessment Survey (SAS), School-Wide Evaluation Tool (SET) and office discipline referrals (ODRs)	3 2 1
Data	2. Can assist schools to develop other data systems as needed; e.g., ISS, OSS, attendance reports, observations	3 2 1
Data	3. Can teach and support leadership team's use of data to guide decision-making; e.g., PBIS assessments, ODRs, achievement, safety, attendance, suspension, expulsion	3 2 1
Practices	1. Knows and can define the essential features of schoolwide PBIS	3 2 1
Practices	2. Understands features of effective classroom instruction and management	3 2 1
Practices	3. Can guide schools in identifying and adopting evidence-based practices	3 2 1
Practices	4. Knows strategies to increase appropriate behavior and decrease inappropriate behavior of groups of students	3 2 1
Practices	5. Can provide schools with models and examples of other schools implementing PBIS	3 2 1
Practices	6. Understands basic principles of applied behavior analysis; e.g., reinforcement, punishment, stimulus control, extinction	3 2 1
Systems	1. Can facilitate effective team meetings	3 2 1
Systems	2. Can provide effective consultation and technical assistance to school teams	3 2 1
Systems	3. Able to effectively communicate within and across schools, district, region, etc.	3 2 1
Systems	4. Can assist schools to establish systems that support staff and increase sustainability of PBIS efforts	3 2 1

Adapted from the work of Timothy J. Lewis and Susan Barrett for the OSEP Technical Assistance Center on PBIS. Copyright © 2004. Reprinted with permission from the authors.

Coach's Self-Assessment Summary and Action Plan for Professional Development and Support

On your coach's self-assessment, add up your scores within each area (data, practices, systems). Add the three area scores together for a composite score; fill this in the blank. Use the scores to identify current coaching strengths as well as areas of need. Within each area (data, practices, systems), identify professional growth goals and the resources and support needed to accomplish each goal. Fill in the timeline for completion.

Current coaching level: _____   Composite score: _____

Area	Goal/Outcome statement: WHAT needs to be accomplished?	Resources/Support needed: HOW will this be accomplished?	Timeline
Data			
Practices			
Systems			

Action-Planning Sheet

Key PBIS Feature	Action/Activity	Who Is Responsible?	Start Date	Completion Date	Review Date

Writing a Purpose or Vision Statement

A purpose statement for your school sets the climate for everything else. In the business world this is called a tagline. The statement should be printed and posted widely: on a big banner in the hallway, on school web pages, and on the newsletter, school handbook, and programs for school concerts and athletic events. Incorporate the following into your process for creating a purpose or vision statement:

1. State positively in two or three sentences (*We are . . . , We will . . . , Our purpose is to . . . , etc.*)

2. Focus schoolwide: all students, all staff, all settings

3. Relate to academic achievement

4. Agree upon by at least 80 percent of school staff

Evergreen School's Purpose Statement

The Evergreen School is a community of learners. With school staff supporting us, we come to school to become our best selves by studying hard and becoming good citizens in a safe and friendly school environment.

Brainstorm some ideas for your purpose statement here:

Writing Schoolwide Behavioral Expectations

Your schoolwide behavioral expectations should expand on your purpose or vision statement. They explain how your school will support the statement. Expectations are better than rules because they allow more flexibility and expandability, and, unlike a rule, expectations can't be broken.

> *Evergreen School's Behavioral Expectations:*
>
> *We come to school to learn.*
> *We respect ourselves and others.*
> *We are responsible for our actions.*

Brainstorm some ideas for schoolwide expectations here:

Data Drill Down for Creating Precision Statements

- Choose a current schoolwide behavioral problem (versus an individual student problem).
- Create an example of a precision statement for the identified behavior. See below for examples.
- Be prepared to show and discuss how you drilled deeper into your data to define the problem with precision.

Drill-Down Questions

1. Where (nonclassroom) are the most problem behaviors occurring in general (top location)?
2. Who is receiving the most referrals in the identified location (top grade)?
3. What are the two most frequent problem behaviors for the identified group in the identified location?
4. When is the problem behavior most likely to occur for the identified group in the identified location (top time)?
5. Why is the problem behavior happening for the identified group in the identified location at the identified time (consider a 30-minute time span, including 15 minutes before and after the behavior)?

Primary Versus Precision Statements About the Current Problem

Primary Statements	Precision Statements
Last year we had an increasing trend of problem behaviors during first 3 months (0.5–2.2/day above national median) and 0.5–1.0/day above national median for remainder of the school year.	Inappropriate language, disrespect, physical aggression, harassment, disruption in class and common areas (hall, cafe, playground, commons) are taking place at 9:45, 12:45–1:30, 11:30–12:15 involving many 6th and 7th graders. Behaviors appear to be driven by a need to gain peer or adult attention.
Gang behavior is increasing.	Bullying (verbal and physical aggression) on the playground is increasing during the first recess, is being done mostly by four 4th-grade boys, and seems to be maintained by social praise from the bystander peer group.

PBIS Action Plan

Include only those items from the Team Implementation Checklist (TIC) that are marked "in progress" or "not yet started."

Activity	Tasks/Action Steps (What)	Who	By When
1. Administrator's support and active involvement			
2. Staff support			
3. Representative leadership team established			
4. Regular meeting schedule and effective operating procedures in place for leadership team			
5. Audit is completed for efficient integration of PBIS team with other committees or initiatives addressing behavioral support			
6. Team self-assessment is completed to identify current PBIS practices used in the school			
7. ODR data is summarized by leadership team			
8. Self-assessment information is used to build action plan for implementation of immediate areas of focus			
9. 3–5 schoolwide behavioral expectations are defined and posted in all areas of building			
10. Schoolwide behavioral matrix developed			
11. Teaching plans for schoolwide expectations are developed			

continued >

PBIS Action Plan, continued

Activity	Tasks/Action Steps (What)	Who	By When
12. Schoolwide behavioral expectations are taught directly and formally			
13. System in place to acknowledge and reward behavioral expectations			
14. Consequences and procedures for undesirable behaviors are developed, clearly defined, and applied consistently schoolwide			
15. Classroom systems summary is completed by leadership team			
16. Action plan addresses any classroom systems identified as a high priority for change			
17. Data system is in place to monitor ODR rates from classrooms			
18. Discipline data are gathered, summarized, and reported at least quarterly to all staff			
19. Discipline data are available to team at least monthly in a form and depth needed for problem-solving			
20. Personnel with behavioral expertise are identified and involved			
21. At least one staff member of the school is able to conduct simple functional behavioral assessments			
22. Intensive, individual student support team structure is in place to use function-based supports			

SUBSIST PBIS Sustainability Checklist

Self-Assessment and Action-Planning Tool for PBIS Leadership Teams

Purposes: This self-assessment has been designed to assist leadership teams in identifying the presence of key PBIS features related to sustainability of schoolwide PBIS and to guide action planning for sustainability.

Guidelines for Use:

- Complete the self-assessment as a team.
- Consider existing efforts, initiatives, and programs that may be integrated with PBIS systems and structures.
- Use results to identify strengths and areas for action planning.

Date:

Team Members Completing Self-Assessment:

Instructions:

1. Identify the extent to which items are fully in place, partially in place, or not in place.
2. Circle items that will be priorities for the upcoming year (identify the smallest changes that will make the greatest impact).
3. Add each circled item to the action plan, identifying *who* will do *what* by *when*.

	Feature	In Place?		
		Yes	Partially	No
Priority	**1.** There is agreement that PBIS serves a critical and shared need for the school.			
	2. PBIS addresses outcomes that are highly valued by school personnel.			
	3. A vast majority of school personnel (>80%) support PBIS.			
	4. PBIS is integrated into new school or district initiatives (e.g., renamed to new needs, shown how PBIS can meet the goals of the new initiatives as well).			
	5. Parents are actively involved in the PBIS effort (e.g., as part of leadership team or district committee).			

continued >

McIntosh, K., Doolittle, J. D., Vincent, C. G., Horner, R. H., & Ervin, R. A. (2013). *SUBSIST PBIS Sustainability Checklist (Version 1.1)*. Eugene, OR: Educational and Community Supports, University of Oregon.

Feature		In Place?		
		Yes	**Partially**	**No**
Building Leadership	**6.** The school administrators actively support PBIS.			
	7. The school administrators describe PBIS as a top priority for the school.			
	8. The school administrators actively support school personnel when implementing and aligning initiatives (e.g., shield staff from competing demands, change language to align PBIS with new initiatives) to allow PBIS to continue.			
	9. The school administrators ensure that the PBIS team has regularly scheduled time to meet.			
	10. A school administrator regularly attends and participates in PBIS team meetings.			
External Leadership	**11.** There are adequate district resources (funding and time) allocated for PBIS.			
	12. The district administration actively supports PBIS (e.g., describes PBIS as a top priority, provides clear direction).			
	13. State/provincial officials actively support PBIS (e.g., promotion, publicity, providing infrastructure).			
	14. PBIS is promoted to important organizations (e.g., school board, community agencies, businesses, parent groups) at least yearly.			
	15. PBIS is embedded into school and/or district policy (e.g., school improvement plans, mission/vision statements).			

continued >

McIntosh, K., Doolittle, J. D., Vincent, C. G., Horner, R. H., & Ervin, R. A. (2013). *SUBSIST PBIS Sustainability Checklist (Version 1.1)*. Eugene, OR: Educational and Community Supports, University of Oregon.

SUBSIST PBIS Sustainability Checklist, continued

Feature	In Place?		
	Yes	Partially	No
Effectiveness			
16. The practices and strategies implemented as part of PBIS are evidence-based (i.e., published research documents their effectiveness).			
17. School personnel perceive PBIS as effective in helping them achieve desired outcomes.			
18. School personnel celebrate the positive effects of PBIS at least yearly.			
19. PBIS has a "crossover effect" in other areas (e.g., improved academic achievement scores, attendance).			
20. PBIS is effective for a large proportion of students.			
21. PBIS has been expanded to other areas (e.g., classrooms, buses, students with intensive needs, parenting workshops).			
22. PBIS is implemented with fidelity (i.e., it is used as intended).			
23. Data are collected that show the critical features of PBIS are being implemented fully.			
24. The leadership team implementing PBIS is knowledgeable and skilled in PBIS.			
25. The PBIS team is well organized and operates efficiently (e.g., regular meeting schedule, process, agenda, and minutes).			
26. The school PBIS team meets at least monthly.			
Efficiency			
27. PBIS becomes easier to use with continued experience.			
28. PBIS is considered to be a typical operating procedure of the school (it has become "what we do here; what we've always done").			
29. PBIS is viewed as part of system already in use (as opposed to being an "add-on" system).			
30. Implemented PBIS strategies are cost-effective (in terms of money and effort).			
31. PBIS is viewed as at least as cost-effective as other approaches to this problem or area of the building (e.g., zero tolerance policies, character education, social-emotional curriculum).			
32. Data for PBIS are easy to collect and do not interfere with teaching.			
33. Materials related to PBIS (e.g., handbook, lesson plans, posters) are used and adapted across school years.			

continued >

McIntosh, K., Doolittle, J. D., Vincent, C. G., Horner, R. H., & Ervin, R. A. (2013). *SUBSIST PBIS Sustainability Checklist (Version 1.1)*. Eugene, OR: Educational and Community Supports, University of Oregon.

SUBSIST PBIS Sustainability Checklist, continued

	Feature	In Place?		
		Yes	**Partially**	**No**
Data-Based Decision-Making	**34.** Needs assessments (e.g., SAS) are conducted.			
	35. Data on the fidelity of implementation are collected at least yearly (e.g., TFI, SET, BoQ, TIC, SAS).			
	36. Student outcome data are collected at least yearly (e.g., ODRs, academic achievement data, school safety survey, student/parent satisfaction survey).			
	37. Data are reviewed regularly at each team meeting.			
	38. Data are presented to all school personnel at least 4 times per year.			
	39. Data are presented at least once per year to key stakeholders outside of the school (e.g., district officials, school boards, community agencies and groups).			
	40. Data are used for problem-solving, decision-making, and action planning (to make PBIS more effective or efficient).			
Capacity Building	**41.** All school personnel have a basic understanding of PBIS practices and how and why they work.			
	42. There is a high level of schoolwide PBIS expertise within the school.			
	43. The school PBIS team has regular access to district PBIS expertise (e.g., external/district coaches or consultants).			
	44. School teams and new personnel are provided with professional development in PBIS at least yearly.			
	45. The school team is connected to a "community of practice" (e.g., network of other PBIS schools, local/regional conferences).			
Overcoming Barriers	**46.** Efforts are taken to build consensus on the school's core values, beliefs, and goals as they relate to PBIS.			
	47. To overcome shifting priorities, the team and school administrators review new initiatives and identify how PBIS can contribute to or be integrated with those initiatives.			
	48. To address general school turnover, the PBIS team is representative and communicates with groups across the school (e.g., administration, grade-level teachers, specialists, staff, students).			
	49. To address "champion" turnover, the leadership and expertise for implementing PBIS is shared among a number of school personnel.			
	50. Administrators have created FTE positions with job descriptions for PBIS-related activities.			

McIntosh, K., Doolittle, J. D., Vincent, C. G., Horner, R. H., & Ervin, R. A. (2013). *SUBSIST PBIS Sustainability Checklist (Version 1.1)*. Eugene, OR: Educational and Community Supports, University of Oregon.

Free or Inexpensive Rewards for Students

For Individual Students at the Elementary Level:

- Assist the custodian.
- Assist with morning announcements over the PA system.
- Be a helper in another classroom.
- Be featured on a photo recognition board.
- Be recognized during announcements.
- Be the first one in the lunch line.
- Be the leader of a class game.
- Be the line leader or the caboose.
- Be the scout (the person who goes ahead of class to tell the specialist teacher they are on the way).
- Be the teacher's helper for the day.
- Borrow the principal's chair for the day.
- Choose a book for the teacher to read aloud to the class.
- Choose any class job for the week.
- Choose music for the class to hear.
- Choose the game during physical education.
- Choose which homework problem the teacher will give the answer to for a freebie.
- Coupon for free test answer from teacher.
- Dance to favorite music in the classroom.

For Individual Students at the Secondary Level:

- Have an adult volunteer write you a job recommendation.
- Attend an all-school party on the weekend, sponsored and chaperoned by parents, with different areas for all interests:
  - Dance area
  - Basketball area
  - Board game area
  - Conversation pit
  - Graffiti wall (piece of sheetrock decorated with colored markers)
  - Karaoke area
  - Computer animation area
- Act as assistant coach for any sport.
- Assist parent-teacher organization to develop ways to reward teachers who go out of their way to help students.
- Call in a request to a radio station, which the teacher will play in the classroom.
- Go to the grade school and teach students about a topic of interest.
- Present a PowerPoint for the class on a particular subject of interest.
- Choose what assignment the class does for homework.
- Design a theme for a school dance, ice cream social, or game night.
- Dress as the school mascot during a sporting event.
- Apprentice on a Saturday at a local store or business.
- Be the water/towel person at a sporting event.
- Do stagecraft for any school performance (lights, stage design, props).
- Assist with the scoreboard at a sporting event.
- Eat lunch with a preferred adult.
- Get free entrance to a dance or sporting event.
- Get a library pass to research a topic of interest.
- Paint a ceiling tile to go in the hallway.

continued >

Courtesy of Laura A. Riffel, Ph.D. Used with permission

Free or Inexpensive Rewards for Students, continued

For the Whole Class:

- Earn the "Golden Plunger Award" for the cleanest classroom.
- Earn the "Gold Record" for the best behavior in music class for the week.
- Earn the "Golden Maracas Award" for the best behavior in Spanish class.
- Earn the "Golden Mouse Award" for the best behavior in computer class.
- Earn the "Golden Paintbrush Award" for the best behavior in art class.

- Earn the "Golden Spoon Award" for the best behavior in the cafeteria.
- Earn the "Golden Sports Trophy" for the best behavior in physical education.
- For all of the above, the next level is the platinum award, which is even more prestigious.
- For the best manners in the library, have the "Shelf Elf" sit in the student's classroom for a week.

Group Incentives with Group Rewards:

1. If there is a zero ODR day, the next day "Zero the Hero," the good behavior mascot, visits classrooms and eats lunch with students.

2. If there are zero tardies, absences, or other issues that have been a problem, instate a homework-free night for the whole school.

3. If the school has ten days with zero ODRs, the principal does something silly, like sit on the roof, get taped to a wall, wear a funny costume, or dress in a competing school's colors.

4. Draw a giant football field on the wall in the hallway. Each class has a football on the field. Every day that a class has zero absences, zero ODRs, zero tardies, etc., its football moves forward five yards. As each class makes a touchdown, it earns a homework-free night or an extra recess. Its football size is then increased and it starts all over again, while others continue toward a touchdown.

5. Play appropriate student-chosen music during the class transition period. Continue with the reward as long as tardies or other issues remain low (set the criteria).

Sample Menu for PBIS Reinforcement of Positive Behaviors

	The Evergreen School Menu for "Caught Ya" Tickets
2 tickets	Choose a prize from the trinket box.
3 tickets	Wear slippers for the day (must be approved by principal for safety).
3 tickets	Wear your hat for the day.
3 tickets	Bring a stuffed animal to school for a day.
3 tickets	Gain special recognition—either a phone call home or a certificate.
5 tickets	Get a picture of you and 2 friends on the front bulletin board.
5 tickets	Trade chairs with your teacher for a day.
5 tickets	Move your desk to a different location in your classroom for one day.
5 tickets	Read aloud in class a book of your choice.
5 tickets	Assist the teacher of your choice for 15 minutes.
10 tickets	Sing a song or tell a joke at the beginning of a class.
10 tickets	Get 15 minutes of extra reading time as agreed upon with teacher.
10 tickets	Get 15 minutes of extra computer time as agreed upon with teacher.
10 tickets	Get 15 minutes of drawing time as agreed upon with teacher.
10 tickets	Eat lunch in the classroom with a friend.
10 tickets	Get a free homework pass on an assignment.
10 tickets	Eat lunch with a staff person of your choice.
10 tickets	Wear jeans on Friday instead of your school uniform khakis (must still wear uniform shirt).
10 tickets	Dance in the music room for 20 minutes with 2 friends and Ms. Maher. You choose the music.
12 tickets	Serve as a workroom assistant for 20 minutes.
12 tickets	Serve as a custodial assistant for 20 minutes.
12 tickets	Shoot baskets in gym with any staff member for 20 minutes.

continued >

Sample Menu for PBIS Reinforcement of Positive Behaviors, continued

12 tickets	Design a bulletin board with Ms. Woods for 20 minutes.
12 tickets	Listen to music during a class for 20 minutes during silent work time.
15 tickets	Make cookies with Ms. Carr after school.
15 tickets	Eat a snack and play a board game with Ms. Kaufmann after school.
15 tickets	Serve as a library clerk with Mr. Olson for 20 minutes.
25 tickets	Create a special welcome with sidewalk chalk for 30 minutes.
30 tickets	Have the assistant principal as your own personal assistant for one hour.
30 tickets	Enjoy a free restaurant lunch with the principal.
30 tickets	Get 15 minutes extra recess for your entire class.
50 tickets	Dye Mr. Anderson's hair with pink stripes.
50 tickets	Take Ms. Nowak's hamsters home for the weekend.

Tips for Creating a Reward Menu:

1. Include a variety of prizes—some kids want things, some kids want time with a person, some kids want to be special, etc.

2. Some schools equate tickets and trinkets with money. For example, 1 ticket may be worth $1 in trinkets, 5 tickets may be worth $5 in trinkets, etc.

3. Hand out the prizes once a week—any more than that and they may start losing their appeal.

4. Survey the staff in your building and see what they will contribute to the list of rewards.

5. Keep all the prizes in one place and designate a specific "prize time" during the week, for example, Fridays during advisory. Have students put their names in a bucket if they have tickets. Choose one student from each advisory to go to the prize room. The names stay in the bucket for the next week's drawing.

Glossary of Terms and Acronyms

action plan: A written plan that uses data to identify goals and determine specific action steps, timelines, and resources needed to reach each goal. The action plan includes *who* will do *what* by *when* and *where*, and *how* it will be accomplished and evaluated, or measured.

behavioral matrix: The behavioral matrix is a chart accompanying a schools' three to five school-wide behavioral expectations that specifically defines the expected behaviors in different settings throughout the school.

Benchmarks of Quality (BoQ): An annual self-assessment tool for universal Tier 1.

capacity building: Refers to the process of developing widespread skills, knowledge, and abilities among individuals and organizations to support the infrastructure in any new or existing system.

core reports: There are seven reports automatically available on the SWIS dashboard, based on the types of data schools commonly use: Average Referrals Per Day Per Month, Referrals by Location, Referrals by Problem Behavior, Referrals by Time, Referrals by Student, Referrals by Day of the Week, Referrals by Grade.

fidelity: The extent to which the core features of PBIS are implemented according to their original design and focus. Fidelity measures whether everyone is doing the same intervention in the same way and whether that intervention aligns with one of the eight key features of PBIS.

implementation science: The science of a "specified set of activities designed to put into practice an activity or program of known dimensions"

(Fixsen et al., 2005); includes the what and how of implementation.

Multi-Tiered System of Supports (MTSS): Used in general and special education to refer to a framework for delivering practices and systems for enhancing academic and behavioral outcomes for all students.

National Implementation Research Network (NIRN): The mission of NIRN is to contribute to the best practices and science of implementation, organization change, and system reinvention to improve outcomes across the spectrum of human services.

office discipline referral (ODR): One of the primary outcome measures of student behavior in PBIS. An ODR represents and measures specific student behavior through the use of an electronic or paper behavioral incident report that contains specific defined fields.

PBIS: Positive Behavioral Interventions and Supports

PBIS assessment coordinator: A designated leadership team member (sometimes the coach) who obtains a PBIS online assessment account; assists leadership teams in using PBIS assessment tools and data to measure progress, to facilitate problem-solving, and to determine what supports may be most beneficial. Assessments include the TFI, TIC, SAS, SET, and BoQ.

PBIS coaching: A set of responsibilities, actions, activities, and personnel resources (i.e., coaches) organized to train, facilitate, assist, maintain, and adapt local PBIS implementation.

School-Wide Evaluation Tool (SET): An assessment designed to evaluate the features of SWPBIS across each academic year. It provides a good measure of implementation and fidelity. It is conducted by an outside evaluator and was created as a research tool.

Schoolwide Information System (SWIS): A digital application for efficient collection, analysis, and reports of ODR data.

Schoolwide Positive Behavioral Interventions and Supports (SWPBIS): A systematic framework and set of evidence-based practices for improving behavioral and academic outcomes for all students and all staff in all school settings.

Self-Assessment Survey (SAS): Solicits feedback from all staff members on the status of SWPBIS implementation and the priorities for action planning (formerly known as the EBS Survey).

sustainability: The ongoing, long-term practice of SWPBIS after formal training ends and at a level of fidelity that continues to produce valued outcomes.

Team Implementation Checklist (TIC): A progress-monitoring tool completed monthly or quarterly by the school PBIS Leadership Team to measure implementation of the Tier 1 universal system.

Tiered Fidelity Inventory (TFI): The TFI gives teams a single, efficient, valid, reliable survey to guide implementation and sustained use of SWPBIS. Using the TFI, teams measure the extent to which school personnel apply the core features of SWPBIS at all three tiers.

References and Resources

Print

Aguilar, E. (2016). *The Art of Coaching Teams: Building Resilient Communities That Transform Schools*. San Francisco: Jossey-Bass.

Algozzine, B., Barrett, S., Eber, L., George, H., Horner, R., Lewis, T., Putnam, B., Swain-Bradway, J., McIntosh, K., and Sugai, G. (2014). *SWPBIS Tiered Fidelity Inventory*. Eugene, OR: OSEP Technical Assistance Center on PBIS.

Algozzine, B., Horner, R.H., Sugai, G., Barrett, S., Dickey, C.R., Eber, L., Kincaid, D., Lewis, T., and Tobin, T. (2010). *Evaluation Blueprint for School-Wide Positive Behavior Support*. Eugene, OR: OSEP Technical Assistance Center on PBIS.

Allday, R.A., Hinkson-Lee, K., Hudson, T., Neilsen-Gatti, S., Kleinke, A., and Russel, C.S. (2012). "Training General Educators to Increase Behavior-Specific Praise: Effects on Students with EBD." *Behavioral Disorders* 37(2), 87–98.

Balfanz, R., Byrnes, V., and Fox, J. (2015). "Sent Home and Put Off Track: The Antecedents, Disproportionalities, and Consequences of Being Suspended in the 9th Grade." In D. J. Losen (ed.) *Closing the School Discipline Gap: Equitable Remedies for Excessive Exclusion*. New York: Teachers College Press.

Bandura, A. (1977). "Self-Efficacy: Toward a Unifying Theory of Behavioral Change." *Psychological Review* 84(2), 191–215.

Barrett, S., and Duda, M. (2011). "Coaching for Competence and Impact." PBIS Leadership Forum.

Barrett, S., Eber, L., and Weist, M. (eds.) (2013). *Advancing Education Effectiveness: Interconnecting School Mental Health and School-Wide Positive Behavior Support*. Eugene, OR: OSEP Technical Assistance Center on PBIS.

Blad, E., and Harwin, A. (2017). "Black Students More Likely to Be Arrested at School." *Education Week*.

Cameron, J., and Pierce, W.D. (1994). "Reinforcement, Reward, and Intrinsic Motivation: A Meta-Analysis." *Review of Educational Research* 64(3), 363–423.

Coffey, J.H., and Horner, R.H. (2012). "The Sustainability of Schoolwide Positive Behavior Interventions and Supports." *Exceptional Children* 78(4), 407–422.

Cotton, K. (1990). "Schoolwide and Classroom Discipline." *School Improvement Research Series: Close-Up #9*. Office of Educational Research and Improvement, US Department of Education.

Crone, D.A., Hawken, L.S., and Horner, R.H. (2010). *Responding to Problem Behavior in Schools: The Behavior Education Program*. New York: The Guilford Press.

Doran, G.T. (1981). "There's a S.M.A.R.T. Way to Write Management's Goals and Objectives." *Management Review* (AMA FORUM) 70(11), 35–36.

Elias, M. (2013). "The School-to-Prison Pipeline: Policies and Practices That Favor Incarceration over Education Do Us All a Grave Injustice." *Teaching Tolerance* 43, 39–43.

The Equity Project (2015). "Discipline Disparities Highlights." The Discipline Disparities Research-to-Practice Collaborative. http://www.indiana.edu/~equity/docs/Highlights011415.html.

Fenning, P., and Rose, J. (2007). "Overrepresentation of African American Students in Exclusionary Discipline: The Role of School Policy." *Urban Education* 42(6), 536–559.

Filter, K.J., Sytsma, M., and McIntosh, K. (2015). "Staff Buy-In to SW-PBIS" (presentation at symposium, SW-PBIS: Measuring Outcomes and Input Factors).

Fixsen, D.L., Naoom, S., Blase, K., Friedman, R., and Wallace, F. (2005). *Implementation Research: A Synthesis of the Literature.* Tampa, FL: University of South Florida, Louis de la Parte Florida Mental Health Institute, National Implementation Research Network (FMHI Publication #231).

Freeman, J., Sugai, G., Horner, R., Simonsen, B., McIntosh, K., Eber, L., Everett, S., George, H., Swain-Bradway, J., and Sprauge, J. (2016). *Tier 2 Systems Readiness Guide.* Eugene, OR: OSEP Technical Assistance Center on PBIS. Online at https://www.pbis.org/resource/1068/tier-2-systems-readiness-guide.

Froelich, K., and Puig, E. (2007). "The Magic of Coaching: Art Meets Science." *Journal of Language and Literacy Education* 3(1), 18–31.

Gilbert, T.F. (2007). *Human Competence: Engineering Worthy Performance.* San Francisco: Pfeiffer.

Gilliam, W.S., Maupin, A.N., Reyes, C.R., Accavitti, M., and Shic, F. (2016). *Do Early Educators' Implicit Biases Regarding Sex and Race Relate to Behavior Expectations and Recommendations of Preschool Expulsions and Suspensions?* New Haven, CT: Yale Child Study Center.

Gilliam, W.S., and Shahar, G. (2006). "Preschool and Child Care Expulsion and Suspension: Rates and Predictors in One State." *Infants & Young Children* 19(3), 228–245.

Goodman, S. (2013). "Implementation of a District-Wide Multi-Tiered System of Supports Initiative Through Stages of Implementation." *The Utah Special Educator* 35, 20–21.

Green, A., Nese, R., McIntosh, K., Nishioka, V., Eliason, B., and Delabra, A.C. (2015). *Key Elements of Policies to Address Discipline Disproportionality: A Guide for District and School Teams.* Eugene, OR: OSEP Technical Assistance Center on PBIS.

Gregory, A., Ruzek, E., Hafen, C.A., Mikami, A., Allen, J.P., and Pianta, R.C. (2017). "My Teaching Partner-Secondary: A Video-Based Coaching Model." *Theory into Practice* 56(1), 38–45.

Hardin, C.D., and Banaji, M.R. (2013). "The Nature of Implicit Prejudice: Implications for Personal and Public Policy." In Shafir, E. (ed.), *The Behavioral Foundations of Public Policy.* Princeton, NJ: Princeton University Press, 13–31.

Hollie, S. (2018). *Culturally and Linguistically Responsive Teaching and Learning: Classroom Practices for Student Success.* Huntington Beach, CA: Shell Education.

Horner, R. (2011). "Coaching for Effective Implementation." Third Annual KY PBIS Network Conference.

Horner, R., and Sugai, G. (2006). *Policy Brief: Scaling Up Effective Educational Innovation.* Prepared at the request of the US Department of Education, Office of Special Education Programs, Washington, DC.

Horner, R., Sugai, G., Smolkowski, K., Eber, L., Nakasato, J., Todd, A.W., and Esperanza, J. (2009). "A Randomized, Wait-List Controlled Effectiveness Trial Assessing School-Wide Positive Behavior Support in Elementary Schools." *Journal of Positive Behavior Interventions* 11(3), 133–144.

Joyce, B., and Showers, B. (1995). *Student Achievement Through Staff Development: Fundamentals of School Renewal.* White Plains, NY: Longman.

Knoff, H.M., Reeves, D., and Balow, C. (2018). *A Multi-Tiered Service & Support Implementation Blueprint for Schools & Districts: Revisiting the Science to Improve the Practice.* Irvine, CA: Illuminate Education.

Leverson, M., Smith, K., McIntosh, K., Rose, J., and Pinkelman, S. (2016). *PBIS Cultural Responsiveness Field Guide: Resources for Trainers and Coaches*. Eugene, OR: OSEP Technical Assistance Center on PBIS.

Lohrmann, S., Forman, S., Martin, S., and Palmieri, M. (2008). "Understanding School Personnel's Resistance to Adopting Schoolwide Positive Behavior Support at a Universal Level of Intervention." *Journal of Positive Behavior Interventions* 10(4), 256–269.

Mathews, S., McIntosh, K., Frank, J.L., and May, S.L. (2013). "Critical Features Predicting Sustained Implementation of School-Wide Positive Behavioral Interventions and Supports." *Journal of Positive Behavior Interventions* 16(3), 168–178.

McIntosh, K., Doolittle, J.D., Vincent, C.G., Horner, R., and Ervin, R.A. (2013). *SUBSIST PBIS Sustainability Checklist (Version 1.1)*. Eugene, OR: Educational and Community Supports, University of Oregon.

McIntosh, K., Frank, J.L., and Spaulding, S.A. (2010). "Establishing Research-Based Trajectories of Office Discipline Referrals for Individual Students." *School Psychology Review* 39(3), 380–394.

McIntosh, K., Girvan, E.J., Horner, R., Smolkowski, K., and Sugai, G. (2018). *A 5-Point Intervention Approach for Enhancing Equity in School Discipline*. Eugene, OR: OSEP Technical Assistance Center on PBIS.

McIntosh, K., Horner, R.H., and Sugai, G. (2009). "Sustainability of Systems-Level Evidence-Based Practices in Schools: Current Knowledge and Future Directions." In Sailor, W., Dunlap, G., Sugai, G., and Horner, R.H. (eds.), *Handbook of Positive Behavior Support*. New York: Springer, 327–352.

McIntosh, K., Mercer, S.H., Nese, R., Strickland-Cohen, M.K., Kittelman, A., Hoselton, R., and Horner, R. (2018). "Factors Predicting Sustained Implementation of a Universal Behavioral Support Framework." *Educational Researcher* 47 (5), 307–316.

Mercer, J.R. (1973). *Labeling the Mentally Retarded*. Berkeley: University of California Press.

Mercer, S.H., McIntosh, K., and Hoselton, R. (2017). "Comparability of Fidelity Measures for Assessing Tier 1 School-Wide Positive Behavioral Interventions and Supports." *Journal of Positive Behavior Interventions* 19(4), 195–204.

Mikami, A., Gregory, A., Allen, J.P., Pianta, R.C., and Lun, J. (2012). "Effects of a Teacher Professional Development Intervention on Peer Relationships in Secondary Classrooms." *School Psychology Review* 40(3), 367–385.

National Center for Education Statistics (2018). "Fast Facts: Back to School Statistics." https://nces .ed.gov/fastfacts/display.asp?id=372.

Nayar, Vineet (2013). "Three Differences Between Managers and Leaders." *Harvard Business Review*.

Noltemeyer, A.L., Ward, R.M., and Mcloughlin, C. (2015). "Relationship Between School Suspension and Student Outcomes: A Meta-Analysis." *School Psychology Review* 44(2), 224–240.

Office for Civil Rights (2016). *2013–2014 Civil Rights Data Collection: A First Look*. Washington, DC: US Department of Education.

OSEP Technical Assistance Center on PBIS (2010). *Implementation Blueprint and Self-Assessment*. Eugene, OR: OSEP Technical Assistance Center on PBIS.

OSEP Technical Assistance Center on PBIS (2015). *PBIS Implementation Blueprint: Part 1— Foundations and Supporting Information*. Eugene, OR: OSEP Technical Assistance Center on PBIS.

OSEP Technical Assistance Center on PBIS (2017). *PBIS Implementation Blueprint: Part 2— Self-Assessment and Action Planning.* Eugene, OR: OSEP Technical Assistance Center on PBIS.

OSEP Technical Assistance Center on PBIS (2014). *Using Discipline Data Within SWPBIS to Identify and Address Disproportionality: A Guide for School Teams.* Eugene, OR: OSEP Technical Assistance Center on PBIS.

OSEP Technical Assistance Center on PBIS (2017). "What Are the Organizational Systems for Tier 3?" https://www.pbis.org/school/tier-3-supports /what-are-the-organizational-systems-for-tier-3.

Penn Wharton Public Policy Initiative (2015). "The Dangers of the 'School-to-Prison Pipeline.'" University of Pennsylvania. https://publicpolicy .wharton.upenn.edu/live/news/831-the-dangers -of-the-school-to-prison-pipeline.

Romano, N., and Nunamaker, J.F. (2001). "Proceedings of the 34th Annual Hawaii International Conference on System Sciences."

Ross, S.W., Romer, N., and Horner, R.H. (2011). "Teacher Well-Being and the Implementation of School-Wide Positive Behavior Interventions and Supports." *Journal of Positive Behavior Interventions* 14(2), 118–128.

Sailor, W., Dunlap, G., Sugai, G., and Horner, R. (eds.) (2009). *Handbook of Positive Behavior Support.* New York: Springer.

The Sentencing Project (2017). http://www .sentencingproject.org.

Skiba, R.J., Chung, C., Trachok, M., Baker, T., Sheya, A., and Hughes, R. (2012). "Parsing Disciplinary Disproportionality: Contributions of Behavior, Student, and School Characteristics to Suspension and Expulsion." Paper presented at the Annual Meeting of the American Educational Research Association, Vancouver, BC, Canada.

Skiba, R.J., Simmons, A.B., Ritter, S., Gibb, A.C., Rausch, M.K., Cuadrado, J., and Chung, C. (2008). "Achieving Equity in Special Education: History, Status, and Current Challenges." *Exceptional Children* 74(3), 264–288.

Stanford Center for Education Policy Analysis (2013). "Racial and Ethnic Achievement Gaps." Stanford University. https://cepa.stanford.edu /educational-opportunity-monitoring-project /achievement-gaps/race.

Strickland-Cohen, M.K., McIntosh, K., and Horner, R.H. (2014). "Sustaining Effective Practices in the Face of Principal Turnover." *Teaching Exceptional Children* 46(3), 18–24.

Sugai, G. (2013). "Arranging for Seats at the 'School Reform Table.'" PBIS Leadership Forum, Chicago Plenary session.

Sugai, G. (2008). "RTI & SWPBS." PDF document retrieved from the PBIS website. Online at www.pbis.org/common/pbisresources/presenta tions/0708gsrtiandpbisDC.pdf.

Sugai, G., and Horner, R. (2009). "Defining and Describing Schoolwide Positive Behavior Support." In Sailor, W., Dunlap, G., Sugai, G., and Horner, R.H. (eds.) *Handbook of Positive Behavior Support.* New York: Springer, 307–326.

Sulik, L.R. (2012). "Anxiety in Children: An Update for Professionals." Keynote. Minnesota Children's Mental Health Conference, April 2011.

Swain-Bradway, J., Johnson, S.L., Bradshaw, C., and McIntosh, K. (2017). *What Are the Economic Costs of Implementing SWPBIS in Comparison to the Benefits from Reducing Suspensions?* Eugene, OR: University of Oregon.

Todd, A.W., Lewis-Palmer, T., Horner, R., Sugai, G., Sampson, N.K., and Phillips, D. (2012). *School-Wide Evaluation Tool (SET) Implementation Manual, Version 2.0.* Eugene, OR: OSEP Technical Assistance Center on PBIS.

Todd, A.W., Newton, J.S., Algozzine, K., Horner, R., and Algozzine, B. (2013). *The Team-Initiated Problem Solving (TIPS II) Training Manual.* Eugene, OR: University of Oregon.

United States Government Accountability Office (2018). *K–12 Education: Discipline Disparities for Black Students, Boys, and Students with Disabilities.* Washington, DC: US Government Accountability Office.

Online

State PBIS Websites

Many websites represent the accomplishments and resources developed across the country in various states. Those presented in this listing have a long history of SWPBIS implementation and have developed resources that others can use.

Regional PBIS Websites

PBIS Regional Technical Assistance Centers include:

midwestpbis.org: Midwest PBIS Network in Illinois

midatlanticpbis.org: Mid-Atlantic PBIS Network in Maryland

neswpbs.org: Northeast PBIS Network in Connecticut

pbisnetwork.org: Northwest PBIS Network in Oregon

CASEL

casel.org

This website promotes teaching social-emotional skills to students in all grade levels. The social-emotional learning domains are self-awareness, social-awareness, self-management, relationship skills, and responsible decision-making. You will find videos about how teaching social-emotional learning has improved schools as well as the CASEL guide to many curriculums that teach social-emotional skills, rated according to the program design and the effectiveness of each curriculum according to research.

Center for Culturally Responsive Teaching and Learning

www.culturallyresponsive.org

Cultural responsiveness is an approach for validating and affirming different cultures. The Center aims to promote cultural responsiveness through professional development, community development, and school development. The website features many resources, including videos, handouts, a list of culturally responsive books, articles, and more.

Florida's Positive Behavior Support Project

flpbis.cbcs.usf.edu

This website offers multiple resources for schools, school and district coordinators, and PBIS coaches. Florida developed the Benchmarks of Quality (BoQ), an assessment that is now used across the country. You will find resources for teams (team development) and for coaches (knowledge, skills, entry information), a Microsoft Excel template for an ODR calculator, and the 2013 online publication *Systems Coaching: A Model for Building Capacity.*

Michigan's Integrated Behavior and Learning Support Initiative (MIBLSI)

miblsi.org

This website for the state of Michigan includes multiple resources of interest and value to others, including resources for PBIS coaches, for evaluation processes, and for implementation strategies.

Missouri SWPBIS

pbismissouri.org

This website represents the statewide efforts of Missouri. Among the various resources offered are complete team workbooks for Tier 1 and Tier 2.

OSEP Technical Assistance Center on PBIS

www.pbis.org

The internet home for the OSEP Technical Assistance Center on PBIS, this national PBIS website is referenced throughout this book. You will find everything related to PBIS, such as research, information for parents and families, training videos and resources, and tools needed to successfully implement PBIS in your school or district.

PBIS Apps

www.pbisapps.org

This online application includes a number of tools specifically designed to assist schools, districts, regions, and states in achieving high fidelity and sustained implementation of SWPBIS. This website is designed to support schools' use of data by improving the efficiency and accuracy with which assessment tools are used. Tools are included for all three tiers of PBIS.

PBIS Maryland

www.pbismaryland.org

The state website for PBIS Maryland has archived many resources and materials. In addition to illustrating examples for schools across Maryland, this website offers resources that can be used in other states. One example is a template for a Cost-Benefit Analysis Worksheet that calculates the instructional and administrative time reclaimed as an outcome of PBIS implementation. In addition, PBIS Maryland has extensive online resources for PBIS coaches.

PBIS World

www.pbisworld.com/tier-2/reward-system

In addition to tons of information on tiered interventions for all kinds of behaviors, this website also provides information and articles on recognition and rewards programs. Download the customizable School Rewards Dollars PDF to create rewards dollars your students can earn and use to purchase prizes or privileges.

Project Implicit

implicit.harvard.edu

Project Implicit is a nonprofit organization with the goal of educating people about hidden biases. The website offers the Implicit Association Test that can help you discover implicit attitudes and beliefs you may hold.

Teaching Tolerance

www.teachingtolerance.org

This website offers many free classroom resources, including film kits and lesson plans. The Social Justice Standards provide educators a road map for anti-bias education at all grades. Also download the classroom guide *Face to Face Advisories: Bridging Cultural Gaps in Grades 5–9* for activities to help students understand and analyze diverse perspectives.

YouTube/TeacherTube

YouTube

www.youtube.com

Find PBIS teaching videos, such as this one: www.youtube.com/watch?v=GJROcj2qG9E

Find videos about cultural responsiveness and bias, including this one: https://www.youtube.com/watch?v=RcakaN5rn1o

TeacherTube

www.teachertube.com

A free community for sharing instructional videos and content for teachers and students. TeacherTube is education focused and is a safe venue for teachers, schools, and home learners.

Index

About the Authors

Char Ryan, Ph.D., is a PBIS coach and evaluation specialist. She has been a Minnesota state SWIS and PBIS trainer working with school teams. Char was formerly the Minnesota state PBIS coordinator and PBIS coach for a regional PBIS project. She was an assistant professor at St. Cloud State University and an adjunct professor in teacher training at the University of St. Thomas. Char works and lives in Minneapolis, Minnesota.

Beth Baker, M.S.Ed., is a teacher and advocate for students with special needs. During her twenty-plus years in education, Beth has taught in self-contained special education classrooms, implemented and coached PBIS teams, and worked as a behavior specialist. She was also a district program facilitator assisting staff with professional development around social-emotional learning and coaching them in supporting students with emotional-behavioral needs. Recently she has been teaching abroad and implementing PBIS at international schools. Beth loves creating positive paths to behavior change, whenever and wherever she can. She presents frequently on social-emotional learning and PBIS, both in the US and internationally. She lives in Minneapolis, Minnesota.

Follow her on Twitter @PBIS_Beth.

Download the free PLC/Book Study Guide for this book at freespirit.com/PLC.

Other Great Resources from Free Spirit

RTI Success
Proven Tools and Strategies for Schools and Classrooms
(Revised & Updated Edition)
by Elizabeth Whitten, Ph.D., Kelli J. Esteves, Ed.D., and Alice Woodrow, Ed.D.

For teachers and administrators, grades K–12.
264 pp.; PB; 8½" x 11"; includes digital content.
Free PLC/Book Study Guide freespirit.com/PLC

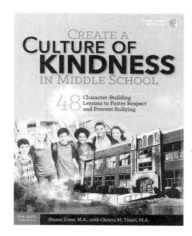

Create a Culture of Kindness in Middle School
48 Character-Building Lessons to Foster Respect and Prevent Bullying
by Naomi Drew, M.A., with Christa M. Tinari, M.A.

For middle school educators.
272 pp.; PB; 8½" x 11"; includes digital content.

Self-Regulation in the Classroom
Helping Students Learn How to Learn
by Richard M. Cash, Ed.D.

For eachers, administrators, and counselors, grades K–12.
184 pp.; PB; 8½" x 11"; includes digital content.
Free PLC/Book Study Guide freespirit.com/PLC

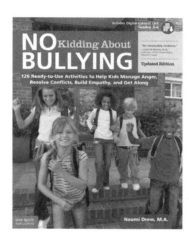

No Kidding About Bullying
126 Ready-to-Use Activities to Help Kids Manage Anger, Resolve Conflicts, Build Empathy, and Get Along
(Updated Edition)
by Naomi Drew, M.A.

For educators, grades 3–6.
304 pp.; PB; 8½" x 11"; includes digital content.

The School Climate Solution
Creating a Culture of Excellence from the Classroom to the Staff Room
by Jonathan C. Erwin, M.A.

For administrators, teachers, and counselors, grades K–12.
200 pp.; PB; 8½" x 11"; includes digital content.

End Peer Cruelty, Build Empathy
The Proven 6Rs of Bullying Prevention That Create Inclusive, Safe, and Caring Schools
by Michele Borba, Ed.D.

For administrators, teachers, counselors, youth leaders, bullying prevention teams, and parents of children in grades K–8.
288 pp; PB; 7¼" x 9¼"; includes digital content.
Free PLC/Book Study Guide freespirit.com/PLC

Boost Emotional Intelligence in Students
30 Flexible Research-Based Activities to Build EQ Skills (Grades 5–9)
by Maurice J. Elias, Ph.D., and Steven E. Tobias, Psy.D.
For teachers and counselors, grades 5–9.
192 pp.; PB; 8½" x 11"; includes digital content.

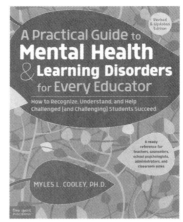

A Practical Guide to Mental Health & Learning Disorders for Every Educator
How to Recognize, Understand, and Help Challenged (and Challenging) Students Succeed
(Revised & Updated Edition)
by Myles L. Cooley, Ph.D.
For educators and counselors, grades K–12.
256 pp.; PB; 8½" x 11"; includes digital content.

The Hands-On Guide to School Improvement
Transform Culture, Empower Teachers, and Raise Student Achievement
by Evelyn M. Randle-Robbins, M.A.
For principals, administrators, and school leaders, grades K–12.
208 pp.; PB; 7¼" x 9¼"; includes digital content.

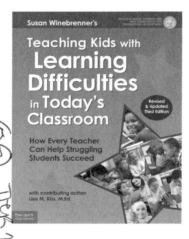

Teaching Kids with Learning Difficulties in Today's Classroom
How Every Teacher Can Help Struggling Students Succeed
(Revised & Updated 3rd Edition)
by Susan Winebrenner, M.S., with Lisa M. Kiss, M.Ed.
For K–12 teachers, administrators, and higher education faculty.
288 pp.; PB; 8½" x 11"; includes digital content.
Free PLC/Book Study Guide freespirit.com/PLC

The Principal's Survival Guide
Where Do I Start? How Do I Succeed? When Do I Sleep?
by Susan Stone Kessler, Ed.D., April M. Snodgrass, M.Ed., and Andrew T. Davis, Ed.D.
For principals and administrators, grades K–12.
208 pp.; PB; 7¼" x 9¼".

Teaching Gifted Kids in Today's Classroom
Strategies and Techniques Every Teacher Can Use
(Updated 4th Edition)
by Susan Winebrenner, M.S., with Dina Brulles, Ph.D.
For teachers and administrators, grades K–12.
256 pp.; PB; 8½" x 11"; includes digital content.

For pricing information, to place an order, or to request a free catalog, contact:

Free Spirit Publishing Inc. • 6325 Sandburg Road, Suite 100 • Minneapolis, MN 55427-3674
toll-free 800.735.7323 • local 612.338.2068 • fax 612.337.5050
help4kids@freespirit.com • www.freespirit.com